Doing Teaching

Doing Teaching

The Practical Management of Classrooms

Edited by
G.C.F. Payne and E.C. Cuff

BATSFORD ACADEMIC AND EDUCATIONAL LTD
LONDON

© G.C.F. Payne and E.C. Cuff 1982
First published 1982

All rights reserved. No part of this
publication may be reproduced, in any form
or by any means, without permission from
the Publisher

Printed in Great Britain by
Billing & Son Ltd
Worcester

for the publishers
Batsford Academic and Educational Ltd
4 Fitzhardinge Street
London W1H 0AH

British Library Cataloguing in Publication
  Data

Doing teaching: the practical management
  of classrooms.
  1. Teaching
  I. Payne, G.C.   II. Cuff, E.C.
  371.102   LB1025.2

ISBN 0-7134-4380-4

Contents

	Preface	vii
	Transcription symbols	ix
	Editors and contributors	x
1	Introduction: some theoretical considerations for practical research *George Payne and Ted Cuff*	1

PART ONE
Familiar Teaching Routines in their Context: The Primary School

2	Telling a story: teacher and pupil competence in an infant classroom *Dave Hustler and Ted Cuff*	14
3	The social organization of reading assessment: reasons for eclecticism *James Heap*	39
4	The social organization of space and place in an urban open-plan primary school *Graham Hitchcock*	60

PART TWO
Familiar Teaching Routines in their Context: The Secondary School

5	Dealing with a late-comer *George Payne*	90
6	Adolescent-adult talk as a practical interpretive problem *Carolyn Baker*	104

Contents

PART THREE
Some Practical and Theoretical Issues

7	The teacher as classroom researcher: a modest method for a new opportunity *Digby Anderson*	130
8	A first try: starting the day *Carol Cummings*	148
9	Talking and teaching: reflective comments on in-classroom activities *Wes Sharrock and Bob Anderson*	170

Prospect: what happens next? — 184

References — 187

Index — 191

Preface

This book has been brought together from two broad sources of interest and concern. All contributors would like to see more teachers doing their own research, but at the same time believe that such research must have a sharp methodological focus for it to have sufficient rigour to be of any practical use at all. The methodological focus favoured by contributors to this book is 'ethnomethodological'. Bob Anderson, Ted Cuff, Graham Hitchcock, Dave Hustler, George Payne and Wes Sharrock have all been developing their interest in ethnomethodology in various institutions – schools, college, polytechnic and university – over a number of years. Carol Cummings has more recently interested herself in this approach. Digby Anderson has been working in the same field of research, previously from Nottingham University, now from the Social Affairs Unit in London.

Although ethnomethodology originated as an approach in the United States of America, it has developed and expanded in other countries. Apart from Great Britain, we find in this book examples from Canada and Australia. Carolyn Baker in Australia and James Heap in Canada are both involved in studying schools in their own countries, using an ethnomethodological approach.

Whatever our interest, we would not have been able to produce this book without the help of other people. First and foremost, we wish to thank all the teachers and pupils who have both wittingly and unwittingly enabled this book to be written. Without their talk and willingness to let others hear it, the book would simply not have been possible.

The manuscript was most diligently and expertly typed by Jean Davies, Pauline Curvis, Edith Jones, Lyn Meehan, Doreen Morris and Joan Naylor. We are most grateful for the care they have taken in the face of some formidable handwriting and some atrocious amateur typescripts.

Earlier versions of two contributions to this collection have appeared elsewhere. The major part of Digby Anderson's chapter has been previously

Preface

published in his *Evaluation By Classroom Experience*, Nafferton Books, 1979. Chapter 5 is a revised version of 'Communicating the features of an occasion to a late-arrival' which appeared in *Language for Learning*, vol. 2, no. 3, 1980.

The transcription used in Chapter 2 has been analysed elsewhere (French and Mclure, 1981), but the treatment here has been radically revised.

James Heap's chapter arises out of a Project on Social Organization of Reading Activities which is one of four related projects within the Social Sciences and Humanities Research Council for Canada Program Grant No. 431-770006, 'The Problem of Self-Reflection and the Study of Children's Culture'. He wishes to thank William Bryant, Mary Farrar, Judy Horn, John McQuade, Peter Weeks, Beverly Bingham and especially Joey Noble for their comments, efforts and support.

Transcription symbols

//	talk overlapped at this point by next utterance
wh—	word started but not completed
yes-I-know	words run together quickly
—	untimed pause
(1.0)	timed pause (of one second)
( )	something said but not transcribable
(yes I know)	transcriber thinks 'yes I know' was said
((laughter))	description not transcription
yes	indicates emphasis
YES	capitals indicates loud volume
:	indicates prolongation of syllable
(hh)	indicates aspiration – usually laughing sound in a word
T	teacher
C	unidentified child
CC	unidentified children speaking together

Editors and contributors

Digby Anderson has taught in further and higher education. His research in health education involved visiting schools and discussing observations with panels of teachers. His research interests include the problems of youth in and out of school. He is currently Director of the Social Affairs Unit.

Bob Anderson trained as a teacher at Southampton University and spent several years teaching in secondary schools and in teacher training. He has continued his close association with teaching through his work as 'A'-level, then Chief, Examiner with JMB in sociology. Currently, he teaches sociology in the Department of Social Sciences, Manchester Polytechnic.

Carolyn Baker trained as a teacher at Lakeshore Teacher's College, Ontario and has taught in intermediate levels. Her research interests involve visits to secondary schools, particularly conversing with students about adolescence and schooling. Currently, she teaches courses in adolescence and sociology to pre-service and practising teachers in the Faculty of Education, University of New England, Australia.

Ted Cuff trained as a teacher at the Central Institute, University of London and has taught in further education and in teacher training. His research interests include the sociological study of natural language and ethnomethodology. He is Head of the Department of Educational Studies, Manchester Polytechnic.

Carol Cummings trained as a teacher at Didsbury College of Education, Manchester and has taught in infant schools for ten years. Her research interests include teacher-pupil classroom interaction, and teacher self-evaluation. She is currently teaching in a vertically grouped reception-middle infant class in a Trafford infant school.

Editors and Contributors

James Heap trained as a teacher and sociologist at the University of California, Santa Barbara and has taught at the secondary level. He is researching into reading activities at the Ontario Institute for Studies in Education where he teaches sociology in education at the graduate level.

Graham Hitchcock trained as a teacher at Padgate College of Education, Warrington and specialized in the intermediate age-range. He studied sociology and the sociology of education at the University of Manchester and is currently teaching at Doncaster Metropolitan Institute of Higher Education.

Dave Hustler trained as a teacher at the Central Institute, University of London and has taught in schools in London and Borneo. He currently teaches education and sociology to in-service teachers and his research interests involve him in observing and teaching in infant and secondary schools. He is a member of the Department of Educational Studies, Didsbury School of Education, Manchester Polytechnic.

George Payne trained as a teacher at Goldsmith's College and has taught in primary and secondary schools. He has continued to study education and sociology at the Central Institute, London and at the University of Manchester. Currently he teaches in the School of Education, Manchester Polytechnic. This work brings him into constant contact with schools and practising teachers.

Wes Sharrock trained as a sociologist at the Universities of Leicester and Manchester. His research interests include theories and methods of sociology with special reference to the study of everyday life. He has long been associated with teacher training as External Examiner in sociology for both the Teacher Certificate and the degree of Bachelor of Education for the Universities of Manchester and Hull. He is currently Senior Lecturer in Sociology, University of Manchester.

1 Introduction: some theoretical considerations for practical research

George Payne and Ted Cuff

Ordinary life and ordinary teaching

Teaching is a job like any other; and so is 'being ordinary'.

Clearly, no one would allow us to get away with such a bald, bold statement without some further explication. Let us begin then by justifying such a statement. The character of that justification will take us right into the nature of this book.

Harvey Sacks pointed out some time ago that the world we live in is much more finely organized than most of us imagine and that it takes a considerable amount of work on anyone's part to achieve even the mundane ordinariness of everyday life. He argued that we work at displaying our ordinariness by finding and reporting on the world as a pretty ordinary place. For example we routinely characterize films we have seen as 'really good', or television programmes as 'appalling rubbish', people we have met as 'quite nice' or even 'very nice', weekends away as 'we went to the Lake District' or 'we had a fabulous time in London'. Characterizations or reports such as these describe the ordinariness, the usualness of the scenes, the activities or the persons. They do not go into all the detailed constituent elements or aspects. If we were to provide all the details, all the constituent attributes and our criteria for judging them for all such occasions, it would not be long before we found no one listening to us, or more probably people avoiding us. Of course, there are persons who go about making their lives an 'epic' so that everything they do and see has poetic or adventurous or incredibly complicated features. In everyday life such persons can be made ordinary, i.e. can be 'normalized' by categorizing them as 'eccentrics', 'actor-types', 'bores' and so on.

This normalization of those who would make their lives an epic gives us some indication that recognizing and producing ordinariness requires work from persons describing what they are doing in the world. It requires work, it is a job to be done. Scenes simply do not present themselves as 'usual'; they

Introduction

have to be found that way and finding them that way demands skills of selection, presentation and description. In finding and reporting on the world as ordinary, we simultaneously indicate to others that we too are ordinary. Finding the ordinary in others is to present ourselves as usual persons, it is to see the world as 'anybody' does, peopled and organized in ordinary ways.

It is an important part of the argument, however, that the necessary work or skill is deployed effortlessly. That is to say, although it requires work to find scenes and occasions ordinary, doing that work presents members of society with no great problems. Ordinary, competent members of society can all do that work without great anxiety and without much trouble.

The two strands of the argument produce a most fascinating paradox, yet truly describe a world which we experience daily. First, it is simply true that situations cannot speak for themselves, they have to be worked on and, secondly, it is just as true that in our daily experience we routinely have no trouble whatsoever finding, for example, this person 'pleasant', that person 'boring', this film 'good', that programme 'rubbish', that weekend 'enjoyable' and so on. In sum we have no trouble in 'doing being ordinary'.

This approach to understanding the social world has direct relevance for a study of teaching. Doing teaching, like doing being ordinary, requires work yet it is overwhelmingly accomplished effortlessly. Now before all teachers rise up in anger, or stop reading at this point, let us immediately explain further what we mean. Clearly we are not saying that teaching is not demanding; we know that it requires planning and organization, physical and mental effort, and a deal of emotional involvement. What we are saying, however, is that some aspects of teaching activities become so much a part of the ordinary day's work that they can often be accomplished, albeit expertly and efficiently, without great anxieties, without too much trouble, sometimes almost without thinking about them. Additionally, and perhaps more importantly than is usually recognised, there are a multitude of ordinary, routine day-to-day activities engaged in by teachers in such a taken-for-granted manner that they go unnoticed. Dealing with late-comers, starting lessons, telling stories, hearing children read, sending them out to play – these are all activities which are seen, but go unnoticed as anything special. Similarly teachers can effortlessly find lessons 'satisfying', 'terrible' or 'very good'; they can characterize classes as 'typical fourth years'. 'timid first years', 'nice reception classes'; they can report '4B is as unruly as usual', 'nothing happened all morning', or a whole day as having been 'bloody awful'.

In finding and reporting on their world in these ways, in doing things routinely and unproblematically, teachers can display themselves as 'ordinary teachers', as doing 'ordinary teaching'. If they are unable to present themselves that way, if they do have great anxieties about the consti-

Introduction

tuent elements of an ordinary day's teaching, then they are unlikely to be teachers for very long.

In this book it is our intention to focus upon the routine, the taken-for-granted, the seen-but-unnoticed elements and aspects of ordinary teaching. Whereas studies of teachers and teaching all too frequently tend to gloss over these routine mundane features in their constant orientation to wider educational issues, we have made them the very focus of our scrutiny. We have done so because we believe there is a great deal to be discovered about the activity of teaching from detailed investigation. Somehow, we have to get behind the sweeping generalizations, the broad glosses, and see how things work in detail and on a day to day basis.

The fact of the matter is that whatever else may happen in schools, whatever far-reaching or revolutionary educational issues may be exhibited or addressed there, the routine, mundane practical activities are fundamental. For teachers and pupils in schools the mundane is inescapable; whatever else may be going on, whatever else may be consequential for wider educational matters, the mundane makes up most of what goes on day by day. In our opinion, study of the accomplishment of the mundane can often illuminate aspects of wider educational concerns in unexpected ways. Most of the researches reported in this book have been selected to give some substance to this view.

Ethnomethodology: a way of studying the everyday world

To make the routine, the unnoticed, the taken-for-granted aspects of the social world the focus of study is not a particularly new idea. Schutz advocated it some 50 years ago, Garfinkel demonstrated how it can be empirically explored around 20 years ago, and since then a growing collection of sociologists has produced a wide range of research material in that area. The sociological studies into this aspect of social life are broadly characterizable as 'ethnomethodology'. Readers should not be put off by this title. Just as ethnobotany is merely the study of the methods botanists use in working in their field, so ethnomethodology is no more than a label coined by Garfinkel (1968) to describe the study of the methods or methodology that people use in taken-for-granted ways to find the obvious sense, the unproblematic features, of day to day living in society. Briefly, ethnomethodology is the study of 'people's methods'.

The characteristics of the approach as a strategy for research include an assumption that the social world is a continuously achieved reality. As we have already noted, work on the part of those who live in and through the social world is required to make it what it is. People have to create their social world through their activities. Thus, just as presenting oneself as ordinary, or finding others as ordinary, requires work, so does any other routine and taken-for-granted activity such as telling stories, cracking jokes, being

Introduction

boring, reprimanding, praising, insulting and so on. Further it is assumed that the work is methodical work, i.e. it involves the employment of general practices, procedures or methods which any competent member of society uses to achieve these activities; and in achieving them he is simultaneously displaying this competence.

Members of society use these methodic practices unthinkingly and in taken-for-granted ways. Yet just as a proficient speaker of English may well not be able to describe this achievement in any technical detail, similarly members of society are unlikely to be able to outline the mechanics of what they are doing as they live out their daily lives. As analysts of the social world, it is our task to uncover the methodic practices by which members of society shape up and live through their everyday activities.

The task is complicated by the fact that although we can talk of 'practices' and 'social activities' as if they were separate 'parts' of social life, in reality they are not so easily separable. Thus members of society have to use methods to produce activities; but these methods are only visible through the activities. Further, the analyst has himself to utilize the very same methods of making sense of the world which he is also attempting to study. Exactly how these seeming methodological paradoxes can be tackled is a major interest for ethnomethodology in general and for this book in particular. Detailed examples and illustrations will follow in subsequent chapters. In this Introduction we simply wish to underline a few key theoretical points which can give guidance towards a fuller understanding of some practical applications in everyday teaching situations.

One such key theoretical point stems from the frequent reference to 'members' of society which we have already made. Ethnomethodologists use the concept of 'member' instead of 'actor' intentionally. Through their use of that concept they are invoking the traditional sociological concept of culture in that to be a member is to be thoroughly familiar with the concepts and beliefs which constitute what 'anyone' in a particular society should know about the social world. Membership involves seeing the social world as a 'factual reality' which is seen and experienced the same way by everyone. Should it happen that someone does not appear to see what everyone else does, members scrutinize him for what is wrong with him rather than doubt their own sense of the social world. Importantly, however, the notion of membership goes beyond that of culture in that it emphasizes that the common stocks of common sense knowledge, the concepts and beliefs about the social world, have to be *used* by people and they have to be used in ways that others can see as appropriate. One's membership is something that is continuously being demonstrated in everyday living through producing appropriate behaviour and activities which indicate to others that common factual realities are being seen.

Another key theoretical point that we wish to express here is that common sense knowledge is not literally what everyone knows. Rather, it is what 'everyone knows' in a particular context or milieu. Thus there is some stock of knowledge which is shared by all in a particular culture; other stocks of knowledge may not be so widely disseminated, as in the case of our interest, the teaching profession. What makes such stocks of knowledge 'common sense' is simply that anyone professing to be a member of the context, professional milieu or whatever has to know and be able to operate with such knowledge in quite taken-for-granted, unconscious ways. Not to do so is to be identified as a 'stranger', a 'foreigner', an 'outsider' and, worse, a 'spy', and 'imposter', 'losing one's grip' and so on. Thus an outstanding feature of common sense knowledge is its normative character, i.e. it entails notions of propriety, of what persons ought to know, ought to be, and ought to do. There can be penalties for not appropriately displaying the common sense knowledge of a context, i.e. displaying what is obvious, what should be taken-for-granted in that context.

The taken-for-granted status of common sense knowledge and the uses members make of it is in no way irretrievable. We can be made aware of what routinely goes unnoticed and that is precisely what ethnomethodological studies take on as their research concern. They are interested in exploring common sense knowledge to uncover its content, organization, and practical usages by members in society, i.e. they seek to describe members' methods of organizing and bringing off their social world.

The usual (but not only) research strategy employed to this end is to focus upon the talk that people produce as they accomplish their activities. The basis for this strategy is the assumption that the common understandings and routine accomplishments of practical activities are largely brought about through language. It is through members' use of language that social phenomena, activities and settings are seen to be accomplished and constituted. As members are assumed to put together social occasions and activities in, by, and through their talk, it follows that the organization of that talk can be worthwhile material for analysing the methodic production and achievement of the social world. Studying the naturally occurring talk produced in schools is one fruitful way into an exploration of teachers' and pupils' routinely taken-for-granted practical reasoning and common sense knowledge.

Generalising from research

Readers will find that many of the studies reported in this book are based on materials collected from a single classroom, or one particular school, or an individual teacher. We are aware of the view that generalizations cannot be made from such single instances, but vigorously deny the validity of such a claim. The argument really hinges on the nature of the generalizations being sought. Statistical generalizations require the study of many situations, which have to be reduced and simplified to make them amenable to numerical manipulation. Not surprisingly, the validity of the results is very often queried because it is frequently difficult, often impossible, to relate them to what actually happens at the 'nitty-gritty' level of everyday life. Consider, for example, the considerable debate around the reported results of Rosenthal and Jacobson's study, *Pygmalion in the Classroom*, and, more recently, over Bennett's *Teaching Styles and Pupil Progress*. Unfortunately, generalizations from the basis of a statistical methodology appear to enjoy a high status in educational research even to the extent that their problematic features are frequently overlooked. As we have suggested, their main problematic feature is in simplifying and reducing the social world to manipulable proportions, yet still wanting to generalize about it in terms of the detail it has had to jettison.

Fortunately, statistical generalizations are not the only form available to researchers and analysts. Neither are they always the most appropriate path to knowledge. For example, if we want to know something about the structure of a language, an hour spent talking to a Navajo Indian would tell us more than all the statistical counts and surveys of the Indian population. Thus generalizations can have a structural form, such as those standardly produced by linguists. Linguists have generally argued that the use and structure of language observed in a small corpus of utterances can be validly generalized to the entire language and in some cases even to all languages. The nature of the generalizations that ethnomethodological analysis can provide is somewhat similar. Any individual member has, through his membership, a repertoire of methods for making that membership observable to others. How these methods are displayed and put together in any one particular occasion will of course be contingent to that occasion, but it is assumed that the appropriateness of activities therein produced will be recognized by others through similarly organised methodic practices and procedures. It is then the methodic procedures which are generalizable.

What should be strikingly distinctive about any generalizations made available in the studies reported in this collection is their embeddedness in the taken-for-granted routine activities of ordinary teaching. They are integral features of a teacher's common sense knowledge about classrooms, teaching, schools and society. The researchers have sought to emphasize the methodic accomplishment of what the teachers and pupils, as members participating in their routine daily lives, consider as simply doing what they obviously have to do, i.e. what 'any' teacher and 'any' pupils would do. In orienting to what they do in that way, they are operating as members who have no need to attend to producing a description of the organization of their routine practices. It is for us as analysts to bring out in fine detail the members' methods and organization of their everyday teaching activities. The analyses presented in this book attempt to do so. It is in that sense they

Introduction

are ethnomethodological; they are interested in the aspects of teaching which are clearly constituent elements of doing ordinary teaching, but which routinely go 'unnoticed'. Most other kinds of studies of teaching do not regard these aspects as 'newsworthy', preferring to study the occasional 'epic' item rather than the wealth of everyday materials.

The practical nature of our researches

Although we have taken some trouble to outline some key theoretical points, we wish to emphasise that the studies in this collection have not been brought together out of some idle curiosity in the taken-for-granted, nor out of some desire to satisfy an idealistic notion to try to extend the frontiers of knowledge just for the sake of doing so. Rather, we believe that each contribution has something to say which can be of practical relevance to teachers.

In the past, ethnomethodology has been criticized on a number of grounds. It is not our task here to take up such criticisms save to say two things. First, in social science there is altogether too much theoretical debate, too little meaningful empirical study. Secondly, work in social science, largely as a consequence, seems to have little practical relevance to the real world. We claim that the studies in this book are both theoretically relevant and empirically directed, thereby avoiding the extremist dangers of sterile theory and 'dustbowl empiricism'. These studies, by giving detailed and careful attention to some of the seen-but-unnoticed aspects of teaching, can help both to develop a greater understanding of what is happening in our classrooms, and also to contribute to the improvement of teaching performances.

We are making strong claims and our readers will have to evaluate them through their consideration of the studies in relation to their own practical experience. They are nevertheless claims we make with serious conviction.

The practicality of what we have to say should not, however, be oversimplified. As we know only too well, telling is not doing. Thus simply telling student teachers over a period of one, three or even four years of a course in teacher training how to teach, or how to control a class, or how to maintain the interest of a class, does not ensure that they will be able to do those things or display those skills when actually involved in the activity of teaching. In drawing out the practical implications involved in the various contributions, we are not advocating a set of cook-book recipes; the outcomes cannot simply be lifted out of context and mechanically applied. Of course, it is open to anyone to try them out, and if they do result in an improved performance all well and good. It would, however, be more in keeping with our intentions and would indicate a more sophisticated understanding of classroom skills if the practical implications are seen as possibilities, as initial suggestions on the part of observers and analysts. Certainly it is hoped that they are seen as

Introduction

fruitful possibilities. Taken together they are meant to be seen as illustrations of how practical possibilities for improving teaching performances can arise from tape recording and analysing one's own teaching and from listening to what teachers and pupils actually say.

Teachers as researchers

What provides the most exciting potential is the fact that the kinds of analyses presented here are accessible to the ordinary teacher. Students and teachers alike can begin from where they are now. They can begin to tape record their own performances and make observations on them. They do not have to be statisticians nor do they require elaborate equipment. They do not have to spend long periods of time collecting data nor become trained in sampling theory or the techniques of questionnaire production and interviewing. What they will have to develop, if they do not already possess it, is an attitude of mind. That attitude of mind requires them to suspend their unthinking reliance on the common sense knowledge of teaching and to make their routine practice anthropologically strange. This procedure of viewing routine practices and unproblematic sense as unfamiliar is a strategy all our contributors have employed in the production of their analyses. Some ingenuity is required to make visible and analysable the taken-for-granted, the seen-but-unnoticed features of our everyday life.

The studies reported here show some exercise of this ingenuity. They range across a wide variety of teaching situations – from infant, junior and secondary schools to higher education. They analyse such routine activities as dealing with a pupil who comes late to a lesson, handling a collection of pupils as a class, telling a story, listening to pupils read, organizing the use of space in an open plan school, talking to adolescents about school and about themselves, and starting the day in an infant classroom.

In each chapter the authors have drawn out some practical implications of their analyses of the usually taken-for-granted features of doing teaching. Readers may well be able to see additional or alternative practical possibilities; it is hoped that they will. For that reason we supply as much as possible of the transcriptions usually used as the 'raw data' for the analyses. Further, the analyses themselves are not curtailed, but reproduced as fully as possible. Through the presentation of the transcription and analyses in full, readers can become aware of the rich potential of this kind of research. We are not in the business of producing findings, conclusions and implications divorced from both the analytical work and the raw materials which can generate them, and Digby Anderson's contribution makes this methodological point in some depth. He outlines in clear and practical terms how teachers may set about studying their own practices and performances. It is there, perhaps, that the central purpose of this book lies. So often teachers are urged to become their own researchers, but they are given little or no practical advice on fulfilling that aim. With this collection, we have set out to indicate to teachers the availability of a particular research strategy, to provide a wide range of illustrative examples of the practical implications and possibilities generated by that strategy, and to offer some down to earth advice on how to get involved in the work straight away. We would be delighted to hear from readers on how they get on.

PART ONE

Familiar Teaching Routines in their Context: The Primary School

Introduction

Telling stories, assessing children's reading ability and organizing the space in school are unquestionably routine activities for a primary school teacher. In infant schools a story is told by the teacher most days; it is part of the taken-for-granted daily routine. Similarly hearing children read is a daily activity for most teachers of the young. And in any primary school the space has to be organized and teachers routinely manage that organization day in, day out. This problem becomes particularly noticeable in an open-plan school such as the one we study in Chapter 4.

In Chapter 2 Dave Hustler and Ted Cuff consider the activity of storytelling. The authors begin by giving the transcript to some colleagues, asking them to comment as professionals on the teaching represented. Readers too might find it useful to make their own comments about the quality of teaching represented by the transcript before proceeding further with the chapter, which contrasts the 'professionals' ' accounts with those of the authors. The authors suggest that the 'ethnomethodological' account they have produced makes visible and accessible certain happenings and issues which the professional accounts tend to obscure and *vice versa*. Specifically, they look at that part of story time which follows the telling of the story when the teacher is checking out the children's understanding and encouraging them to talk about themselves and what they have heard. They show how collaborative interactional skills involved in producing stories are largely everyday conversational skills and imply that children are probably much more competent then teachers generally recognize. In fact, they suggest that the routine organization of story-time can restrict the development of 'everyday' abilities and, in so doing, might even generate resources for the construction of inappropriate educational identities.

In Chapter 3, James Heap considers how routine classroom practices employed by teachers in their assessment of reading comprehension can be self-defeating if too much weight is placed on specific approaches. Broadly,

Introduction

he argues that it is methodologically impossible for anybody to assess with certainty a pupil's skills in reading comprehension because of the inevitable problems inherent in the social organization of any classroom test of understanding. His analysis is generated out of materials from seven classrooms of 5–7 year olds in inner city schools in Canada. Through an extended example he shows how the organization and sequence of a teacher's utterances can produce 'misunderstandings' which may be interpreted as lack of ability. But the principled reasons go much deeper. Once aware of the nature of these reasons it becomes clear that a variety of assessment formats are advisable and that teachers in the classroom are in a better position than administrators or external experts to make valid judgements about children's reading skill.

In Chapter 4, Graham Hitchcock takes us into an open-plan primary school and studies the seen-but-unnoticed ways in which spatial arrangements of a school without classrooms are organized. His analysis comes out of eighteen months of participating in the daily life of the school. He describes the sorts of problems the spatial organization of an open-plan school generate for the teachers and how they and the pupils have evolved ways of getting around both these problems and the school. In fact, they create their own 'walls' or boundaries from the mundane objects available to them and the author shows how these boundaries are used to accomplish the routines of everyday life in the school. In 'normalizing' these routines, the whole question of employing suitable categories is vital and the author explores in some depth how teachers and pupils categorize, thereby making sense of, the social world of the school.

It is generally recognized that teachers are very much aware of the gaps between theory and practice in education and the teachers in the open-plan school appear to be no different in this respect. For the procedures and practices they develop for dealing with their daily teaching involve a translation of professional ideologies and academic theories into practical possibilities. Often the process of translation amounts to a subversion of the intended ethos of open-plan schooling. The author concludes that the accomplishment of routine teaching in an open-plan primary school presents an inevitable professional contradiction which can only disappear when our conventional wisdoms about classroom practices are jettisoned.

2 Telling a story: teacher and pupil competence in an infant classroom

Dave Hustler and Ted Cuff

I

Woven into the school day for every child in almost every infant school is an occasion usually known as 'story-time'. This occasion nearly always involves the teacher in telling or reading a story, which may be preceded and followed by some story-related activity.

Not only is story-time often the final event of the day for many schools, it is also one of the few times when teachers gather together their children as a class. Story-time, then, is both a scheduled activity and also a somewhat distinctive one in comparison with the individualized and group-based activities making up the rest of the school day. For readers whose experience of education lies elsewhere, story-time may thus seem a more familiar part of a school timetable than other parts of the infant day. It should also be noted that for the children themselves, story-time provides an experience of a teacher-class relationship which will become increasingly familiar as they move through the school system.

For some time we have been studying from a broadly sociological orientation the interactional organisation of the everyday world, i.e. ordinary settings in social life. Story-time in an infant classroom is such a setting and our transcription* represents one of a number which have been recorded for study.

The manner in which we have made use of this particular transcript however, differs from our usual practice. We made the transcript available to some colleagues who have considerable expertise in teaching infant children and in the training of others to become infant teachers. These fellow lecturers were asked to give their professional views in the space of 2–3 sides of paper. Six responses were forthcoming (Cuff, ed., 1979).

---

* The transcription is printed at the end of this chapter, beginning on p. 31. For a key to the symbols used in transcription throughout the book, see p. ix.

Telling a Story

In this chapter, we shall outline some of the features of these six responses and shall also add a seventh response in terms of how we see the story materials from our own stance. It is hoped that this procedure will enable readers to make ready comparisons and thereby to be able to recognize clearly the distinctive character of our own approach. At this stage, however, we strongly press readers to study the transcript and actively respond to it with written comments, if possible, before proceeding to read the description of our responses. The only orientation which we would like to prescribe for this exercise is that the reader should at least in part be concerned as to whether good or bad teaching is taking place. We suggest that this preliminary work will prove rewarding by making for a more informed, critical and, hence, livelier reading of what follows.

II

We now look at some of the features of the six responses to the transcription. At the outset, we wish to be quite clear that this presentation has neither critical nor ironic content or intention. We have no interest in criticizing the responses in any attempt to arrive at some more 'reliable' and 'valid' description of reality. We have no means of saying what is 'really' happening, or what the children or the teacher are 'really' like. Rather, we regard these responses as 'accounts'. As such, they make sense of the transcription through the very process of reporting on it and any comments produced by the reader can be viewed as accounts in similar fashion. Our interest lies in examining these accounts as presentations of professionals' common sense knowledge about everyday teaching situations.

For five of the six responses, the main connecting thread is the question of whether or not good or bad teaching is taking place. More accurately, this thread is not so much a question, but rather an observation made quite effortlessly. For these respondents, their extensive professional experience enables them to see what is happening 'at a glance'. Now it is far from easy to specify in detail the exact nature of good or bad teaching. By contrast, the recognition (as opposed to the description) of good or bad teaching can be accomplished quite readily, as can be seen in these five responses.

This focus on good or bad teaching struck us as worthwhile to pursue, since 'doing good teaching', presumably a difficult task for many, might benefit from a more detailed consideration of the observations of those who can most easily recognize it. From a content analysis of the five accounts we notice that in arriving at their assessments of teaching skill all five address three similar broad themes; teacher's competence, children's competence and attitudes, and purposes of story-time. The sixth response gives a rather different account of the story materials and we shall return to that later.

The Primary School
The Themes
A TEACHER COMPETENCE/INCOMPETENCE

Throughout the five responses there are several observations concerning the teacher's competence, or usually incompetence, in terms of the choice of story, the telling of the story and the follow-up work. Below we give some indication of the nature of these observations by presenting selected extracts. These extracts are examples only and it is in no way intended that they should be taken as complete coverage of the respondents' observations on this theme.

A(i) The choice of story
Respondent 2 for example, poses a question and rapidly answers it:

> Is this a good choice of story? – characteristics of good stories for infants. Yes – simple plot which can be related to children's experience. Possibilities of identification.

From Respondent 4 we find:

> The story is itself trivial and difficult to justify in terms of time and energy expended on it.

and, with reference to utterance 32:

> A very poor book/story. Ill chosen. The main intention is now revealed – the listener is to identify with the lonely donkey.

Respondent 5 concurs:

> In this case the entertainment for the children was short-lived as the story was very babyish with little content.

Also Respondent 3:

> I found the story to be trivial, to have a weak story-line, unconvincing characterization... .

A(ii) The telling of the story
Respondent 2 poses this question at the very beginning of the response and then answers it:

> Does the teacher tell the story well?
> Yes – the children are involved, few interrupted during the story itself. The depth of emotional response from some children suggests that they were stirred and touched by the story.

Respondent 4 does not agree:

> The teacher did not prepare the way for the story in such a manner as to rouse the children's interest

And with reference to utterance 32,

> appears to break the rules of story-telling – and something teachers normally avoid in order to maintain interest and the thread of the story – story-telling should be a series of magic moments uninterrupted by asides.

Respondent 5 is also critical:

> When the story got going there was little attack and the children soon lost interest. There were no visual or oral aids and so the story should have been told much more graphically. There should have been a word picture of the field with the little shed etc.

Respondent 1, with reference to utterance 37, says

> The children obviously wanted to join in here, and the teacher could have encouraged the children to describe Father Christmas and his sleigh.

A(iii) The follow-up work
Respondent 5 says:

> For the age of the children the pleasure of having company and the unhappiness of being without it could have been made ... but to ask the children in turn to give examples of loneliness was a mistake and led to disturbance. An experienced teacher would have passed on swiftly to another story... .

Respondent 4, with reference to utterances 79–106, says

> The questions and answers seem to be adding little of value.

And with reference to utterance 115:

> Paul's comments were the opening for a real discussion on loneliness perhaps? This opportunity was not seized and one doubts whether it could have been.

These observations on the choice and telling of the story and on the follow-up work all concern the readers' competence. They are inextricably linked to two other themes, B and C below, by these five respondents.

B CHILDREN'S COMPETENCE AND ATTITUDES
In large part, the nature of the teacher's competence is seen to revolve around the level of awareness of the needs, cognitive states and interests of infants. There are two strands here: the respondents make comments about what children of this age are like; and they make observations on particular children in the transcription. These two strands are commonly woven together in one sentence or paragraph in the text, together with observations

The Primary School

about what the teacher should or should not have done. For example, the extracts below illustrate this pattern.

Respondent 4, referring to utterance 115, says,

> At this stage (7) children are not deeply interested in other children's traumas. They are not at the stage of development where they can see things from another's point of view. If they believe the story – even if it is a case of suspended disbelief – then they are incapable of the level of thought required to deal with abstractions such as loneliness. Paul had, one imagines, an experience to relate, the relating of this would probably have been beneficial to him and informative for the teacher. But this was not the time to relate it – a dialogue would have been better.

Respondent 5 makes several points under this heading:

> Children of this age can take quite a long story – they enjoy a serial continued over several days. But they need something much more robust with pace and excitement and a strong story line.
> The intention seemed to be to discuss the problem of loneliness.
> The concept was beyond the children's comprehension.

And, with reference to utterances 64–66,

> The expectations of the modern child for Christmas presents were sadly underestimated.

Respondent 3 concurs with the previous views almost in the same terms:

> If the story were intended to stimulate discussion about loneliness it was ill chosen since the comprehension level required to appreciate the story would hardly match that required to discuss such a concept as loneliness. The transcript raised questions about the teacher's attitude to and understanding of children. How much did she know about children's cognitive development?

C   THE PURPOSES OF STORY-TIME
The third major theme on which five respondents concur consists of comments concerning what story-time is for, what its purposes are. The teacher's competence, or lack of it, is once more spotlighted, but now with reference to the ways in which this occasion did or did not relate to these purposes.

Thus Respondent 5 states:

> (Story-time) affords: 1. A period of entertainment, mutual enjoyment and relaxation for children and teacher ... . 2. An opportunity to develop

the children's language by listening and responding to good English ... .
3. A stimulus to the children's imagination and creativity.

And Respondent 4 says:

> The story provided so weak a base for questions, for developing understanding, for enlarging of horizons, for any of the purposes of storytime... .
> This transcript illustrates the pitfalls which are ahead of teachers who do not select material very carefully with specific objectives in mind. These might include:
> a) The revelation to children that their own experiences, problems, traumas, are not unique
> b) Exposure of children to the literary heritage of Western Civilization
> c) Extension of children's vocabularies ... (there follows a further seven objectives)

As we have noted the five respondents interrelate themes A, B and C with a central focus on teacher competence. This focus, however, is directed at the specific teacher in the setting of the transcript. Teacher competence is not addressed as a general and problematic issue. Rather, items from the transcript, together with comments on what we know about infants and the purposes of story-time, are used to document the observations about this teacher.

The sixth response differs from the others. It begins by commenting on the methodological shortcomings of transcripts and then gives an account of the transcript in five sections: affective development, cognitive development, moral development, language, and learning. The focus is on children's competencies in these areas and the major theme concerns how the transcript relates to the work of various researchers and theoreticians, including Piaget, Bruner, Kohlberg and Vygotsky. The account also involves discussion more directly on teacher competence, e.g.

> These examples suggest that the concept of loneliness has not been fully grasped by these children, but concept formation is a slow developmental process, and acceptance of the idea of a 'spiral curriculum' (Bruner) suggests that the approach adopted by the teacher is the correct one. If children are to understand 'loneliness' their understanding must start at a very concrete level with incidents and experiences that they can grasp. Perhaps it is inevitable, therefore, that 'lonely' is synonymous with 'alone' at this stage. A deeper, more adequate understanding may emerge when this concept is returned to at a more advanced level, but it can be argued that for the moment the teacher is introducing it in a way which is appropriate to the children's present level of thinking (i.e. in relation to concrete experiences of aloneness).

The Primary School

One striking feature of this viewpoint is the careful and qualified nature of the comments, e.g. 'can be argued that', 'suggests' etc. The contrast with the accounts of the other five respondents is sharp. This contrast highlights one of the outstanding and recurring problems for teacher education: the theory-practice debate. For students and teachers concerned to improve their teaching, the problem is acute. At times, it can boil down to deciding who is worth listening to: those who confidently know what teaching is about and who can easily recognise good and bad teaching on the basis of their own practical experience; or those whose starting point is seen to lie in theoretical debates.

On our reading of the first five accounts, we see their authority derive from the underlying knowledge of who is producing them. They are produced by teachers with extensive experience of infants and of infant schools. The authority underpinning the sixth account is somewhat different. It derives from a command of a body of literature which can be used to re-describe practical situations in theoretical terms. Here the practical aspects of the setting are seen to be of much less significance than the theories themselves.

Another interesting slant on this question of authority and the nature of professional expertise comes from a closer examination of the three major themes, A, B and C, which we examined above. When stripped of their infant context and generalized as in the second column below, we obtain a message which many experienced teachers might regard as essential, viz:

The Themes	The Themes Generalized
A (i) The teacher's choice of story	The teacher's choice of materials, subject matter
A (ii) The teacher's telling of the story	Presentation of materials, subject matter etc.
(iii) The follow-up work	ditto
B The teacher's awareness of what infants are like in general	Awareness of pupils' stage of development, attributes at that age
The teacher's awareness of particular children – their needs, problems etc.	Awareness of particular pupils in the class, etc.
C Teacher's awareness of and specification of the purposes and story-time.	Knowledge of and specification of particular aims, objectives, purposes of a lesson.

The right hand column gives a list which can be read as indicating what any professional knows are the essential dimensions of teaching. Further, these dimensions are relevant in *all* teaching contexts. In the left hand column, we

Telling a Story

have a concrete display of these dimensions in terms of what any professional in the context of the infant school knows is important for good teaching to take place in story-time.

What we hope to have made clear so far is how a given body of materials – story-time in an infant classroom – can be described and made visible by these six accounts. The construction of these accounts displays something in the nature of professional expertise by showing what expertise looks like not merely as a claim, but as a practice. That is to say, we can see what professional expertise looks like in practice through the appraisals of the story materials. As the professional concerns and expertise differ, so does the nature of the accounts and also the practical possibilities for improving teaching.

A question we cannot answer, but which is of relevance here, concerns how any account produced by readers of this book relates to the responses we have described. We did argue that 'doing good teaching' might benefit from the observations of those who can easily recognize it, given their extensive professional experience of the particular settings involved. For readers who did perceive good or bad teaching as taking place, one natural line to pursue is the straightforward comparison of accounts. This can be done in terms of both the concrete details of the accounts and the dimensions which played a part in arriving at recognition of competence or incompetence. We would argue, however, that accounts which focus throughout on the quality of the teaching performance serve not only to make visible what is happening in fruitful ways, they also systematically render certain happenings and issues more inaccessible.

In the next section we attempt to make visible what is happening in the infant classroom by producing yet another account. This account derives from ethnomethodological research and, from close analysis of the talk, tries to show how the everyday setting, story-time-in-an-infant-classroom, is brought about by the activities of the relevant parties. Of course, these everyday settings are so extremely mundane and ordinary that we, as analysts, have somehow to make them 'anthropologically strange' in order to uncover their workings and organization.

Our account differs from the six we have just examined in refraining from taking a critical or ironic or corrective attitude to the materials. Such an attitude would be inappropriate as we have neither a long-standing professional commitment to infant schools, nor do we have an investment in highly developed psychological theories on the nature of children and their cognitive development. Neither do we wish to take the teacher's view or the children's view. Instead, we wish to show how the talk works, how the talk is organised, in our classroom setting. We do so by focussing on certain structures of talk which can be found in the story materials. Although we do not lose sight of the nature of the setting – the identities of its parties, their

The Primary School

purposes, their location, and so on – we concentrate particularly on these structures.

III

Our account derives from work on the organization of natural conversation initiated and developed by Harvey Sacks. In the broadest terms, he was concerned to describe how members of society interactionally collaborate to produce any particular occasion, event or setting, e.g. a conversation about X, a debate on Y, a radio programme on Z. He pursued this study of the 'sense assembly procedures' of members of society by examining transcriptions of talk in 'natural' settings such as our own story materials, i.e. settings which are not a product of contrivance, experiment or ingenuity, but, rather, represent routine and mundane everyday activities of ordinary members of society.

For Sacks, (1972; and unpubl. lectures esp. 1970–1972), 'stories' in natural conversation are best approached in terms of their functions in talk. Thus, a speaker may wish to talk at length about something he has done, heard, or knows. To talk at length, he requires to secure both the cooperation and attention of the other parties to the talk in order to avoid interruption until he has finished what he has to say. In more technical terms, there are questions of possible completion points and speaker-change and such matters are vital not only for stories, but also for much wider considerations of turn-allocation in the organization of talk (Sacks et al 1974). Here, we focus on those stretches of talk which both member and analyst alike can recognize as 'stories' and Sacks (1970) suggested that they have an interactional structure, which we schematize as follows:

(a) STORY-PREFACE   e.g. A Something terrible happened on
    (REQUEST)   the way here
(b) ACCEPTANCE   e.g. B Oh dear, what?
(c) STORY   e.g. A ((A tells what happened))
(d) HEARING/SECOND   e.g. B Oh, that's terrible ((and B may go
    STORY   on to tell a similar story))

To clarify, a prospective story-teller uses the story preface (a) in order to seek permission to tell about something that has happened, i.e. to tell a story involving what may well be a lengthy piece of talk. The story-preface also indicates the kind of story it will be and what its ending (the possible completion point) might look like. Thus in our example, hearers may wait until they know that something terrible has happened. The story-preface therefore also indicates what an appropriate hearing will look like. If the request embodied in the story preface is accepted (b) and not declined, diverted, avoided, then speaker A can embark on his story (c). Although others may properly speak in the course of the story (e.g. to produce 'continuers' like 'Hmmm', 'Yes', 'I

Telling a Story

see' etc., or 'clarifiers' like 'he did what', 'pardon' etc), such interventions need not come off as 'interruptions' or 'subversions' if hearers continue to honour the story acceptance (b) by returning the conversational floor to the story teller to continue his story. Finally, hearers are interactionally required to monitor the story in order to take up the talk when its completion is reached, i.e. to discover an appropriate completion and speaker-transition point – see (d). As we have noted, the materials of the story preface can provide a useful resource for this purpose.

Simply to take up the talk at an appropriate place and to repeat the materials of the story preface might indicate minimal listening, i.e. hearers have been monitoring the story sufficiently only to recognize a possible completion point. Interactionally, hearers can display interest, involvement and close attention by producing further stories which build on the one they have just heard. Sacks called these further stories 'second stories' and gave several reasons for their strong interactional relationships. 'First stories' can be found to provide basic resources for the production of 'second stories'. Not only do they appear to stimulate and organize the memories of hearers, they also provide structural models for the production of 'second stories'. For example, the relation of tellers to events and activities in 'second stories' tends to resemble that initially presented in the 'first story'. A party to the talk can strongly display his close attention to and understanding of the 'first story' through his construction of an appropriate 'second story'. Moreover, a 'first story' often generates a 'round' of stories in multi-party conversation; and the stories in the round which have been touched off by the 'first story' have in common these topical and structural features.

We can now return to our story materials. It is useful and convenient to present them as being in three stages:

Story-time
   Stage 1 Pre-story period.   Build up to the story, utterances 1–23
   Stage 2 The story   The teacher tells the story about the lonely donkey, utterances 24–76
   Stage 3 Post-story   The teacher asks (utterance 79) 'Have you ever felt lonely' and teacher-pupil talk ensues.

On the face of it, the materials in stage 3 appear to reflect some of the features of stories as outlined by Sacks. For example, there is a round of stories; there is topical coherence (loneliness); and there is structural similarity (the relationship of each teller to these activities) within the round of stories. Not much effort is required, however, to reveal major differences from Sacks's analysis of stories in natural conversation.

One obvious basis for differences is given by the nature of the setting, 'story-time-in-an-infant-classroom'. For in such a setting, some or all of the

The Primary School

parties are aware of and orient to the fact that there is an 'agenda' to be got through, i.e. there is a story to be told and all that it entails on such occasions. Further, there is a specified time in which to do the activity entailed by the agenda, i.e. the time before going home. Finally, there is the knowledge that someone is assigned to steer and control this agenda, namely the teacher. Secondly, the talk is partitioned between speakers so that alternate slots are occupied by teacher and pupil respectively. Furthermore, next-speaker is usually, although not invariably, selected by the teacher. There are no examples in the transcription of publicly available, i.e. 'classroom', talk being conducted between the children.

In view of these differences, there can be no straightforward application of Sacks's analysis. For example, the teacher's long story about the lonely donkey does not produce from the pupils any volunteering of 'second stories'. Nor does the teacher appear to expect her story to have this effect for she goes on immediately to ask (in utterance 79), 'Have you every felt lonely have you ever felt lonely' and then, after a chorus of apparently affirmative responses, the talk continues with what appears to be a different organization for the production of stories, i.e.

(a) STORY INVITATION	82 T	When did you feel lonely Colin
(b) STORY-ACCEPTANCE AND STORY TOLD	83 C	Uhm ... we went out one day ... ... and I stayed in the tent.
(c) HEARING AND CLOSING OF STORY	86 T	You stayed in the tent on your own – and then you felt lonely.
(d) STORY INVITATION (for new teller)	88 T	Yes (Sarah) when did you feel lonely

This pattern appears to persist through a round of stories in which the children respond to the invitation to tell about when they felt lonely.

We can contrast this pattern with the one we outlined from Sacks's work above. The pattern here seems to exemplify a class of stories found in natural conversation which has been termed 'invited stories' in research by Cuff and Francis (1978) into the talk of persons invited to tell the story of their marriage breakdown. Their 'invited' stories differ from 'volunteered' stories in terms of the organization and functions of turns to talk. They also differ in terms of some important interactional features. First, the teller (or, rather, invited teller) may not be as ready, willing or able to produce a story at the request of the inviter as someone who has remembered and wishes to volunteer a story at that place in the talk. Secondly, in trying adequately to fulfil the terms of the inviter's request, the teller of an invited story may have difficulties in knowing exactly what these terms are, how they might be achieved

Telling a Story

and when 'enough' has been produced. Thus the teller might offer only a possible closing and the onus of finding it adequate might be regarded as the responsibility of the inviter. For example, the inviter can seek to extend the story by asking for more detail, clarification etc. Although such interactional work can and does occur in 'volunteered' stories, all sorts of interactional troubles can result insofar as such probings can more readily be seen as impugning, subverting or undercutting both the story and the character of the teller. As we have indicated, such interactional troubles can be avoided by demonstrating both understanding and agreement or sympathy by means of an appropriate second story, but this method might not be available for an inviter who is seeking to generate a round of invited stories.

We now turn to our materials to examine these points in relation to stage 3 (utterances 79–127), i.e. when the teacher has finished her story about the lonely donkey and moves into eliciting talk from her pupils. She cannot be confident that they have available a story about feeling lonely, but her question, 'Have you ever felt lonely have you ever felt lonely', serves to produce a number of affirmative responses from the children. These responses can be used to indicate the availability of a pool of possible story-tellers about this experience. We note, however, that the brevity of most of the children's responses to the invitation seems more to resemble 'answering a question' than 'telling a story'. Of course, such a characterization cannot be ruled out as 'incorrect'; but it gives less analytical purchase on the materials and is therefore less useful. For a 'story' does not simply consist of what the child produces. Rather, in terms of describing the organization of talk, a 'story' is made up of the linked sequences of utterances of inviter-teller-inviter, and this pattern can itself be taken as a 'natural unit' of talk. Its shape, the fact that it has a beginning, a middle and an end, is manifestly generated by the interactional collaboration of the parties involved. It is a unit of talk which demarcates who can properly talk and who should properly await a suitable completion point before gaining the right to hold the conversational floor. Further, a story can itself be seen to be incorporated into an even wider organization of talk, namely, a 'round' of stories (Sacks, 1970; Atkinson et al 1978). Such an organization of talk has to be interactionally achieved by the parties concerned.

We can take up some aspects of this collaborative interaction through noting that of the stories in stage 3, only one story, the seventh, appears to produce what can be heard as a closing of the story, i.e. 127 Kevin ('N) I was lonely.

In the other stories, regardless of their length and complexity, it is the teacher who effectively produces a closing both in terms of providing a topical, relevant ending and also of effecting a change in speakers. She effects this change by reiterating the substance of her initial story invitation and by nominating next-speaker:

25

The Primary School

86/88	Colin's story	....and then you felt lonely ... . Yes (Sarah) when did you feel lonely
90/92	Sarah's story	and you felt lonely on your own what about you Wendy
104	Wendy's story	and you felt lonely – yes Melanie
109	Melanie's story	Oh I see — what about you Richard have you never been lost or felt lonely — never what about you Paul
124	Paul's story	and-that's-when-you-felt-lonely what about you Kevin

In this way, the teacher provides a possible story ending, thereby displaying her hearing that what the children have been saying is something which has appropriately met the terms of her invitation. An apparent exception in this round is her reply to Melanie which might indicate her inability (possibly as well the reader's inability) to follow it. We note, however, that even though she cannot apparently find it to be an *appropriate story* about being lonely, nevertheless she does seem to accept Melanie's production as being at least a *story*.

There are some further features of the utterances closing off each story which are of interest. We noted earlier that a potentially problematic issue in story-telling is achieving a completion, and that completions to 'invited' stories present different interactional requirements from completions to 'volunteered' stories. As completions, utterances like 'and then you felt lonely' are continuations of the talk in two senses: as linguistic constructions and as developments in a chain of events. In these ways, they are particularly economical devices. First, as leading to a proper possible completion. Secondly, they themselves provide a completion to an invited story. Finally, they provide continuations to a chain of events, by displaying monitoring and understanding of the previous talk. For such utterances do more than *claim* an understanding (as in 'Oh I see'); they go on to *demonstrate* understanding by their actual use of the previous materials (as in 86, 'You stayed in the tent on your own – and then you felt lonely').

We are suggesting, then, that it is useful to consider stage 3 as a round of invited stories and we draw attention to the economical features of teacher-initiated utterances which can serve not only to conclude a particular story, but also to help to signal the imminence of a next story in a continuing round of stories. Thus utterances like 'and-that's-when-you-felt-lonely, what about you Kevin' (124) simultaneously can (a) discharge these functions, (b) show understanding and (c) continue to constitute the occasion as a 'round of invited stories about loneliness'.

Although we note the economical nature of these productions, whose basic format is (i) 'and then you felt lonely' plus (ii) nomination of next-speaker, we must also draw attention to the fact that the teacher usually provides even more materials for the production of the stories. For example, Colin's offer of a closing (85 'and I stayed in the tent') is incorporated and extended in the teacher's closing and recycling to a new speaker (86 'You stayed in the tent on your own – and then you felt lonely'). Here, it appears that staying in a tent is not of relevance until it is made explicit that being on one's own is involved. Thus 'and then you felt lonely' serves as a continuation/completion to Colin's-story-as-developed-by-the-teacher. In short, the previous talk which is being brought to a completion and for which understanding is being displayed is, in part, the teacher's talk.

Considerations such as these lead us to suggest that at least the first six of the stories in stage 3 can be seen to display as an integral aspect of their production the feature that they are *joint-productions* in a very strong sense. Although clearly any story produced in natural conversation can reasonably be described as a joint-production because it has to be collaboratively achieved and also because it generates resources for subsequent talk, the stories in our materials accentuate this feature.

We suggest that potential problems for the teacher like, for example, 'agenda control' and 'topic control', are in part resolved by means of this feature of joint production. One story which amply illustrates the strong sense of joint-production which we have been discussing is 'Wendy's story':

92	T	What about you Wendy
93	Wendy	Well uh – I got lost // (one day)
94	C	Kathy
95	T	Yes
96	Wendy	and uh — and — I can't remember (the rest)
97	T	You got lost did w— were you going shopping
98	Wendy	Uhm – yes I (was with) Mummy ( ) a— a— no I wasn't going shopping with ( ) and uh she uhm she was in the shop and I went down and no she wasn't in the shop
99	C	hahhhh
100	Wendy	and I went and looked in the shop and she wasn't there ( ) and she (caught) up ( )
101	C	hahhhhh
102	T	and did you think for a moment you'd been left on your own
103	Wendy	Y(hhh)es
104	T	and you felt lonely — Yes Melanie

Here the teacher undertakes fairly extensive interactional work by way of continuers/questions to assist in the generation of talk which is recognizable both as a story and as an appropriate story. It can be argued that the joint-production of this story is not only a consequential feature of the 'invited story' format, but it is also a necessary feature, given Wendy's 'inadequacies' as a competent story-teller. However, some care must be exercized in making such a judgement. Competence in terms of talk-production is very much a contextual matter. Hearings of utterances are made in terms of their location in the on-going talk, in the immediate particulars of the sequential organization of the talk. Hearings are also made, however, in terms of more general orientations to the talk, deriving from the parties' background knowledge and experience concerning what the setting is and should be. In making this point, we are reinvoking the occasioned nature of the talk in our materials. The talk does not simply occur 'in' story-time, but, in occurring, is part-and-parcel of what we mean and understand by 'story-time'. Certainly, in our account of the materials, story-time is what happens, not what we feel ought to happen.

Wendy's 'Well uh — I got lost // (one day)' (utterance 93) can be heard to be thematically relevant since being lost is presumably a good basis for the possibility of feeling lonely. It rapidly becomes clear, however, that for the teacher at least, her utterance is insufficient and, we would argue, its insufficiency lies in its not being recognizable as an 'adequate' story, i.e. it does not give as an account a sequence of events culminating in getting lost. In short, it not only fails to be an 'adequate' story, it is not even a recognizable story (Sacks, 1972), although elsewhere it might be adequate as a story preface and here it might be adequate as an answer to a question. Its inadequacy, therefore, appears to stem from its inappropriateness as a recognizable story in response to an invitation to tell such a story. Of course, the teacher *could* continue and complete with 'and you felt lonely' and it is not difficult to imagine circumstances which might warrant such action for herself, e.g. her identification of Wendy as a 'very shy child', as 'someone who has done well to produce even that talk' etc. In fact, in our materials she goes on to invoke the sort of common sense knowledge that an adult can employ to find the sort of situation in which a six-year-old child could get lost. In other words, the teacher provides, as a possible prompt, an example of what Wendy is required to do: locate the sequence of events leading to being lost and thus produce a story. The fact that the teacher's utterance 97 ('You got lost did w— were you going shopping') seems to provide Wendy with problems should not prevent us from noting that in her next utterance, although parts are untranscribable, the pupil seems to be trying to construct a sequence of events appropriate for a story about getting lost.

Wendy's story can be interestingly contrasted with a later story in this round of invited stories, namely, the one produced by Paul (utterances 111–123). It may be that the materials of Paul's story seem largely irrelevant in relation to the teacher's invitation, whereas, as we have noted, Wendy's first utterance has strong topical coherence. Yet Paul clearly recognizes that a story is called for and he is also able to keep it going by building up an extending sequence of events, culminating in a proffered candidate for conclusion and completion. We further note that he is able to include within this sequence of events a story funny enough to evoke a response from his peers and that this funny story seems to have been touched off by the talk of a previous child about ice-cream. In addition, we can speculate about the dual directionality of his talk in that he appears to be addressing *two* audiences, his peers and the teacher. The central feature of Paul's talk is that he can construct stories. Story-time has as one of its routinely possible occurrences a time within it for the production of such stories by the children. That certain of these stories seem to us as hearers to have minimal bearing on the themes nominated by the teacher may not be a central issue if competence is viewed in terms of acquiring methods of telling stories rather than the ability to produce an appropriate utterance or story in terms of topic. As noted much earlier, even Melanie's production (utterance 105–107) would appear to be accepted by the teacher. It would also appear that it is less important for Wendy to tune into the topic as defined by the teacher than to produce something that can be heard as a recognizable story during this stage of story-time.

IV

From our account we trust that readers may notice aspects of the transcript which the other accounts, produced from different professional stances, did not illuminate. We reiterate that in no way are we claiming any superiority for any aspects brought out by our account. We do claim, however, that our account makes visible different features which might otherwise remain unnoticed. We conclude by pointing to some issues which our analysis raises for discussion and further thought for practising teachers and by indicating the kinds of practical possibilities it generates.

Primarily we note that we have presented two contrasting though non-competitive approaches in this chapter. The first shows how the events in and making up the setting are viewed by persons professionally engaged in them. To describe their stance was to display something of what professional expertise in this area might look like. At the same time as this expertise was context-specific, bound to the infant school setting, it also seemed to have more general characteristics associated with professional expertise across a range of educational settings. This leads us to speculate briefly on the advantage that might be gained from a closer association between those involved with children of differing ages and in different schools. For both long-standing professionals and for student teachers, the issue of just what 'doing good teaching' consists of might be fruitfully explored through such a collaboration.

In asking readers to study carefully the transcript at the outset, our intention was twofold. In the first place, it was precisely to provide for a more fruitful encounter with our own respondents. In our view, the most impor-

The Primary School

tant issue here concerns just how it is that good teaching or bad teaching can often be so readily recognized by experienced professionals, and what sort of knowledge is being used to arrive at that recognition. If it is the case that the expertise involved has some characteristics which are not restricted to particular contexts, then the collaboration suggested above could provide us with a clearer picture of these characteristics. In the second place, we assumed readers would produce accounts largely contrasting with our own particular account.

One general intention in presenting our own account was to show how mundane, ordinary happenings like the story-time represented in our transcript can be subjected to scrutiny and analysis. Despite the possible shortcomings of transcript materials, e.g. the absence of visual cues, the difficulty of showing intonational contours etc., there is interest, even fascination, in trying to display the interactionally achieved organization of everyday life and its settings. The richness of these materials as a source for analysis should be readily apparent.

More specifically, through our concern to describe that interactionally achieved organization in this setting we have pointed to some activities and 'happenings' which the 'professional' approach tended to render invisible or at least more inaccessible. Through an examination of how large-scale organization of talk in terms of rounds of stories is interactionally achieved in this setting we brought out the competences of the parties in their various identities: as teachers/adults, as pupils/infants.

It is through this aspect of identities that we can perhaps bring the two approaches closest together. The 'professional' approach partitions the parties to the setting in terms of teachers/pupils, whilst the 'conversational' approach sees 'conversationalists' at work. Thus in relation to the question of competency of the parties, the frame of relevance differs. Broadly, the professional approach asks what the pupils are getting from the teacher, what they are learning, whereas the conversational approach tends to focus on the competence of the children to do everyday activities such as telling appropriate stories. In addition, this latter approach points to a variety of ways in which this teacher, apart from 'doing good teaching' or 'doing poor teaching', displays her competence in remarkably sensitive collaboration with the children.

It is possible, however, that the collaboration displayed, through for example the joint productions of stories and of story completions in particular, can inhibit children in developing the skills of story telling themselves. It may be that the teacher's apparent concern to have as many contributions as possible from the pupils in the short time available restricts the development of desirable or appropriate skills involved in story telling.

The analysis in our account does make clear this teacher's efforts to cooperate with these children in producing an 'adequate' story. Other teachers may conduct their story-times differently. However they do it, it would seem that a detailed consideration of their efforts to collaborate could generate practical possibilities for improving teaching performances and childrens' conversational competence.

In any such consideration, however, it is important not to lose sight of the skills, in some ways highly developed, which even young children bring to the infant school. Perhaps the young teacher in our materials can be viewed much more favourably in the light of the sensitive and painstaking interrelation with the children in the third stage of story-time. We suggest that somewhat greater attention to children in terms of their everyday conversational skills might prove beneficial in the educational task of helping the eventual development from 'child' to 'adult'.

We stress again that the two approaches are neither competitive nor antithetical. The parties are not children *or* pupils, teachers *or* adults. The everyday skills learned in the world outside the classroom have to be brought to bear and utilized to organize the setting, story-time-in-the-infant-classroom. It is a setting with its own relevances, purposes, activities and relationships – all of which require new learning and new adjustments vis-à-vis other everyday settings.

Finally, our account generates for discussion some wider issues. First, a question emerges regarding the sorts of knowledge which young children are working with concerning the everyday routines of infant school life, and whether professionals can benefit from a more detailed consideration of that knowledge as displayed in teacher-child talk. A second question is the need to ask how different children come to terms in differing ways with settings such as story-time. In particular, even if we accept their skills as conversationalists, we can go on to ask the reasons why some children still find particular problems in this somewhat distinctive context involving talk between the teacher and the children as members of a class. This last question is significant in at least two senses, given the increasingly important role that the teacher-class relationship comes to play as children continue their education. On the one hand, children's early experience of participation in such settings presumably provides some basis for the nature of their participation at a later stage; on the other hand, through their participation, children are providing teachers with materials upon which attributions of competence and incompetence can be based, and which can lay the foundation for children's future educational identities.

Transcription

1 C   (   )
2 T   That's a nasty cut isn't it
          Did you fall over
3 C   Don't know

The Primary School

4	C	(nasty cut)
5	C	I think my mummy and days says ( ) fall over – or anything
6	C	(//)
7	C	(//)
8	T	Anyway – it's time for your story now // ( )
9	C	( )
10	T	Look this way — Look this way — that's right the story I'm going to tell you today is about – rather ( ) Christmas (about a donkey) do you know anyone that rode on a donkey at Christmas. Yes (//)
11	C	Mary and – Joseph
12	T	Yes well Mary rode on a donkey didn't she //
13	C	Yes
14	T	( ) Very tired on her legs
15	C	Bethlehem
16	T	Yes
17	C	( ) my brother and me and my cousin made an ( ) and I made an angel
18	T	Did they
19	C	Uhm it took 5 weeks to get back
20	T	Did it take 5 weeks
21	C	and ( ) going to make a donkey when I get home
22	T	You made them at home
23	C	Yes
24	T	Well this story isn't about a donkey a long time ago it's a story about — a donkey that's — around today a little donkey and it lived in a field — a little black donkey in a little green field — at the time of the story snow was falling — the little donkey in the field were all covered with snowflakes — he wasn't cold though because he ran round the field – but he was lonely — whenever he stopped he threw back his head he said EE-AW EE-AW – there was no other little donkey to say ee-aw back so he was a lonely donkey — two little girls came past the field and they stopped and they looked over the gate – and they stroked him and patted him — a : nd they said well we must be off now – donkey we've got to hurry home – it's Christmas Eve we must hang up our stockings — we must hang up our stockings — sto:ck:ings // hh Christmas E:ve — what's that
25	C	uhhhhhhh
26	T	he hadn't heard of Christmas Eve — why said the little

Telling a Story

		girl – Father Christmas will come tonight — Father Christmas (he will) *Father Christmas* said the donkey who's he
27	CC	he hhhh
28	T	Well he's a very old man and he has a red jacket shiny black boots and a long white beard and he visits children at Christmas time
29	CC	hehhhh
30	T	and when they're all asleep in bed he fills their stockings with things – just the sort of things they want most
31	CC	( )
32	T	Oh you're the Father Christmas in the play aren't you Kevin – and is that what you're doing to do in the play
33	C	Yes
34	T	Yes — well this little donkey had *never* heard of Father Christmas – does he come to *don*keys as well as to children
35	C	hehhhh
36	T	asked the little donkey – we don't know said the little girls and then ran off down the lane – to get ready — it's Christmas Eve — the little donkey didn't run round his field any more — he stood still – he thought — he thought — I wish Father Christmas would visit me — I wish he'd some and visit me and bring me a present — a stocking with a present in it anything I wouldn't mind what it is was – cos I like the sound of presents — then he went to sleep in his little shed — in the middle of the night the donkey woke up – and he heard jingling and the sound of be:lls – he went out of his shed – and *there* coming through the sky
37	C	Father Christmas – // Father
38	T	Yes
39	C	Father Christmas
40	T	Yes on a silver sleigh — it was pulled by reindeers — ( ) Father Christmas with his merry blue eyes – and his bright rose cheeks was pulling
41	C	( )
42	T	the sleigh the reindeers were pulling as well he landed in the field – the little donkey jumped to his feet and *ran* out into the snow
43	CC	Hehhhh
44	CC	Hehhhh ha ha
45	T	Hello there – said Father Christmas – my youngest

33

The Primary School

		reindeer – Springer has gone lame – what does that mean gone lame – Yes (Marianne)
46	C	( )
47	T	She can't she can't walk
48	C	( )
49	T	and I wondered if *you* could help – you look a strong and sturdy little donkey said Father Christmas – Well – the little donkey can hardly believe his ears he jumped up and sprang about of course I'd love to help you Father Christmas – and Springer your youngest reindeer can rest in my shed — Well Father Christmas was very pleased — he unharnessed Springer – the little reindeer and led him into the shed and he lay down on the straw to rest and then Father Christmas harnessed the little donkey – in place of Springer so there were three reindeers – yes
50	C	Was these uh were there ( )
51	T	Yes just a
52	C	(baby) Christmas stocking
53	T	This is this is Christmas Eve we're talking about now and then — they uhm — they harnessed the donkey to the to the sleigh and they took off into the sky – the donkey was very surprised because he'd never seen a donkey fly before have you
54	CC	No
55	T	On a special day of course because it was with Father Christmas he took off in the sky with the reindeer
56	C	What day was it
57	C	and went through the sky — and Father Christmas landed — on the
58	C	( )
59	T	rooves of the rooves of the chimney, can you sit down a bit and then every can ( )
60	C	Kevin
61	C	( )
62	T	it landed on the rooves of the houses and Father Christmas pops off the sleigh and went down the chimney with his sack
63	C	huhhh
64	T	and in each stocking he gave the children *just* what they wanted most – he even visited the house of the two little girls and he gave them an *ap*ple, an *o*range and some *n*uts — and one little girl got some be : : : *ads* and the other

Telling a Story

		little girl got a jigsaw puzzle
65	C	is that all
66	T	Well that's all they got yes they didn't get a lot of toys but they were very happy — the donkey was very excited — but he was feeling tired because it was quite a heavy sleigh that he had to pull – he was very happy when he saw that at last they were coming down into his own field – back again – and Springer the little donkey who'd had a rest – was feeling much much better – and didn't limp at all – and Father Christmas unharnessed the little donkey and harnessed Springer back onto the sleigh – and turned – Father Christmas turned to the little donkey and said HO HO HO, well my young fellow — you deserve a very big Christmas present – what would you like most – well the little donkey didn't have to think twice about it – straightaway he said – please I should like a friend – you see – I have no one to run round the field with me
67	C	//(Betty)
68	T	and no one to share my little – shed – well go to sleep – and see what awaits you in the morning – said Father Christmas
69	C	haha
70	T	Well the litle donkey went to sleep and the very next morning he woke up and the *first* thing that he saw//was
71	C	a donkey
72	T	a snow-white donkey
		((tapping on a desk))
73	T	( )
74	C	oohh
75	T	The little donkey said hello what's your name — my name is Snow Queen and I come from Father Christmas to be your friend said the white donkey – and the donkeys rubbed noses and galloped out over the snow round and round the field together – and then when they got tired they came back and sat in the shed and told each other stories
76	CC	hahhhh
77	T	the little girls came past the field — and they saw that there were two donkeys — and said to each other – We:ll it looks as though Father Christmas comes to *don*keys as well as people — and so both the little donkeys and the little girls had a very — happy — Christmas

35

The Primary School

		((whispered)) – and so the little donkey wasn't lonely any more
78	C	( )
79	T	Have you ever felt lonely have you ever felt lonely
80	CC	Mmmmmmmhh ((several children make similar type utterances))
81	C	Yeh yeh
82	T	When did you feel ( ) lonely Colin
83	Colin	Uhm — we went out one day and – me dad said uhh we're going to (bridge) you want to come with me now
84	C	Hahh
85	Colin	and I stayed in a tent
86	T	You stayed in the tent on your own – and then you felt lonely
87	C	( ) ((very softly))
88	T	Yes (Sarah) when did you feel lonely
89	Sarah	( ) ((very softly))
90	T	and you felt lonely on your own
91	Sarah	(Yes)
92	T	What about you Wendy
93	Wendy	Well uh – I got lost // (one day)
94	C	KATHY
95	T	Yes
96	Wendy	and uh — and — I can't remember (the rest)
97	T	You go lost did w— were you going shopping
98	Wendy	Uhm - yes I (was with) Mummy ( ) a— a— no I wasn't going shopping with ( ) and uh she uhm she was in the shop and I went down and no she wasn't in the shop
99	C	hahhhh
100	Wendy	and I went and looked in the shop and she wasn't there ( ) and she (caught) up ( )
101	C	hahhhhh
102	T	and did you think for a moment you'd been left on your own
103	Wendy	Y(hhh)es
104	T	and you felt lonely — Yes Melanie
105	Melanie	Wh—when my mummy - when we were going to the shopping and then my— my mummy — when (//)
106	C	hehh ice cream
107	Melanie	and then she (forgot) it to bring him and then when my mummy come for us she said you you ( ) Eleanor — Eleanor // and we will go and get that ice cream

Telling a Story

		// ((someone enters the room and speaks in the background)) ((further child taking right through this stretch of talk))
108	?	hehhh
109	T	Oh I see — what about you Richard have you never been lost or felt lonely — never what about you Paul (1.0)
110	C	hehhh
111	Paul	I have uh — I have once when I was in the house fast asleep — and uh I woke early in the morning looking around for them ( ) in the house I jumped up up in the air and uhh I thought that was Mommy and Daddy in bed (somebody else)
112	C	HA HA
113	T	Hehhh
114	C	Hehhh
115	Paul	and so: : o — i the - uh me Aunty and me aunty said to me cos me mummy went to uh — me mummy went to hospickle to get a baby ((one child laughing throughout))
116	T	Was that when you had a new baby
117	C	Yes
118	Paul	and m - then me dad was poorly he had to go to hospital (as well) because he couldn't e:at *well* and then -
119	C	// ( )
120	C	// ( ) Aunty ( )
121	Paul	do you know what happened when I came downstairs — well hehh something really funny — came downstairs - I turned round me head and then I turned round - and me aunty ((laughs and talks)) me aunty stuffed me head in the ice *cre: : :am* ((rising crescendo of laughter by Paul through last part of his utterance)
122	T	// uhhh
123	Paul	hehh and then I went outside to play and came back in - an went in bed and noone was in the ouse ((one child in laughing throughout the utterance))
124	T	and-that's-when-you-felt-lonely what about you Kevin
125	Kevin	(Well) One day when I when I was at Huyton ((one child is laughing through his utterances)) I went out and I had my flippers and my snorkle and my goggles in my bad and there was a river so so I get them (on)// then I went in the river ((school bell rings))

The Primary School

126 T You did
127 Kevin (N) – I was lonely
128 T Were you – well does anybody *know* — of anybody that lives on their own perhaps
[Story-time continues for a further 83 utterances in which the children tell more stories]

3 The social organization of reading assessment: reasons for eclecticism

James Heap

Ordinarily, teaching children is difficult, demanding work. Teaching children to read is especially difficult if viewed from the theoretical assumptions of those disciplines which are thought to furnish the grounds for teachers' practical efforts. There are three lines of thought in social science and the humanities which are particularly relevant. The first takes it that reading is essentially an activity of mind. Following this line of reasoning psychology has made impressive contributions to knowledge by studying reading behaviour as cognitive processes. The second line of reasoning is a venerable one in philosophy: we do not and cannot have direct access to the minds of others. Thus research and theory here have tried to devise means to overcome this problem of others' minds and to offer us dependable ways of indirectly discerning the cognitive processes of others. The third line is only a few centuries old, yet is deeply rooted in common sense and supported by social science: children are persons whose minds are in the process of development. Psychologists speak here of cognitive development and have generated sophisticated and well received theories about the character and stages of such development.

While persuasive and perhaps obvious when taken individually, these lines of reasoning intersect in a rather paradoxical way when viewed from the vantage point of the classroom. If reading consists of cognitive processes which are not directly available to an observer, and if children have minds which are not fully developed, then teaching reading to children looks *theoretically* to be a most difficult task, fraught with uncertainty. Yet children learn and are taught to read virtually every day they spend at the primary level (and beyond).

Our concern as analysts of practical, everyday settings is with the social organizational 'machinery' – the systematic presuppositions, beliefs, commitments, procedures, conventions and rules – which makes the teaching of reading both feasible and defeasible. At the professional and common

The Primary School

sense levels much has been written about the teaching of reading. Every year more (though rarely new) advice is forthcoming in the form of reading programmes, textbooks, lectures, articles and scholarly books. Usually the recommendations are for some clearly drawn tasks, guided or at least monitored by the teacher. Provided that the tasks are content valid, i.e. they measure what they purport to measure, then task performances or outcomes are taken as transparent displays of the target reading skills. Successful task performance is repeatedly taken as the defining criterion of reading competence.

While work is under way on how the teaching of reading is made interactionally feasible, here we wish to report on how it is defeasible, i.e. how judgements of skill can be defeated, can go wrong for social organizational reasons. Specifically, we wish to outline two types of incurable problems in the social organization of assessment, the resource problem and the frame problem. From this outline we will go on to illustrate how the two problems can often be found to be intertwined in classroom lessons. In offering our outline and illustration we shall focus on the interactional work of assessing reading comprehension in a primary school group setting.

The practical consequence of our work is that systematic grounds are furnished for making a recommendation which runs counter to most advice given to teachers. We recommend an eclecticism of method in the assessment of reading. To give good grounds for this recommendation we need now to turn to the organizational assessment problems facing teachers and administrators.

The problems and a negative condition

In the very way reading related tasks are socially organized, they provide limits to certainty for claims about reading skill. This is so because the proper circumstances which the organization of the task furnishes and arranges are themselves mental phenomena which cannot be detected with certainty.

Our examination of classroom material will allow us to state a negative condition for any claim about children's skills, or knowledge claimed to be present in task performances or outcomes. To claim with certainty that a particular task outcome is related in a particular way to a specified reading target skill, teachers/assessors must establish the absence of any organizational assessment problem. From our examination of classroom material we will argue that such a requirement cannot be met. The most that can be done is to establish the certainty that an organizational assessment problem is *present*, not that it is absent. The consequence of this argument for assessment and measurement is that we can establish with certainty only that a particular empirical claim is invalid; we cannot establish with certainty that it is valid.

Our examination will be based on a selection of samples from four years of research on the social organization of reading activities, involving classroom observation, audio-taping and transcription of reading activities of 5-7 year olds. The seven classrooms observed during the past four years have all been in inner-city schools in a large Canadian city. The children are of working class, immigrant backgrounds, very mixed ethnically and racially. The problems we shall detail, however, are in no way limited to settings where teachers/assessors face children with this type of background or location in society.

Before turning to classroom materials, we need to distinguish between organizational 'problems' and organizational 'difficulties'. 'Difficulties' are faced or possibly faced by the children, and teachers/assessors have to detect when, where, and how these difficulties are organizationally present. 'Problems' are what we, as analysts, have to come to terms with and to explain. In reading assessment, we wish to explore two such problems: the resource problem and the frame problem.

Resource problem

The first problem concerns the meaning of a correct performance or outcome, what it signifies or displays. In a test or task with high content validity (cf. Ebel, 1972, Guion, 1974) a correct outcome is presumably a display of the test or task's target skill(s). In any actual single case, however, can the teacher/assessor know with certainty that the child's only resource for producing a correct outcome was the target skill? If the assessor cannot know with certainty that this was the only resource, the circumstances are not proper for claiming to know with certainty that the target skill was displayed. From our research, we see that there is always the *possibility* of two other resources for producing correct outcomes. One resource is provided by the test or task itself, which sets up the 'internal resource problem'. The other resource is provided by phenomena or circumstances 'outside' the task itself, which sets up the 'external resource problem'.

We begin with the internal resource problem. From the very ways that a task is constructed or administered, the children may be offered internal resources for producing correct outcomes without the aid of the task's target skill. In such cases, a correct outcome could be an artifact of the way the task is constructed or administered, raising the principled, abiding problem for assessors: how to decide whether a correct outcome displays the target skill or is an internal artifact, a by-product of the way the assessment activity is organized.

An illustration of the unintended internal resource possibility is derived from our own research on the actual organization of reading activities. The following account is of an advanced oral reading group, consisting of five

The Primary School

second-graders. Our focus is on the actions of one pupil whom we shall call Brenda.

The reading group had been introduced to the new words for today's story on a basic reader and was into the reading aloud section of its lesson. Brenda had been the second reader. She had read while lying on her stomach, as had the first reader. As the reader after Brenda was reading aloud, Brenda began playing with her book, moving one leaf up and down, turning to the pages ahead of the story being read, and apparently looking at the illustrations in the book. The teacher caught this behaviour, reached down and closed Brenda's book, interrupting the turn of the boy reading aloud, and said, 'If you're not interested in reading, don't bother!' meaning, presumably, 'Don't bother with the book at all'. Brenda said nothing, but continued to lie on the floor. The lesson continued. The last person in the group had read, by which time Brenda was lying on her side, with her back to the first reader. The story had not been completed so the teacher directed the first reader, the boy at the left, to read. After he read a paragraph the teacher asked the third reader in the circle to read, skipping Brenda's turn. From what we could see, Brenda did not pay attention to the story. At times she seemed merely to be moping. The reading aloud came to an end at the end of the story.

The teacher said, 'Well let's talk about the story', and began asking questions related to the story. The story had been about a little boy who liked baseball and had begun listening to a game on the radio when his mother asked him to take the clothes to the laundromat. It all turns out well, as the boy gets to hear the game. Also, a home run ball flies over the fence and lands in his laundry basket when he is walking past the game.

When the second question was asked about what the boy was doing when his mother asked him to do a chore, we were surprised to see Brenda's hand go up to answer the question. Someone else was called upon. Then the teacher asked, 'How did he hear the game?' Brenda's hand shot up again; she was called on and answered, 'From the stores along the way', which was the correct answer. In the story, each of the stores along the way to the laundromat had their radios on and tuned to the ball game. The little boy in the story was thus able to hear the game.

There are important grounds for being surprised by her answer. The teacher had closed Brenda's book before the children got to the part of the story that Brenda needed to know in order to correctly answer the question. After the lesson we spoke to her and she said she had been listening to the whole thing.

What is of analytic interest here is that Brenda displayed what counts procedurally as reading comprehension in terms of the organization of the lesson. Yet she did so without having read the relevant part of the story. There is more, though. Look how she was able to do this, by listening to the other children read aloud. As a task organized to make reading skills observable and assessable, the reading lesson provided an unforeseen resource, reading aloud, for a participant to continue to participate in the task and display comprehension in its terms. This points to the possibility that other, and indeed any, participants in such a task at one time or another make use of reading aloud as something to listen to when it is not their turn. In pedagogic terms there is the likelihood in a task organized in this way that comprehension questions tap both reading and listening skills. Thus, no direct inference from correct reading performance (question answering) to reading comprehension competence or skill can be made.

It is, of course, the case that the teacher in the previous example could have noted what we researchers noted. It is hoped that the teacher did see these things. Our concern, though, is not what the teacher actually saw or noticed. What is important is the problem which this example features: the *possibility* that correct answers are artifacts of task organizations. To see this possibility in any particular case requires dropping the assumption that because tasks are carefully designed to allow assessment of particular skills, the task outcomes in fact always reflect the presence (or absence) of the target skills. Having dropped this assumption, we need to reflect on the organization of the task as it was carried out, to see whether it offered unforeseen internal resources for producing correct outcomes.

In our classroom examples, reflection allows us to see that the correct answer by Brenda is *definitely* an organizational artifact. As Mehan (1974, p. 114-124) shows, in some cases it is quite probable that correct answers are artifacts. In examining completed written tests and worksheets, however, we simply *cannot decide* whether or not any particular correct outcome is an artifact. Thus, throughout, we see that any correct outcome could be an artifact, though it may not be.

The moral of this (part of our) story is that if we never reflect on task organization and instead merely assume that a task which is content valid in general will be content valid in particular, then we shall never know if outcomes are artifacts. However, if we stop treating outcomes as defining criteria and begin to reflect on task organization, we still may not be able to decide whether or not an outcome is an artifact. The best we can hope to discover is that a correct outcome *is* an artifact, for we cannot discover (with certainty) that a correct outcome *is not* an artifact.

We now turn to the external resource problem, i.e. how to decide whether a correct outcome displays the target skill or is the result of the child's use of a resource external to the task. This is a principled problem encountered whenever the response to a task demand is intended to depend on information internal to the task.

This problem, like the internal resource problem, only becomes noticeable when it is least troublesome, i.e. when we can recover the resource that the child probably used. The difference between this problem and the internal resource problem is sometimes simply an issue of where the boundaries of a task are drawn. We can see this in the case where a child answers a comprehension question in a test based on information in a previous part of the text or based on classroom discussion prior to the commencement of the test. In other uses, though, the distinction marks a clear difference. When a child copies answers from a classmate's workbook he is guilty of using a resource that is not internal to the organization of workbook completion. Even if the organization of seatwork is such that pupils have the opportunity to copy, teachers typically take exception to such behaviour. Yet they do not take exception to them listening to each other read, even though an unintended (internal) resource for answering reading comprehension question is provided.

An example that raises the external resource problem comes from a lesson (Heap 1979) observed on Rumpelstiltskin. The reading group consisted of six second-graders. The following question-answer-comment sequence, excerpted from the transcript of that lesson, occurs after part of the story has been read aloud. Presumably, comprehension is being assessed. (T stands for teacher, C for child).

T: No. Who helped her Mineen?
C: Rumpelstiltskin
T: Yeah the little man. We don't know his name is Rumpelstiltskin yet, do we? The little man. OK, what was the first thing the Prince said – sorry, that the girl gave to Rumpelstiltskin, to the little man? We better call him the little man because we don't know really he's Rumpelstiltskin yet.

From one perspective, the teacher's assertion that 'we don't know his name is Rumpelstiltskin yet' is wrong, if not absurd. The word Rumpelstiltskin was introduced and discussed during the first part of the lesson, along with other 'new words'. As well, we later learned that five of the six children in the group in the previous year were in the teacher's first-grade class where two different movies of the Rumpelstiltskin story were shown.

From the perspective of the running organization of the lesson, however, 'we don't know his name is Rumpelstiltskin yet' is necessarily true. Its truth derives from the convention that the oral reading section of the lesson provides pupils with all they need to know – or are allowed to know – in order to answer (literal) comprehension questions about the text. Essential to the story of Rumpelstiltskin is the mystery of the little man's name. His name is not revealed until the end of the story. In the lesson above, however, the end of the story had not yet been read. The intended and warranted resource for answering comprehension questions in this lesson was the oral reading so that the teacher legitimately could say (and teach) that 'we don't know his name is Rumpelstiltskin yet'.

Organization of Reading Assessment

When we reflect that the name Rumpelstiltskin and its referent had been discussed in the new words section of the lesson, and when we discover that five of the six children were probably exposed to the story of Rumpelstiltskin, we can conceive of the difficult work that children had to do in order to carry out the lesson in the way it was run by the teacher. In orienting to the convention that the oral reading section provides what they need to know, the children must suspend use of any other resources for answering comprehension questions.

Because such a suspension is difficult if not impossible, task constructors seek to design tasks in ways that allow the teacher/assessor to assume that the task information is new to children. The task constructor's success is a condition for valid claims about the display of target skills. The problem for teachers is that of knowing whether children have access to information resources external to task organization. In the case of the Rumpelstiltskin lesson, the teacher did know that they had access to external sources — the two movies. Yet, she carried out a lesson on that story anyway, as the next story in the basic reading programme.

The problem which the teacher can be seen to have encountered, whether she realized it or not, was the external resource problem: did correct answers reflect reading comprehension skills or long-term memory skills? In her case we can be certain that the problem was encountered, even though we cannot be certain that any particular answer about the text was the result of long-term memory. In other cases where questions are asked about a text just read in a lesson we cannot be certain that the external resource problem is absent, nor can we be certain, in principle, that a correct answer to a text question reflects the task's target comprehension skill.

Frame problem

The second problem faced in principle by assessors is more complex. Primarily it arises out of the interpretation of incorrect performances or outcomes and we call it the organizational frame problem. It is: how to decide whether an incorrect outcome indicates the absence of the target skill or whether it results from a difference in the pupil's frame of reference for understanding and completing the task. Unless a teacher/assessor can show that a frame problem was *not* present, he cannot claim with certainty that an incorrect outcome indicates the absence of the target skill.

If a child participates in and/or completes a task, we can take it that he or she has understood the task. Understanding what is to be done, e.g. filling in the blank, does not guarantee, however, that a task demand will be interpreted by a child using the same frame of reference as the task designer or assessor. It is a feature of language that its meaning can vary with context. The utterance 'Open your books' means one thing when said by a teacher to a classroom of children and another when said by a revenue auditor to the president of a corporation. The meaning of speech is overwhelmingly context dependent, i.e. indexical (cf. Bar-Hillel, 1954).

The term *context*, however, is a gloss for a larger collection of things, such as: who the speaker and hearers are; who they take each other to be; how much they know about each other; how much they know that the others know about them; their reasons for interacting, for doing whatever they are now doing together; their beliefs and assumptions about what the others believe and assume about the intent of what they are doing together; the literal time and place of the interaction; the figurative time and place of the interaction in relation to the topical structure of their conversation, in relation to social structure, to history, to the body of knowledge organized within some paradigm in some science and the like. Any of this can be part of the context of understanding the meaning of speech in some situation. Rarely would all of it be relevant.

'Relevant' is the key word. *Context* stands for whatever is relevant to producing and deciding the meaning of speech. What a context consists of cannot be known prior to or independently of what is said and meant. Thus, what counts as context in any situation is dependent on the meaning of the speech in that situation. Yet the meaning of the speech is itself context dependent. This *gestalt* character of meaning and context requires us to recognize that deciding the meaning of speech (and writing, of course) is through and through an interpretive affair. The phrase 'frame of reference' is a gloss for all those possible features of the context on which the speaker depends and the hearer draws in order to accomplish a sense of shared understanding in the course of interaction. Thus we distinguish between the frame(s) of reference implied in speech (and required by it) and the frame(s) of reference or interpretive schemes used by the hearer. Given the context dependency of the meaning of speech different frames can be inferred from speech, thus different frames can be used to achieve a sense of what the speaker means.

The fact that different frames are always usable sets up the difficulty for hearers of deciding which frame is to be preferred, i.e. which one the speaker (or task) depends on, or intends. This difficulty of knowing hearers' preferences gives rise to our second problem for assessors. Tasks that allow assessment are typically, and perhaps necessarily, organized to require a single frame of reference (or set of frames). Thus a correct outcome from a well-designed task strongly implies, though it does not entail, that the child interpreted correctly what the task demanded, i.e. used the preferred frame of reference. Any incorrect outcome is essentially ambiguous on this point. With a standardized, written test of reading skills, for example, the child can use the preferred frame of reference, but might not have the skill to complete a task correctly. Indeed, such tests must be organized to allow for just this possibility; they depend on it insofar as an incorrect outcome is treated as showing the absence of the target skill.

Any outcome, however, could be correct given some conceivable frame of reference. A correct outcome is one which is preferred, given one particular frame of reference. An incorrect outcome is one which is not preferred, given that same particular frame of reference. Of course, not all frames in any situation are equally relevant. It requires some quite outlandish thinking to conceive of frames that will make correct each selection on a multiple choice test. All we need to illustrate this point is simply one alternative frame for us to see the ambiguity of the incorrect outcome.

Our extended example of the frame problem comes from a third-grade classroom where one reading group is working through a story entitled 'The Big Big Parade in the Green Green Jungle', in *Carnival*, a reader published by Ginn. The teacher instructs the children to read a page and find the answer to a question she asks. After they have completed reading silently, she begins a sequence of verbal interaction with them that is aimed at having them answer the question she had asked. She also typically asks a few additional questions based on the assigned page. We shall speak of each identifiable question-answer sequence as an 'extraction sequence' (cf. McQuade, 1980) within the longer instructional sequence focusing on the assigned page. Teachers whom we have observed appear overwhelmingly to be concerned with completing and closing each extraction sequence (cf. Mehan, 1979). In the course of completion, outcomes and performances which are criterial for assessment of task target skills are generated.

The excerpt below is from the fourth of six such instructional sequences that make up the day's reading lesson for the group with which we are concerned. The story is about a big parade in the jungle. The question the teacher has asked before they read (page 50) was, 'What other animals are in the parade?'. She began the instructional sequence with this question, and the children and she collaboratively composed and concluded a list consisting of tortoises, kangaroos, goats, donkeys and rabbits. The excerpt begins at the end of the list production on line 15 of our transcript of the fourth sequence. (T indicates teacher, C indicates an unidentified child. Fr and Ra identify the children Franco and Raymond.)

15 T Anything else?
   Fr This is a kangaroo, right?
   T Right. What were the...um...donkeys like? How were they described?
   C A goat
      ((several other comments, indistinguishable))
20 T What were they like? Polite, kind, friendly?
   C Polite
   C Friendly
   C Friendly

The Primary School

	C	Friendly
25	T	Did you read that well?
	C	Yah
	C	Yep
	C	((inaudible)) polite. ((inaudible)) manners you have to have manners
	T	You do, but what about the donkeys?
30	C	Well, they (inaudible) hee haw, hee haw.
	T	Read the bottom paragraph on page 50 and find out what the donkeys were like ((between lines 32 and 33 the children were rereading the paragraph, with some side talk going on))
	T	OK, Raymond?
	Ra	Some are white
35	T	Right, that's one thing
	Fr	Ooh, ooh
	T	Franco?
	Fr	They hee-hawed
	T	Yes
40	Fr	Oh, Oh. They kicked their legs out.
	T	Right. Was that polite?
	C	No, No. ((Several students speak together))
	C	They have to have manners
	T	Right. In other words they don't have any manners. Anything else? Some are white, Mike. What else?
45		

From lines 25 and 31 and 32, we see the children formulated as having failed to produce correct test outcomes. Their failure can be seen from line 25 as a problem of poor reading, which the teacher remedies by having them reread the paragraph on page 50.

A frame problem arises from the frame difficulty that the children can be seen as having with the teacher's turn construction on line 20. That construction can be seen as a reformulation and elaboration of the turn construction on line 17 which began this sub-sequence. Our claim is that 'Polite, kind, friendly?' as a clarification of 'What were they like?' is intelligible and hearable as a multiple-choice question, like those questions which pupils answer in written tests and on worksheets. Under the multiple-choice frame of reference the hearer is justified in assuming that the question 'What were they like?' is answerable and is to be answered by one of the choices offered by the teacher after she had asked the question. Using this frame of reference the children's attempts to answer are sensible and warrantable. Their answers can be seen to fail not because of any deficit of reading comprehension skills, but because they had experienced a frame difficulty.

48

Organization of Reading Assessment

Judging by the conclusion of this extraction sequence (line 44) the teacher can be seen as having wanted the opposite of one of the descriptors she had proffered as an answer on line 20 – an opposite of polite. Thus, in retrospect, we can hear the teacher on line 20 not as limiting the pupils' choices for an answer, but as explicating what she means by 'like' in her question 'What were they like?'. She does so by offering examples of what animals could be said to be like. As sophisticated hearers, we can note that she was also giving some direction to the children. 'Polite', 'kind', and 'friendly' are semantically related and in some contexts would be practically synonymous.

The examples she offers, then, can be analysed for the preference they display collectively within her turn construction. Working from the assumption that the children read the page and would orient to it as the source for answers, the teacher's turn on line 20 appears to be so constructed as to direct them to react against her proferred answers, being the opposite of what the donkeys were like in the story. The difficulty posed by such subtle turn construction by the teacher is that the children did not hear exactly how she was helping them. Instead, they seem to hear her offering them a choice of answer in a multiple-choice format.

Their difficulty continues even after lines 31 and 32, when they have reread the bottom paragraph under instruction to find out what the donkeys were like. A child answers by identifying their colour (line 34). White is an odd answer, which suggests that Raymond perhaps had a frame difficulty. From the point of view of the question the teacher asked, it is odd that she accepts the answer. 'Right, that's one thing'. However, from the point of view of her task of concluding the extraction sequence initiated on line 17, her move is not odd at all. Her acceptance, though, could serve to exacerbate further the children's frame difficulty.

Continuing difficulty is evidenced by Franco's attempt to answer the question of what the donkeys were like by describing what the donkeys did – 'hee-hawed' (line 38), and 'kicked their legs out' (line 42). The teacher displays her organizational skill by turning the latter into the focus of a preclosing question. She accepts the description of what they did – 'kicked their legs out' – and asks for an evaluation of it. The correct answer to 'Was that polite?' (line 41) is the correct answer to her original question (line 17). By constructing her turn on line 41 as a question answerable by yes or no, she increased considerably the chances of closing the sub-sequence. Since the answer of 'polite' was already proffered by a child on line 21, but not used by the teacher to close the extraction sequence, we can see that 'Was that polite?' was virtually certain to provide a preclosing device for concluding the extraction sequence successfully.

As with the other examples of organizational assessment problems discussed in this chapter, this one allows us to claim the presence of a problem. The frame *difficulty* that children can be seen to be experiencing gives rise to

The Primary School

a frame *problem* for any assessor who wishes to claim that the children are not displaying the task's target skill. The fact that a frame *difficulty* is probably or even possibly present for children is the foundation for the fact that a frame *problem* is definitely present for assessment. Thus whenever a frame difficulty is possibly present for children, our negative condition cannot be met: the assessor cannot decide and show that a frame problem is absent.

Problems in relation
While the resource and frame problems are analytically distinct, practically they may occur together in a variety of relations, which ethnomethodological research can be used to discover.

We shall now examine a short excerpt of a reading lesson involving a teacher and a group of six children in a third grade classroom. The children give a wrong answer to a question about a story and are told by the teacher that they are not reading well. What we shall try to do is furnish an account of the children's interpretive work which shows them to be competent interactants, having adequate, lesson-furnished grounds for their answer. In developing this account of their competence we shall illustrate one way in which the organizational frame and organizational resource assessment problems can be co-present and related. If these problems are present and related we cannot be certain that an incorrect answer displays an absence of the lesson's target skill: story comprehension.

STORY AND DATA
'The Story of Olaf' in *Bundle of Sticks*, a basic reader published in the Ginn series, is about the adventures of a page boy, Olaf, who lived with two knights in an old castle. The two knights spent their time riding their horses and being brave while Olaf chased birds with his little red flag. However, all was not well, for the tranquility of the land was disturbed constantly by a fierce dragon. So the two knights asked the local wizard to turn them into dragons, which he did by giving them a bottle containing a magic potion. The fierce dragon loses out in the battle with the two knights-cum-dragons. But then there are two dragons instead of one, and two less knights than there were before!

> Poor Olaf! When he awoke, he was all alone. He knew what dreadful thing had happened but Olaf didn't know what to do about it. Then he saw the potion bottle where Sir Charles had left it. Olaf picked it up. There was still some left in the bottom. If I drink it, he thought, I too will become a dragon! But that would only make another dragon. Suddenly he remembered the words of the wizard: 'Face him as a man' (p. 8).

Olaf takes the bottle, finds the two knight/dragons and sprinkles drops of the potion on each dragon. Then he flees, tires, falls down on the grass and sleeps. The reconstituted knights awake, head home, discover Olaf on their way, pick him up and carry him, still asleep, back to the castle. The tranquility of the land is thus restored. The king orders a celebration and Olaf is made a knight. The story closes with Sir Olaf chasing birds with his little red flag and being very happy.

Apparently using a modified form of Stauffer's Directed Reading Thinking Activity approach (1975) the teacher asks a question before the children read a page. After they read the page the teacher begins with a question and moves them along to answer the original question (or a facsimile). Prior to silently reading the page quoted above they were asked by the teacher to 'find out what's going to happen'.

After the children read, the interaction went as follows:

```
 1 T    Olaf has a problem
   Ra   I know
   T    What's his problem?
   Ra   He's goin— um
 5 C    He ⎡ forgot to ⎤
   Ra      ⎣ to drink  ⎦
   C    turn them
   Ra   –he's going: to drink u: : :m some of the –
   C    Oh no
10 Ra   – u um some of the potion–/
   C    /Oh!/
   Ra   /Magic
   C    Po—/ ((faint))
   Ra   /po—um potion stuff, and then he's gonna become a dragon./
15 T    /Right why would he want to become a dragon?
   Ra   To get the others back
   T    Do you think that he is going to help?
   CC   No: : : ((not in exact unison))
   T    Does he actually decide to drink the potion?
20 C    No ((faint))
   CC   /Yeah
   C    Yeah
   T    How many think he does? (    ) How many think he doesn't?
   T    (    ) How many think we need to read the page again?
25 CC   No: : : ((not in unison))
   T    You're not reading very well today
        ((She re-reads the whole page to them))
```

INTERPRETATION I
Our interest in this sub-sequence of the overall lesson centres around lines

The Primary School

19 to 21. The teacher asks 'Does he actually decide to drink the potion?' All but one of the students who answer say 'Yeah'. One student turns out to be a (faint) dissenter but does not attempt to reassert this dissent. (It may even be the case that the dissenter changes this position on line 22). From the page (quoted in full above) which they read, we know that 'Yeah' is the wrong answer. It is wrong in terms of what actually happens in the story *beyond the page they read*. The correct answer to the question is 'No'. However, in terms strictly of the page they were reading it is wrong in this solely relevant way: the page does not tell whether or not Olaf drinks the potion.

Under this view, the failure of the children is twofold:

1 They have failed to display comprehension of the part-of-the-story that they have read
2 They have failed to understand and orient to the organizational rule that the text should provide the sole accountable source for (factual) answers to comprehension questions.

The first failure is the one which is most obvious and most consequential for the assessment of pupils. That they display the second failure only compounds their incompetence. It does not mitigate or reduce that apparent incompetence. Had the children really comprehended what they read they would have recognized that the teacher asked a question which the text did not answer. In answering correctly, e.g., 'it doesn't say whether or not Olaf drank the potion', they would have displayed reading comprehension as well as an understanding of and orientation to the rule that the text provides all they need to know in order to answer factual questions.

An understanding of this rule resolves any confusion engendered when the teacher asks a question that sounds as if it should have a clear-cut factual answer. When the child understands the rule and has a sense of having understood the text, this rule overrides the assumption that a factual question is answerable from the text just because the teacher asked it. Further, the application of this text-as-sole-source rule in the setting, enables children to recognize a certain type of 'trick' question, given that they do comprehend what they have read. Orienting to the rule, without comprehending what was read, however, will not allow such questions to be recognized as trick questions. A guess either of 'yes' or 'no' will display an absence of comprehension. Hence, the second failure does not prevent the teacher from assigning full weight to the first failure. Were this not so, the type of trick question used by the teacher above would be ineffective as an assessment device.

The first interpretation, then, is that in spite of any frame of reference difficulties which the children who answered may have had, they still displayed an absence of the sub-sequence's target skill: comprehension of the facts of the story.

Organization of Reading Assessment

INTERPRETATION II

An alternative interpretation can be generated by first noting an equivocality in the task the teacher directed the children to satisfy through their reading. 'Find out what's going to happen' can be an injunction to find out what happens in and on the page they read. Or it can be an injunction to read the page to find out what is going to happen *later on* in the story, beyond the page they are to read. The former frame requires the children to be detectives who solve the case by reading the page. The latter frame requires children to be detectives who must read the page to gather clues for the eventual solution of the case. Under the requirements of the latter hearing, line 19 can be heard as a question requiring a reasonable conjecture about what Olaf will do, based on what has been read so far. Heard this way, 'Does he actually decide to drink the potion?' is a question that intends assessment of something like projective comprehension of story development.

Frankly, Interpretation II is weak, as it stands. If one were seeking to assess 'projective comprehension', then the question would have been better put as 'Will he actually decide to drink the potion?' If the sub-sequence is read, however, as seeking to assess 'projective comprehension', then the children still do not come off as very competent. Olaf does not drink the potion.

INTERPRETATION III

The case of Interpretation II can be strengthened. Without taking a position as to the type of comprehension skill being assessed, a different way of hearing the sub-sequence can be furnished. In so doing we can account for the children's answers on lines 21-22 as reasonable, warranted and skilfully achieved. The skill displayed, though, is not that of reading comprehension in any of its varieties.

Begin by noting that the children's answers to the teacher's trick question, line 19, are all the same, with one faint dissent. They are affirmative: 'Yeah'. Since the page does not give the answer to the teacher's question, why are the answers not 'No', or at least an even mix of affirmative and negative answers? An answer comes by attending to the sequence of talk-in-turns prior to line 19.

In response to the question of whether becoming a dragon will help get the other knights back (line 17) several children answer 'No', thereby displaying comprehension of the story. Although we cannot tell from the audiotape of the lesson whether all six children answer on line 18, we can at least remark how odd it is for the children to answer 'Yeah', (i.e. Olaf drinks the potion). After all, it has just been said (and not challenged by the teacher) that after drinking the potion one becomes a dragon (lines 8 and 14) and that becoming a dragon will not help get the others back. It now looks even more curious that several children answer affirmatively on lines 21-22.

Curiosity can be satisfied, perhaps, if we consider lines 1 to 15. The teacher begins by asserting that Olaf has a problem and asks what it is. Raymond answers, saying that Olaf is going to drink some of the magic potion and then he is going to become a dragon. It sounds as if Raymond heard the teacher's original instructions ('find out what's going to happen') as directions to act as a detective who gathers clues, then conjectures as to what will happen, as per Interpretation II.

The key to Interpretation III is the first part of the teacher's turn on line 15. There she comments on Raymond's answer to her question. She says 'Right'. Since in the story Olaf does not drink the potion, what could the teacher mean by 'Right'? One conjecture is that she could be affirming the proposition: if Olaf drinks the magic potion then he will become a dragon. When instruction is viewed as the joint production of propositions by teacher and pupils (cf. Farrar, forthcoming, and Chapter 2 of this volume) through question-answer-comment sequences, we can appreciate the important pedagogic work which the teacher could intend through her 'Right' (see also Payne 1976, on the classroom use of 'Right'). However, the real issue here is not what the teacher meant by 'Right', but what she could have been heard to have meant by 'Right'. What she could have been heard as affirming is the truth of Raymond's claim that Olaf is going to drink some of the potion. If the children heard the teacher's 'Right' in this way, then the question put by the teacher on line 19 can and should be answered in the affirmative: 'Yeah'.

Note, though, that the teacher includes 'actually' in her question: 'Does he actually decide to drink the potion?' That a question is asked to which an answer has already been given, and that the question is marked by 'actually' could suggest that in spite of a prior confirmed answer, 'Yes' is not the correct answer. Perhaps the teacher was making this suggestion through her use of 'actually'. However, if the children are sophisticated enough interactants to recognize the type of suggestion achieved through the use of 'actually', they would also see that in the above sub-sequence the circumstances were not adequate to allow 'actually' to suggest that the prior confirmed answer was wrong. The reason is that the very person who confirmed the prior answer is the one who uses 'actually' in her question on line 19.

A prior answer is suggested to be incorrect when 'actually' is used in restating the question, but only when someone other than the user of 'actually' proffered or confirmed the prior answer. Or 'actually' can be used when the speaker herself proffered or confirmed a prior answer, but only when there has been subsequent discussion which downgrades the likely correctness of the prior answer. Given the absence in the above subsequence of any challenge to the teacher's confirmation of Raymond's assertion (line 14), her use of 'actually' (line 19) cannot (easily) suggest the incorrectness of the answer she previously confirmed. If she believes that the

Organization of Reading Assessment

prior answer is incorrect, the sophisticated child would be right to wonder why she confirmed it in the first place. Perhaps such a child might even wonder whether she really intended to confirm the prior answer at all. Either way, the sophisticated child would be confused by the apparent inconsistencies of the teacher's talk.

Of course, we do not know whether or not the children who answered 'Yeah' on lines 21-22 are sophisticated. Interpretation III, though, does suggest them to be competent interactants. They can be seen as having made use of a resource internal to the sub-sequence (lines 8 and 14), a resource hearably authorized by the teacher as correct (line 15). If they read and understood the page they then have two resources for answering the question on line 19: the text and the talk in the sub-sequence itself.

It seems that some well-read child could have stuck with the text-as-sole-source, following the rule stated above. Such a child could have answered 'it doesn't say whether Olaf drank the magic potion'. To do so, he would have had to see that the teacher in line 19 was actually asking a question about what will happen in the story beyond the pages they have read. (Remember this choice from Interpretation II). Our conjecture is that no child and thus no well-read child answered 'it doesn't say', because 'Yeah' was hearable in *that sequence of talk* as the preferred frame for understanding the teacher's question. 'Yeah' refers to 'what will happen', whereas 'it doesn't say' refers to 'what happened'.

The difficulty of preference between frames is resolved in terms of the available, authorised internal resources for answering the question. For the well-read child, the fact that the teacher apparently confirmed an assertion about a course of events not described in the text-so-far gives adequate, defendable grounds (resources) for hearing 'Does he actually drink the potion?' as necessarily being a question about what will happen later in the story. The 'necessity' of this hearing is founded on the children's assumption that the teacher is a consistently rational person who is aware of what she does and implies, and who intendedly controls what she does and implies. The 'necessity', hence, is founded on a child's conception of his teacher.

Under this assumption of teacher rationality and consistency, the word 'Right' on line 15 became hearable as (1) a positive evaluation of Raymond's answer and therefore as (2) a legitimate internal resource for interpreting and answering future questions in the lesson. If the teacher is formulated as rational and consistent we would have to interpret her 'Right' as not intending positive confirmation of the proposition: Olaf drinks the potion. Instead, we would have to interpret her as perhaps confirming some other proposition, e.g. drinking the potion would turn Olaf into a dragon. While her actual intention cannot be recovered with any certainty, her behaviour is important to note. It illustrates how the sequential placement of a single word in the comment or feedback slot of an extraction sequence can close a sequence, yet render ambiguous exactly what proposition the sequence jointly produced and affirmed. In this case a proposition, which the teacher likely had not intended to affirm, looks to have been taken as a teacher-intended, i.e., legitimate, internal resource. This shows us how the children's use of an apparently authorized resource can enter into the production of incorrect outcomes.

What Interpretation III has sought to show is how well-read children methodically could have produced a sensible, defendable answer which is incorrect in the teacher's terms. Such an answer could be produced through their competence as interactants and through their conception of their teacher. If Interpretation III is correct, then 'Yeah' cannot be treated for purposes of assessment as the absence of the task's target skill: story comprehension, or 'projective comprehension' (whatever that could be). We can thus see how the organizational frame and organizational resource assessment problem could be related, how an unintended internal resource may produce frame difficulties for children as they try to collaborate with the teacher in the joint production of a corpus of classroom lesson knowledge.

Comparing Interpretations

Interpretations II and III are obviously related. Both depend on the possibilities that various utterances in the lesson can be heard as referencing what will happen in the pages beyond what will have been read. Interpretation II simply assserts this possibility. Interpretation III develops it. Where they differ is in how they assess the answer 'Yeah'. Where Interpretation II asserts an absence of the target skill, III argues that absence of that reading skill (however conceived) cannot be warrantably asserted. In terms of this key difference, Interpretations I and II line up on the same side of the issue: III opposes them.

Interpretation III is more complex than the others, but we feel it also to be more persuasive. For purposes of assessment, however, it is not a question of feelings; the sole issue with regard to target skills is what can be made, definitely, of the answer 'Yeah'. On this issue, we need not be certain that Interpretation III is correct. As long as *we cannot be certain that Interpretation III is wrong*, then this possible interpretation is enough to defeat the attempt to treat 'Yeah' as the absence of some target reading skill according to Interpretations I and II.

Conclusion

We cannot be certain that a task outcome displays the operation or absence of a target skill, because evidence for cognitive phenomena offers no guarantees of certainty. What we have done is to show the inevitable principled problems which teachers/assessors face in making claims about the results or

Organization of Reading Assessment

outcomes of socially organized tasks. We now see that to claim with certainty that the proper cognitive conditions have been met in the display/non-display of a target skill, the following conditions are required: (1) that the children attempt to use only the teacher and task-intended resources for completing task demands, and (2) that the children understand task demands in terms of the frame of reference intended in the task design. If these conditions cannot be met, assessors cannot claim with certainty that a target skill has or has not been displayed.

Regarding each of the two conditions, we have argued that they cannot be shown to be definitely present. We can be certain only that these conditions are absent because the mere possibility that children used unintended resources or faced frame difficulties establishes the existence of the resource and frame assessment problems. In finding these problems to exist, we find the two proper conditions for making claims to be absent.

The consequence of these findings is significant. No matter how high a degree of content validity an assessment task is judged to have, empirical claims about the display of target skills are essentially suspect. Of course, as Zaner (1970) shows, all empirical claims are essentially open to revision in part because of the possibility of human error. But with claims about a person's reading processes and other cognitive phenomena we have additional cause for suspicion. While the claim that someone scored in a game can be incorrect, it is incorrect in ways that others can see. They can see that the ball actually did not go through the hoop, though from where you sat it looked as if it did. Or they can note that the ball was never officially put into play, or the scorer was out of bounds when he shot, though you thought otherwise. The point is that, in principle, it is possible for someone to know with certainty that a player did or did not score, though in particular cases no one may actually be certain. With phenomena for which defining criteria are not available, e.g. cognitive phenomena, no one is in a position to know with certainty that someone did or did not display a reading skill. Our suspicions about the validity of the claim that a target reading skill was or was not displayed cannot be allayed by turning to others who could know for certain, e.g. a panel of expert psychometricians, neurophysiologists, teachers, and seers. Our suspicions are incurable, because evidence of cognitive phenomena can never guarantee the presence of the phenomena for which it is evidence.

Of course, there is an arsenal of remedies developed by teachers/assessors. A major weapon is reliability. While the 1965 edition of the Gates-MacGinite Reading Test Technical Manual said nothing about content validity, a great deal was said that showed the test had a high reliability coefficient. Alternate forms of the 'same' test were administered on different days to the same sets of children, with children achieving similar scores on each form of the test. While assuring task reliability is certainly a helpful and sensible procedure, it does not solve the problem of what the task measures, i.e. its content validity. Teachers/assessors may require tests to be organizationally identical in order to establish a reliability coefficient, but in our terms such a procedure simply guarantees that similar resources and especially difficulties will be present for the children who took each alternate form of the tests.

Attentive readers will have noted that we have been careful to unfold the problems surrounding the interpretation of *particular* task outcomes. Another obvious weapon is to aggregate outcomes, as done by all standardized tests. The results of aggregation take the form of scores, e.g. 33 correct out of a possible 50. However, if we cannot decide how many of the 33 correct outcomes result from the use of illicit resources, and how many of the 17 incorrect outcomes result from frame difficulties, then we do not resolve our problems.

Our message is most strongly aimed at those who intentionally or effectively treat task outcomes and scores as certain measures of reading skills. Given the limits to certainty in reading assessment, what can teachers do, besides be sceptical? A recommendation can be developed by noting the character of these limits. These limits hold for the assessment of any particular task and they depend on the nature of the task format and the organization of task completion.

Put in its negative form, our recommendation is simple: do not depend on one format or a set of similar formats. Most emphatically, do not depend (or let administrators depend) on formats whose actual organization of completion is not available to critical reflection, as with workbooks and standardized tests. In its positive form our recommendation is that in assessing reading competence of children, teachers should use multiple tasks having different formats. Current pedagogy offers a wide array of formats relative to different reading skills, from the round-robin to directed reading and thinking activities, and from standardized tests and workbooks to the story writing/reading identified with language experience approaches. Each format offers different resources and barriers to performance and requires different frames of reference. The thoughtful use of multiple formats provides for the possibility of a child's competence showing through the collective differences in format resources and barriers. Phenomenologists like Zaner (1973, p. 34) speak of this as 'coincidence in conflict'.

The use of multiple formats as a method does not provide certainty about the meaning of particular outcomes; no method can do that. In the face of the limits to certainty in assessment, the method provides all that can be provided: a sense of a child's competence as documented through performance on a variety of reading assessment tasks. This sense can best be developed if teachers pay close attention to how teaching and learning are done in the most ordinary ways and as a matter of mundane classroom routine.

We conclude with a note on accountability. Given the cultural and social organizational limits to certainty in reading assessment, there are limits to the accountability of teachers. The success of their teaching strategies cannot be decided by looking at task outcomes on a test or two, for we do not know with any sense of certainty what outcomes actually display. Since the limits to certainty issue from the nature of reading, psychometricians or psychologists of reading can know with no more certainty than a teacher that a child has displayed a reading skill. In fact, since reading competence is shown over time and is best seen through performances on a variety of reading tasks, the teacher is in the best position to see whether or not an outcome documents a child's underlying reading skill. However, what the teacher can see and what he or she can prove to administrators and parents are not always one and the same. A first step in proving what has been seen over time is not allowing others to claim to see more than anyone can be certain of seeing.

4 The social organization of space and place in an urban open-plan primary school

Graham Hitchcock

Introduction

People routinely have to make sense of and get themselves around and through places and spaces. We have to deal with countless combinations of physical artifacts and objects that appear in our society in ways which we understand to be legitimate. By and large we do so without any difficulty. Using spaces and places is important for us in the course of doing our job. As teachers, we have an interest in such matters as coming to terms with and understanding the physical spatial environment, so that we can do our teaching. Yet in the open-plan primary school which is the subject of this chapter, the absence of conventional classrooms means that spaces and places take on a quite distinct significance.

What we will try to demonstrate in this chapter is firstly how spaces and places are interesting topics of sociological interest and, secondly and more particularly, how teachers in an urban open-plan primary school manage, cope with, and make sense of the physical arrangements of their school on a daily routine basis. We hope to demonstrate how the use and understanding of space for teachers is an interactional affair which is defined by the contextual features of the overall social organization of the school. Life in an open-plan school appears to be chaotic and sometimes is. Yet from our ethnographic observations of how teachers and children manage spaces and places in their school an order is clearly discernible. We will examine the nature of this order.

The materials discussed here are drawn from a wider study of the social organization of one urban open-plan primary school. This project was concerned to produce an ethnographic account of a school which we call Cedars Junior. By 'ethnographic', we refer to the work of describing a particular culture whether it be the culture of an 'exotic' tribe or a particular occupation in our modern society. It aims to provide, as far as possible, a description of the group of people under investigation from their own point of view.

Organization of Space and Place

As Malinowski (1922, p. 25), one of the first social scientists to use the technique of ethnography, has written, the goal of ethnography is 'to grasp the native point of view, his relation to life, to realise his vision of his world'. The ethnographer helps to build up a description of a particular way of life or culture from his observations on and participation and involvement in what people in the setting say and do. He asks a series of questions concerning what the people under observation say, know, and do. In getting answers to such questions, the ethnographer spends quite considerable amounts of time with those he is studying. He records his observations and takes notes of the events that happen. He is not only concerned with the extraordinary, but also most importantly with the ordinary, the frequent routine and day-in-day-out occurrences. Of importance here is the fact that the researcher himself becomes a major research instrument, relying on his involvement in the setting for some grasp of what is happening. The aim of this particular piece of research was to produce just such an ethnographic account of an urban open-plan primary school. Our interest was in what teachers and children did on a routine basis: what they talked about, how they interacted with one another and how they understood and made sense of the complex arrangements in which they found themselves. Our interest was in what teachers regarded as ordinary teaching, how they interpreted the behaviour and actions of their children, and the ways in which they had come to understand, use and make sense of teaching in a school without classrooms. This approach required using the method of participant observation, involving the negotiation of an appropriate role with the headmaster, i.e. a role enabling entry to the school, observation of teachers and pupils, participation as far as possible in the day-to-day activities, the opportunity to ask questions in return for 'helping out' and acting like a teacher when called upon to do so. In fact this role was not unlike that of many students who go on teaching practice or observation. The aim was to become as much a part of the furniture as possible so that the feel, the atmosphere and the reality of the life and interactions of those being studied could be grasped. The period of time spent doing participant observation in Cedars Junior and related settings was about eighteen months. Examples of 'related settings' are, school trips, meals and outings with members of staff and the two school holidays which took place outside school.

Cedars Junior is located in an inner city, down-town urban, predominantly lower working class neighbourhood. The school is modern and situated in its own grounds. The distinctive feature of Cedars Junior is that it is open-plan and as such it is not typical of junior schools. We suggest that readers consult Fig. 1, a plan of the main building of Cedars Junior, at this point to get an initial idea of what this particular open-plan school looks like. Basically the main building of the school represents an attempt to create a teaching and learning environment which will facilitate and encourage both

The Primary School

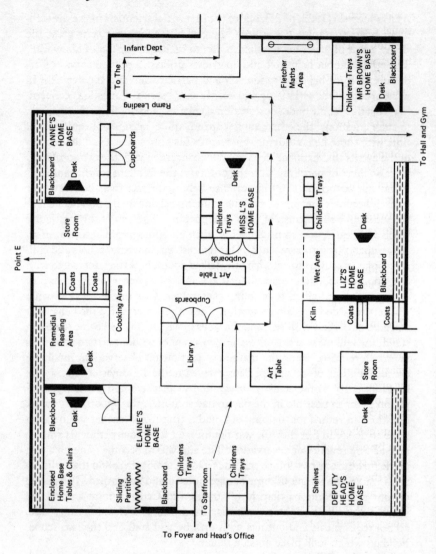

Figure 1 Plan of Cedars Junior – the Junior Department showing main lines of travel

Organization of Space and Place

teachers and pupils to overcome the inflexibility and limitations of conventional classrooms. The sought after outcome of open-plan teaching is the creation of a more 'informal' atmosphere and the adoption of 'progressive' primary school techniques such as 'team teaching' and the 'integrated day'. Instead of classrooms, the main building of the school has a number of 'areas' set aside for particular activities, e.g. art, Fletcher Maths, and cooking. It also has 'home bases', which are distinctive locations for each of the teachers in the main building of the school to call his or her own and in which they carry out administrative tasks.

Some of the basic ideas of English progressive primary schooling of which open-plan is a part, can be traced back to the Plowden Report (1967) and the Leicestershire Plan. Specific statements on open-plan can be located in the literature, for example Rintoul and Thorne (1975, p. 13) suggest that there are two major concepts entailed in the notion of open-plan primary school organization.

1 The organization of classroom spaces so that children can learn as individuals in small groups from time to time.
2 The integration of subjects so that different activities may be going on at the same time.

What in fact does go on in schools which claim to be operating the open-plan system will naturally vary from place to place. As Bennett et al. (1976) have commented from their survey, open-plan schools do indeed display an amazing amount of variation in design, layout and, we might also add, teaching organization. Our concern is: what precisely is it that a group of teachers do in one school which they themselves describe as 'a very open open-plan school'?

One of the important things for members in Cedars Junior to do and to be seen by others to be doing was dealing with, organizing, using and making sense of spaces and places in ways which others can recognize as being not only 'the way-things-get-done here', but also as evidence of competent teaching. This accomplishment involves teachers in actively making sense of a number of things in ways their fellow teachers see as being *adequate*. As an aspect of their professional training, teachers have to consider the professional themes and educational goals of the organization they find themselves in, yet at the same time, they have to get by, to do their job, on a practical day-to-day basis. Our interest is in how they manage to *translate* the professional themes into practical arrangements. Here we want to know how this work is done in the particular setting of the open-plan school.

The chapter is organized in the following way. One of the basic problems for people in Cedars Junior is to be able to get themselves physically around the place. To begin with, then, we discuss this basic problem under the heading of the 'navigational problem'. Next, we look at the ways in which boundaries are created and used by staff and children to handle problems of space and location. Linked with boundaries is the practice of categorizing and describing locations in ways which can provide grounds for what people may or may not legitimately do in them. Finally, we examine teachers' practices for making adaptations in their work in response to some of the professional problems raised by the open-plan nature of the school.

The navigational problem
Fig. 1, showing a plan of Cedars Junior, also indicates the main lines of travel or thoroughfare along which most people get themselves around the junior department in the school. As will be seen from the diagram, the school is a maze of areas, partitions, and chairs and tables. These all have special purposes and functions, but also pose problems in that during the course of the day, ways through and about these objects have to be found. Teachers have to get themselves from one end of the school to another, they have to move around to gather materials and to pick up groups of children. Children have to move from one teacher to another. We are interested in how people manage to avoid colliding into one another and find their way around in a way which also enables them to do their job. Teachers and children have to be able to negotiate, in collaboration with others, these physical arrangements, and they have to do so in a way that enables them to complete their everyday tasks. This problem is very similar to what Ryave and Schenkein (in Turner, ed., 1974, p. 266) describe as 'The Navigational Problem'.

From observation in Cedars Junior, teachers had arrived at fairly methodical and economic ways of getting from A to B. So much so that a main line of travel or a thoroughfare could be identified. Though teachers did not get together to discuss it, nor were any signs needed to point the way, a main line of travel did evolve and was orientated to as such by teachers without making any fuss. For example, a look at the diagram shows a number of possible routes for getting from the staffroom to the hall/gym, or to the infant department, or simply to the other end of the school. The main thoroughfare indicated was not the only one used by members of Cedars Junior for these purposes, but it was the most common one. Also it turned out to be quite economical in the sense that it was fairly direct and avoided taking in many other areas and locations other than those necessary to get from A to B.

One of the problems for teachers in a school like Cedars Junior is to create some kind of order and pattern out of an environment which affords the possibility for endless trouble and chaos. The children are not located in one place all the time and as one teacher put it, 'You really have to keep your eyes on them in this place you know. You could do with eyes in the back of your head'. Teachers have a vested interest in choosing a pattern of travel that facilitates as much control over the situation as possible. Elaine, whose home base is located near the staffroom end of the school, explains the 'procedures' she tries to get her children to follow whenever they have to go to the hall/gym or music room:

> Elaine: You have to watch it here you know. Otherwise this lot will get to the hall only after charging through the cooking area and the loo. So we walk single file slowly past the library, Liz's area and alongside Mr Brown's to the hall!

Clearly, it was not enough for Elaine alone to regard the route outlined in Fig. 1 as being a main line of travel. Obviously, it would have been unworkable for everyone to develop and utilize their own idiosyncratic lines of travel. There would have been literally problems of bumping into one another. Hence a main line of travel had to be recognized by all members as being the way to walk through the school and not a 'subsidiary line', a 'side line', an 'escape line' or an 'alternative line of travel'. If all teachers in the junior department were to employ their own idiosyncratic ways of getting through the school, the order that could clearly be observed there would quickly have deteriorated into chaos.

If we examine Fig. 1, the arrows indicate the main thoroughfare through the school. Starting from the staffroom foyer, headmaster's office and staff toilets, the line passes directly all but two of the teaching areas. To use this line of travel collaboratively offered the staff a number of advantages, but it also carried a number of significant, interactional consequences. These consequences derived from the fact that most of the teaching could be seen and heard from points along this route. In comparison to the conventional classroom, most of the teaching was naked, exposed to passers-by, who were mainly professional colleagues. One important implication of this situation was that professional competence – the ability to control children, to get them to work, to be busy, to present interesting displays – was open for all to see. It is of interest to note, however, that to use an alternative main line of travel involved penetrating the teaching areas even more deeply, thus making the teachers' work even more visible.

This problem of visibility frequently came up in conversation with staff who regarded it as a serious issue. For example, staff often referred to the occasions that the headmaster wandered through the school as 'spying' 'snooping' or 'prowling around', and his appearance generated quite frantic attempts to look busy. The theme of visibility is one which came up throughout the investigation and we will return later to some of the issues it raises. For the time being however, we simply note that for teachers to adopt a main line of travel along which routinely to navigate themselves and the children had both advantages and problematic consequences. It was double edged.

From this description of the orderly, typical and routine ways of navigating through the school and getting from one place to another with the

The Primary School

minimum amount of chaos, we move on to examine what members in Cedars Junior do with the physical objects and arrangements there, in order that we can develop an understanding of how spaces, places and objects in the school are socially organized.

Natural boundaries
Here we want to ask questions about the kinds of barriers and boundaries that members in Cedars Junior seem to be orientated towards and the ways in which these influence both teaching and interaction. We explore the way boundaries can be created out of the physical materials and objects found in the school and the implications they have for everyday life there. Boundaries can be created out of almost anything, but what is interesting is the way in which people orientate to them in common ways. In Cedars Junior, the teachers used the physical layout and design of the building, and also a number of objects to create boundaries. These objects included desks, chairs, art tables, sinks, display boards, doors and the five feet high partitions and hardboard sides of the home bases. In exploring the ways of using these things as boundaries, we begin with the initial issue of how members demarcate where 'school life' and 'non school life' start and finish.

Most institutions have demarcations and boundaries to mark off where organizational life and work begins and ends. In our increasingly bureaucratized society, a whole army of people have been charged with the task of dealing with outsiders on entry to the institution or organization. Such people are secretaries, receptionists, doormen, commissionaires, caretakers and the like. These 'gatekeepers' function symbolically to let the outsider know that he is now 'inside' the organization and secondly to present what Goffman (1971) calls 'front' to the outside world. This front can be used to develop and foster impressions about what the inside is like. In the context of Cedars Junior, these gatekeeping functions were built right into the physical setting by means of a foyer which acted as an effective barrier to the 'inside' of the school. Doors also effectively demonstrated the symbolic distance between this foyer and the staffroom and the head's room. The school secretary was charged with the gatekeeping functions of Cedars Junior. Joiner (1976, p. 228) makes the following remark from his study of small offices.

> Probably the initial introductory ritual in this building, which involved interaction with a receptionist and a secretary, was not only to ensure privacy and freedom from interruption for the occupant, but also a highly conventionalised piece of impression management provided by the organization.

Although in Cedars Junior it was the head's intent to make the parents welcome in school and to open up the school as much as possible (for example the door to his office was frequently left open), it was unlikely that outsiders on entry to the school could feel anything but awareness of their entry into 'The School'. The foyer (see Fig. 1) and the closed doors to the main school building effectively contained outsiders in this area.

As a boundary, the foyer had a number of uses. For example, whenever irate parents arrived in school demanding to see someone, as happened from time to time, they could be effectively contained in this foyer area. Indeed, the secretary seemed to have developed a definite style in dealing with outsiders entering the school. She adopted a fairly formal manner and asked them to wait in the foyer or in her office whilst she went to the main part of the building in search of whoever was required. This manner quickly changed once inside the staffroom, where her formal approach would give way to joking and friendly chat.

We note with interest that the location of the school secretary, both physically and interactionally, put her in the position of being a party to all kinds of interactions and information which were often closed to the rest of the staff. Hence she became an important link in the chain of management and the passing of information in the school. Staff frequently referred to 'getting the gossip from Mrs X' or 'Mrs X heard that' or 'Mrs X tells me'. Such boundaries, though often going unnoticed, could be quite important in conducting everyday affairs in school. More particularly, the foyer could be used to contain visitors, letting them see only what insiders wanted them to see. The situation was rather different when outsiders entered the main building directly by avoiding the main doors and foyer and going straight into the school from the playground (see point E in Fig. 1).

When parents or other 'outsiders' entered the school from this point, the advantages of the boundary to school life created by the foyer or a similar arrangement could not come into play. Once the outsider entered the school this way, he was literally amongst the teachers and pupils and could see and hear what was going on. It was probably as a direct consequence of the visibility of their activities to anyone entering school from this point that staff tended to feel uncomfortable and, in some cases, to complain. For example one teacher said:

Mr Brown: I'm going to see him about this, this morning, there were three parents wandering around at about 9.30 am bringing their children in. I think if they are late they should see the head first, not wander about as if they owned the bloody place...they can have it I don't care really ((laugh)).

The orientation of members to such boundaries varied from group to group. Here one group, 'the parents', posed problems for teachers since they often did not enter the school through the ordinary channels. The result was regarded as problematic by many staff.

At a basic level, natural boundaries provide arenas for routine interaction to take place. The question of boundaries is of special interest in Cedars Junior because not only is it an open-plan school, but for some teachers it was seen as a 'very open' open-plan school.

> Miss E: You know Graham you've got to forget everything you learnt in College here you know. It's no use. This place is just so different. I'm finding it really hard.

and

> Miss L: Yes I have been to a couple of open-plan schools, but they're nothing like this, look I mean it's really open.

But for some, their views went further:

> Mr A (Bill): ((laughs)) Have you seen Mr Brown's area lately ((laughs)) My God, bloody hell, it's a joke, it's an educational disaster area over there you know. I'm serious.

We note that Bill talked from a position quite different from other members of staff. He had a class in one of the prefabricated 'classrooms' located in the playground that were 'added on' to the school.

Cedars Junior does appear, then, to be regarded by most as being highly open. In the main teaching area itself much of what was going on could be seen. The visibility and openness of Cedars Junior was seen as being problematic, often the source of embarrassment and a serious concern for staff. Nevertheless, our research showed that natural boundaries could be so managed and utilized that these problems were minimized and as smooth a flow of events as possible was ensured, given the general possibilities for troubles and chaos offered by Cedars Junior. Let us, then, consider some of the interactional strategies the teachers used to deal with these problems.

One of the most recognizable consequences of staff in Cedars Junior constantly being on view was to respond by 'putting on a show' in order to 'create the right atmosphere', or to 'create the right impression'. Teachers could at least make sure that their display boards were full of good interesting pieces of work, coloured displays and diagrams. The following comment by Liz as she was putting the finishing touches to her display board echoed the views of several staff:

> Liz: I try to keep my displays clean and tidy. I also like to make them interesting and change them often. He's always snooping about.

Such displays as well as appearing educationally desirable also distracted the attention of passers-by from what the teacher was currently doing with the children.

Another course of action resulting in the creation of effective boundaries was to use whatever already existed in the building to gain as much privacy

Organization of Space and Place

and quiet as possible for teaching. In a setting where apparently there was little scope for the creation of barriers and boundaries, the use of the 'enclosed home base' and the 'home bases' became important. The 'home base' was a partially enclosed area used exclusively by a member of staff for doing administrative tasks. The 'enclosed home base' was really a 'homebase' in a corner location, but encloseable by means of a sliding partition, thereby making it rather like a small conventional classroom. The home base was smaller than the enclosed home base. Staff made quite extensive use of these areas and the boundaries which they created. They provided maximum privacy in a school that otherwise seemed to offer little or no privacy for the ordinary teacher.

Another interesting feature of the openness of the school concerned staring and gazing at one another. It soon became apparent that by and large staff did not stare or gaze for lengthy periods of time at what other members of staff were doing. The staff appeared to have developed something like a *'working disregard'* for one another in this respect. This 'working disregard' must not be taken for a suggestion that staff were unaware of what others were doing in the school. They clearly were aware and could comment on another teacher's 'problem' or 'difficult' children based on what they had seen or heard. They were also observed to orientate quickly to the head's presence by looking busy, by making a point of talking to the children and the like and ending such activity once he had passed out of range. The working disregard teachers expressed towards other teachers had become thoroughly commonplace and had important consequences. These consequences can best be seen by examining an example of what followed as a direct result of failing to employ a working disregard, i.e. by failing to put up effective boundaries between what was *properly* seen and not seen. For to dwell on the control or discipline problems of other teachers carried with it the assumption that other teachers could also legitimately stare, gaze at and dwell upon your own control or discipline problems. Indeed, since many teachers in Cedars Junior school echoed the sentiment that 'No one's perfect', and since most were in strong agreement that the school was very open, then for staff to employ the working disregard, or norm of disregard, was to place voluntary boundaries upon their direct visual range. In cases when teachers were clearly having difficulties, the norm involved leaving them to it and getting on with your own work. The application of this norm could even involve teachers physically turning their backs on one another to avoid the possibility of 'staring'. Of course, such action could effectively change the boundary of interaction, e.g. one teacher might turn her back on a fellow teacher who is having problems with her own class or maybe telling a child off, and take up another set of activities, perhaps focusing on her own 'home base' and her own group of children.

A detailed illustration of the norm of disregard for other teachers was provided by Elaine who was generally regarded as having some very difficult children in her class. Also she was herself having difficulties in the school (due in part no doubt to the fact that this was her first job) and on the occasion in question was busy having a row with a group of children in her home base. Liz and her group of children were travelling to the playground near the entrance foyer which necessarily took them right past Elaine's home base and coincided with the moment which she was shouting at two of her third year 'heavy lads'. As this was happening, some of Liz's children stopped, fascinated with what was going on, and were staring at the scene. Whereupon Liz became very irate, looked at Elaine with obvious embarrassment, and rushed back along the line to the offending children to reprimand them and to urge them to 'come along quickly now'. Clearly both Liz and Elaine would have preferred Liz and her class to have passed by without apparently noticing the scene. But things did not happen that way and as Liz explained later:

> Liz: It puts a strain on things you know, relationships, when you see and know that someone's having problems..... you know like Elaine.

Finally, we address ourselves directly to the most obvious features of the open-plan school: the absence of walls between the classes. In this respect, Cedars Junior is part of a current trend in educational architecture. As Bernstein (1967) has commented, 'the very architecture of the new schools point up their openness compared with the old schools. The inside of the institution has become visible'. In Cedars Junior, walls as such did not exist inside the main building, but the partitions, which were five feet six inches high, and also other physical objects were treated by staff like walls. In fact, the teachers created their own walls, barriers and boundaries for their own purposes from the available materials in their environment. From the plan in Fig. 1 it is clear that a wall divided the infant department from the junior department. The infant department was reached from the junior department by a ramp. This ramp had walls on its side which some of the children took great pleasure in hiding behind. Now a commonly stated aim of the head was to develop continuity between the infant and junior departments of the school in terms of exchanging knowledge and profiles of the children, joint activities and so on. Yet in practice, in the course of the day-to-day routine activities of the school, there was indeed very little flow, continuity or interaction between the two departments. Not the least impediment to this aim was the existence of the wall. Indeed, in doing this piece of research we felt that the very nature of the physical/architectural dimension put effective boundaries on it. To move from the junior department to the infant department literally meant going behind closed doors and felt like 'breaking in', so that it seemed advisable to stay put rather than enter into new territory. The infant department, being physically distinct and set apart

Organization of Space and Place

from the junior department, felt like different territory. The creation, understanding and maintenance of boundaries are important in enabling teachers to provide an order to their world which allows them to know where they are going. This order is actively made or accomplished by the routine everyday work of teachers themselves which largely goes unnoticed by them. Here we have attempted to describe the taken-for-granted work involved in their routine practices.

Categorizing locations

In order to operate normally in society, people have to use and to come to some kind of understanding of categories. Whether it be categories of people or categories of places, they have to understand what is involved in, for example, describing someone as this or that kind of person, and hence as someone who can legitimately do certain kinds of activities. The sociological interest of this type of inquiry surrounds the suggestion that for teachers, as for members elsewhere in society, certain categories are seen to 'go together'. Knowing the way categories are used in this way helps to provide members with a sense, or an understanding, of activities and talk.

As far as the world of Cedars Junior was concerned, the actual system for categorising locations provided members with specific understandings of the kinds of activities that (a) went on in locations; (b) were expected to go on in these locations; (c) involved particular categories of persons in relation to these locations. For example, the teachers knew that 'toilets' were the kinds of places that 'kids' could be found 'messing around in'. In contrast, the 'staffroom' was a haven for staff from which the children were normally excluded. Commonsensically, the staffroom was not the same kind of location, as the 'home-base' or the 'Fletcher Maths' area, and the kinds of activities that could legitimately go on there were very often not the kinds of activities that could be allowed to take place in those other locations. The language of the staffroom – its distinctly non-formal character and the frequent use of swearing – was acceptable for the location of the staffroom. For many staff in Cedars Junior, the staffroom was the place to get away from the bustle of school life in order to relax and have a break. It was seen as being 'backstage' and its layout is shown in Fig. 2.

The following incident, recorded one lunchtime, serves to illustrate the kind of thing that happened when the unspoken but accepted pattern of seeing certain types of location linked to certain definite kinds of activities was broken or in some way questioned. Elaine, Miss L and Alex, a twenty five year old School Liaison Officer (a post inaugurated by the job creation programme for unemployed graduates) were talking during the beginning of the lunchtime break in the staffroom about the forthcoming visit to the local museum. Some of the details about the arrangements, things for the children to do and questions to ask them, were being dealt with fairly swiftly. The

71

The Primary School

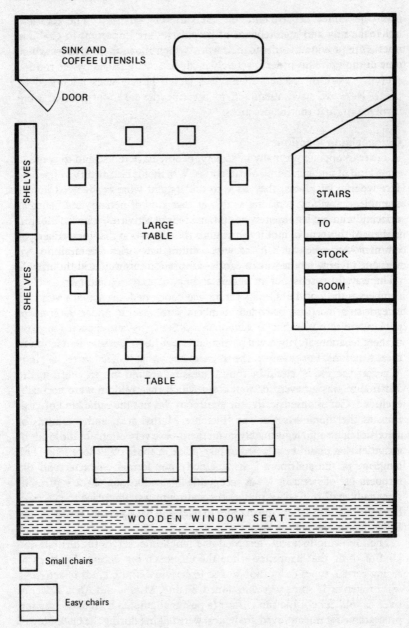

Figure 2 Plan of Staff Room

Organization of Space and Place

topic of conversation ended and the atmosphere of the staffroom changed back to the frivolous 'joking' atmosphere typical of lunch and morning break times. After a period of about five minutes, however, Alex returned to the topic of the museum trip:

> Alex: So you are going to look for something for Mr Brown's class then Jane ((Miss L)). Any ideas or shall I think of something for this trip then?
> Elaine: Oh she's talking work again ((smiles)) Oh shut up Alex for goodness sake.
> ((General smiles, conversation fades out, laughter.))

Here we find Alex, for whatever reason, apparently breaking the accepted assumption about minimizing shop-talk in the staffroom. Indeed, on the surface, Elaine's comment could appear to be something of an insult, though neither Alex nor the others present took it that way. Rather, Elaine's comment was taken in a friendly and joking way. Yet the reminder to everyone present about proper practices in the staffroom was still there.

The ways in which specific locations are generally seen often constrains members to follow the rules for expected interaction in them. Of course, once a system of categorizing locations has developed in a setting, it becomes quite powerful. Consider the differences, for example, between 'kids messing about in the toilets', and 'teachers messing about in the toilets', and 'priests messing about in the toilets'.

One of the major features of the social organizational use of space in Cedars Junior was the differential access to places and spaces between teachers and children. In comparison to the children the teacher could go almost anywhere on the grounds that finding out 'what's going on' was, in effect, doing his job. Despite appearances to a casual observer, children were not permitted to go just anywhere they liked. They were supposed to be found in particular locations, at particular times of the day, for particular purposes.

Let us turn now to specific locations in order to see the kinds of activities that went on in them and were supposed to go on in them. Kate Evans (1974a, p. 30) has commented:

> Within the school the headmaster's authority is manifested in the carving out of a specific bit of territory for his or her occupation. Some heads claimed that they were hardly ever in their rooms but none had permanently abandoned them even in the most informal schools.

We noted earlier that the location of the offices of both the secretary and the head endowed them with special uses. Evans (1974b, p. 199) further notes an interesting contrast with the apparent and presumed openness of the newer primary school she investigated and the nature of the head's room.

73

The Primary School

An unexpected visitor penetrating into the school might see aspects of it which had not been prepared for presentation. Despite the openness of contemporary architecture, there is a widespread use of vision net on head's windows, which makes visibility one-way and helps to keep observability predictable. If you can see who is coming in, you have those few moments of warning, which are often quite important.

The offices of the head, deputy head and the secretary had the net curtains mentioned above. Even in an otherwise extremely 'open', visible school there were still subtle barriers to this visibility, which could be manufactured by the members involved in the setting. The head in a sense commanded at least this foyer area of the school, here he was boss. But not so in the staffroom which the staff saw as belonging to them. Typically, the head would only stay in the staffroom for a few minutes during break time before leaving. It often appeared that staff resented his encroachment on their private territory and regarded the kinds of activities and talk which went on there as for staff ears only. Their break times represented 'between-act-time', not occasions for talking about changes in the script! Interestingly enough, however, though staff could have taken steps to ensure a greater degree of privacy by taking their coffee upstairs in the staffroom, they chose not to do so. On the one and only occasion when Mrs Smith did so, the occurrence was used by staff for doing inferential work on her character, i.e. the action of taking coffee upstairs in the staffroom to drink on her own was seen as 'daft' or 'eccentric' or 'hostile'. For the other staff, this action was noticeable, worth talking about and commenting on. Though moving upstairs to the staffroom could provide good possibilities for distancing oneself from the head and securing some peace and quiet during break time, it was simply not an acceptable thing to do. Thus only certain strategies were regarded as legitimate in dealing with the head's encroachment upon what staff see as their territory and their 'own' time.

On other occasions, certain physical features were used to demonstrate what kind of a place a particular location in fact was, and therefore, the appropriate patterns of action for such a setting. We can take the remedial reading area as an example (see Fig. 1). The location of the remedial reading area and the paraphernalia required for the work of teaching made this area and its interactional properties distinctive. On entering the remedial reading area there was a large poster which said 'Reading can be fun'. The tables and chairs were arranged differently from other areas where the children's tables were characteristically located outside the home base. Inside the remedial reading area, another poster read 'quiet'. These signs helped to orientate members to the kinds of interaction and behaviour deemed appropriate for this location. Interestingly, staff went very infrequently into the remedial reading area itself and interaction between the remedial teacher and other teachers characteristically took place outside it.

These were some of the cases where locations were marked out and understood by the staff, yet, of course, in an important sense, the whole of the school was indeed the headmaster's territory. He had rights of access to all the various areas and could go anywhere. Yet staff could still maintain their own understanding of locations. These understandings in Cedars Junior were worked out by school members themselves, were affirmed and reaffirmed by various symbolic and physical features and had become incorporated into the everyday talk of members of staff of the school. Talk about particular areas and bases was understood by staff and children; they knew what was meant and what implications particular locations carried. The interactional work of linking up in routine, taken-for-granted ways, kinds of places, categories of person and types of actions was the product of an ongoing process of interpretation. In providing teachers with typical people, typical places and typical events, the system of categorizing locations contributed to the social order of Cedars Junior. It was one of the seen but taken-for-granted aspects of routine life in school.

Responses and adaptations: professional themes and practical arrangements

Teachers in Cedars Junior are faced with a problem: a problem which has for a long time interested sociologists who have looked at professions. Cedars Junior is an open-plan primary school which has adopted many of the techniques of so called progressive primary school education, i.e. team teaching, subject integration, discovery learning and so on. In professional terms, then, there is a theoretical ethos concerning what ought to go on in such a school and how open-plan ought to work. Beyond that, there is a set of assumptions which suggest why teaching and, more importantly, learning are best furthered by the adoption of such methods and approaches. Teachers, however, have to come to terms with the world in which they find themselves, they have to deal with the everyday occurrences that befall them on a routine, day in, day out practical basis. The problem, then, surrounds the ways in which teachers manage and accomplish the translation of these professional themes into practical arrangements and therefore bridge the gap, for undoubtedly in many teacher perspectives there is a gap between 'theory' and 'practice'. We are concerned here not so much with what *should* go on in Cedars Junior, but with what actually *does* go on, with what members do in order to get things done. We will show how the practical responses and adaptations of teachers in Cedars Junior bear directly on the organization of spatial arrangements in this open-plan school.

First, there is a great deal of professional/ideological thinking about what Cedars Junior and other 'progressive' primary schools are about. What outlooks, skills and methods are required to sustain such an organization, and

The Primary School

make it *work*? Teachers are instructed in these 'professional themes' and are expected to be aware of their implications for teaching. It is part of their 'professional ideology' to know about such features as 'integration', 'team teaching', 'group learning' and 'discovery methods'. Furthermore they are often trained in and expected to understand the professional/philosophical background to the 'progressive' debate, irrespective of their agreement or disagreement concerning such notions. Most members of staff in Cedars Junior had undergone training which stressed progressive primary school theory and method.

However, in reality what happened was that teachers *translated* these professional/ideological features of the open-plan system *into* the routine, practical, day-to-day realities of school life, thereby demonstrating their competence as *bona fide* teachers. The reality of the situation was that they had to handle matters in school on a routine everyday basis and their solutions might not have borne much relation to the professional themes of open-plan. In terms of our interests here, the teachers in Cedars Junior had to create regions and areas for particular purposes; identifiable locations had to be developed, teachers and children simply had to be able to find things and other people, images had to be managed, an order had to be created, interactional territories had to be evolved, spatial arrangements and behavioural limitations had to be demarcated. The ways that the teachers did these tasks reflected their *translation* of the professional themes into practical arrangements. These arrangements involved members' practices for organizing space and locations in the setting of the open-plan school.

Three such practices stand out for close consideration: firstly, the process of normalization; secondly, the development of a norm of disregard; and thirdly the retreat into the home base.

The process of normalization was a widespread activity in Cedars Junior. It was quite a pervasive practice which teachers drew upon not only when dealing with space in Cedars Junior, but also with a whole range of potentially problematic situations and events.

To become engaged in a normalization process involved the teachers collaboratively learning to recognize and interpret certain features in the life of the school as being normal, and to make non-problematic a whole range of situations. In Cedars Junior, the teachers were often seen to be engaged in making normal what appeared to be clearly unusual, untypical and for some, abnormal spatial arrangements. Evidence for such practices derived from the teachers' suggesting that they had got used to this or that feature of the school by saying, for example, 'Well that's normal for here', or 'That's nothing new here'. The kinds of troubles which emerged and were seen as being the direct result of open plan, for example, the freedom of movement given to the children, were treated as typical, given this kind of situation. Thus the problems of children running around all over the place, being able to 'skive

Organization of Space and Place

off', were not problematic *per se* for the teachers, rather they were seen as routine, and 'typical' for Cedars Junior. Moreover, these problems were presented as being generalizable, i.e. they could be understood as problems *everyone* had to face in a school like Cedars Junior. As one teacher explained, in such schools these problems were nothing new.

> Mr Brown: This place just lends itself to kids skiving off...it's just too much of a temptation for them, you can't always do much about it. You quite often see kids doing nothing much; hanging around the toilets or the cooking area, and it goes on all the time here.

In short, the staff in Cedars Junior simply reworked their notions of the normal and abnormal to include a much wider range of activities. Making normal here what appears to the outsider to be chaotic, provides staff with some kind of interactional hold over and understanding of the school.

Another strategy employed by staff was what we earlier termed 'the norm of disregard'. This norm refers to the situation in Cedars Junior whereby a number of categories of disorderliness, lack of control, disciplinary problems, and the like were interactionally ignored by staff. They were ignored in that staff did not stare at one another, especially when one of them had troubles with the children. Troubles were ignored and not usually made serious topics of conversation by members of staff. This norm was perhaps one of the most direct responses staff made to the visibility and openness of the school. It was an unspoken norm or assumption which clearly had to involve acceptance by most members of staff for it to be effective. Operating the norm had certain practical advantages for teachers in a school like Cedars Junior. For if, as Goffman (1971) has indicated, 'coolness' and remaining in control of social situations are hallmarks of successful interaction in our increasingly bureaucratic, rational, technological society, then the norm of disregard plays a crucial role in the reduction of embarrassment, loss of face and lowering of status in the setting of Cedars Junior. Discipline problems, like reprimanding or losing control of the children, can potentially throw doubt on to a teacher's competence and are highly visible to everyone in the open plan school. To some extent, they can be offset and managed by the collaborative stance of disregard.

We are not suggesting that licence reigned in Cedars Junior. Of course not. When the difficulties, troubles and problems of a member of staff went beyond a certain point, the norm of disregard ceased to operate. Instead the whole machinery of judgmental and inferential work was put into operation as happened in the case of Elaine. Her case and her difficulties with the children are instructive in showing what happened when the norm of disregard ceased to operate. In terms of (a) the main thoroughfare through the school and (b) the relation of her class to that of the deputy head (see Fig. 1),

The Primary School

Elaine was placed in a poor position. People frequently passed her area and could compare her activities with those of the deputy head who was directly opposite. The spatial organization of Cedars Junior provided differential visibility between areas and, in the case of Elaine, the location of her home base right on the edge of the main thoroughfare through the school meant that every passer-by could see what was going on, whereas for most of the other members of staff the home base provided some form of 'cover' for distancing themselves from the main thoroughfare. Elaine's position tended to highlight any problems she had because everyone could witness them. We note, however, that the deputy head's home base was opposite Elaine's and also bordered on the main thoroughfare yet characteristically he had no problems. It is possible that there was something of a comparison going on between the deputy head and Elaine when assessing her problems, involving the general refusal on the part of the rest of the staff to put into effective operation 'the norm of disregard' on behalf of Elaine. This refusal may have had something to do with the status and hierarchical positions of the parties involved in that Elaine was a very junior 'probationer' and the deputy head was regarded as being 'experienced' and as standing 'for no nonsense'.

Finally, we come to the question of 'the retreat into the home base'. This phenomenon was fairly widespread in the school and an examination of this pattern of interaction highlights the ways in which physical and spatial arrangements were practically used by members themselves for their own, as opposed to 'professional', purposes.

The following are some typical comments made by staff concerning the home base:

Liz: I'm going to spend most of the morning with my class in our home base for some peace and quiet.

Mr Brown: Yes, I'm getting them settled down in the home base before we start to do anything, get them reading.

Louise: I'm spending more and more time in the home base these days, it stops them charging about anyway.

Liz: I like it in the enclosed home base, you can draw the partition and no one disturbs you. It's very good for poetry, English, Creative Writing and that kind of stuff, it's more like a classroom.

Comments and remarks like these were indicative of much of staff opinion concerning the home base. For these staff, the home base was in many ways, a 'mini classroom' and the substitute walls – the five feet high partitions – acted as effective barriers within which particularly sought after modes of interaction, notably orderly, stable, relatively quiet behaviour on the part of the children, could be pursued. From the plan of Cedars Junior we can see how these home bases characteristically had three sides with a small gap for

Organization of Space and Place

an entrance. There was, of course, the enclosed home base that could also be used (see Fig. 3). Here we can see the phenomenon of 'the retreat into the home base' as something of a reaction to the almost total openness of the junior department and the characteristic *visibility* which is a consequence of this design. Yet this retreat is indeed in opposition to the ethos of open-plan teaching.

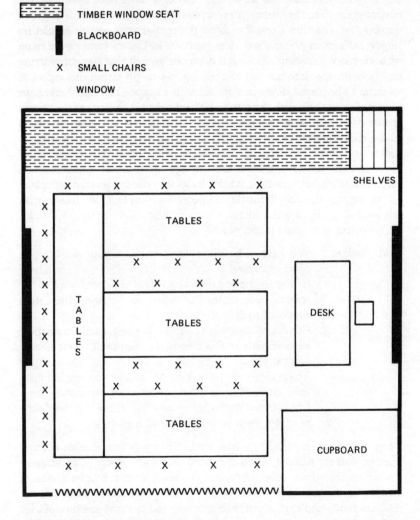

Figure 3 Plan of enclosed home base

Let us look in more detail at what interactional possibilities the use of these home bases provided for the staff of Cedars Junior. On any day in Cedars Junior, apart from first thing in the morning and last thing in the afternoon, a constant flow and movement of both teachers and pupils could be observed. During the course of a typical day, children in Cedars Junior travelled from the Fletcher Maths area to the cooking area, wet areas, the gym, home base and toilets. They may also have visited anything from two to four teachers. This situation is professionally encouraged on the grounds that greater flexibility and movement lead to a more conducive learning environment. Yet the theory may indeed be one thing and the practice another, for as a direct result of both the spatial arrangement of Cedars Junior *and* certain professional ideas, teachers in Cedars Junior were faced with very real problems. Although it can be argued that control is structurally built right into the role of a teacher, we might expect this aspect of teaching to be played down in a school with a supposedly 'open' ethos. In Cedars Junior, however, 'control', 'discipline' and 'being seen to be in charge' were viewed as important and as professional attributes which all teachers should have. Yet the spatial arrangements in a school like Cedars Junior presented teachers with professional difficulties. These difficulties concerned the ability to control and manage children and to demonstrate successful teaching in a setting which, by its very nature, seemed to encourage and exacerbate disorderliness and potential trouble. How to cope with this kind of situation was a frequent topic of discussion for staff. Consider the following comments made by staff:

Mr Brown:	You have to have eyes in the back of your head in this place you know
Elaine:	((After Elaine had found two of her children hiding in the cooking area instead of doing the drawing they were supposed to do)).
	Skiving off again; it's terrible they just wander anywhere and everywhere this bloody lot. You can't blame them I don't suppose.
Mrs Smith:	These kids need some kind of security you need to keep your eyes on them. What you want are classrooms.
Liz:	I've got used to this set up now but it took me a long time to adjust, even now I don't find it easy.

Thus the retreat into the home base could be seen as one possible strategy open to staff for gaining as much control as possible over the children in circumstances which they perceived as minimizing the possibilities of control. It was noticeable that whenever the opportunity occurred, the teachers conducted as much of their teaching and spent as much time with their children as possible within the confines of their home base. This retreat into the home base facilitated easier interaction between teachers and children and helped to reduce some of the problems staff generally complained about. It provided a certain amount of security and, as one teacher, Miss L, pointed out:

> Miss L: It's all right this theory stuff you get at college, but when it comes down to it you have to get on with the job.

The home base was small, the children could be grouped round the teacher, they could sit on the floor. It gave a cosy, quiet environment where most frequently stories were told and discussions held. Yet we do not wish to give the impression that there were explicit rules for 'retreating' into the home base. The staff did not sit down collectively to discuss this matter. Rather, they seemed to take for granted that this kind of response could legitimately be adopted in the circumstances. We also note with interest that staff did not perceive or recognize any contradiction between their actions and the organization of the school. They were able to retreat to their home base whilst at the same time ostensibly preserving the open-school ideology. The retreat into the home base became so complete with some members of staff that they even arranged the furniture in it to achieve a greater control over the children. This was the case with Ann, who explained:

> Ann: My home base isn't bad really but I've organized things so as to make sure they only have a little space to get in and out of. Little buggers. I can keep an eye on them better then, it stops them a bit from messing with Miss L's kids.

Fig. 4 shows the arrangement of furniture in Ann's home base. A very limited entry and exit zone was created by moving cupboards and the blocks of children's trays. The location of the teacher's chair and desk also put her in a good observational position *vis-à-vis* the children.

Generally speaking, the major problem staff seemed to contend with was how to provide interactionally for the equivalent of classrooms and walls. As we have seen, staff employed a number of responses to the open-plan situation of Cedars Junior and of these the retreat into the home base was the most pervasive. It seemed to secure for staff much of the kind of control and intimacy characteristic of conventional classrooms. Staff endeavoured to create their own equivalent of classroom walls out of the meagre raw materials available to them – the partitions and furniture of the home base.

We are suggesting that the practical everyday organization of the use of space in Cedars Junior translated and, in some cases, even subverted the professional ethos of open-plan teaching and integration. The organization of furniture in Ann's home base not only restricted what involvement her children might have had with Miss L's, but also restricted the involvement and integration possible between the two teachers and two groups of

The Primary School

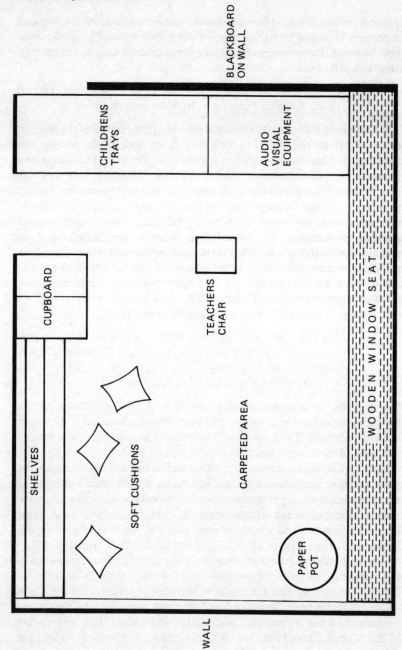

Figure 4 Plan of Ann's home base

children. Similarly Liz's concern to get into the enclosed home base as often as possible reflected her backing and preference for the 'classroom situation'. Some of the staff seemed to want to try and teach as if they were in a classroom. All the same, teachers in Cedars Junior felt it necessary to make this translation of professional themes into these practical arrangements if they were to get through the day. There were in effect 'good-organizational-reasons' for this 'bad', contradictory educational practice.

We have been trying to look at the world of Cedars Junior as being made up of a continuous process of interactions, interpretations and understandings. Human society consists of people engaged in getting on with living and organizing their lives and behaviour in the light of what they find going on around them. Similarly teachers in Cedars Junior have been getting on with doing their teaching in ways which are recognizable by others as being competent. One of the features they had to cope with was the spatial arrangement of the school. Cedars Junior, like other institutional arrangements, is made up of places which are defined territories having boundaries and locations categorized in socially consequential ways. The teachers described spaces and places in particular ways and developed assumptions about what places were about and how they could be used by watching other staff, talking to them and intuitively grasping the situation. In this way, they worked up a sense of what was right and acceptable between themselves. In this sense the use and understanding of space and place in Cedars Junior was just part of the wider social organization, or culture, to be found there.

The discussion of such issues has involved us in looking at the social repertoire of members, their 'folk knowledge' of 'the-way-things-are' in school. However, we stress again that this knowledge was implicitly organized, it was tacit knowledge. Characteristically people in Cedars Junior did not sit down to discuss what they were going to call places, or how they were going to interact in them – they just got on with it. For example, we have seen how there was differential access to spaces and places between teachers and pupils and how also certain locations had specific properties. The following example highlights the implicit nature of some of the assumptions and understandings about spaces and categories in operation in the school. They remained largely unquestioned and were a taken-for-granted part of the teachers' common sense thinking. The scene was a typical lunchtime in the staffroom in Cedars Junior when Jane, a first year pupil, came into the staffroom:

Jane: ((Goes up to Elaine)) Miss, Miss can I get my coat from Mr Armstrong's classroom cos I left it there after games Miss.
Elaine: Jane just get out go on and come in properly ((Jane looking rather worried goes back out of the staffroom and then walks back in))
Jane: Miss
Elaine: No Jane go out and come in again. You're supposed to knock

The Primary School

((Jane goes out once more and Elaine turning to Liz and myself proceeds)) Oh I'm cruel ain't I ((smiles))
Jane: ((knocks on staffroom door))
Elaine: Come in
Jane: ((Walks in)) Miss please Miss can I get my coat from Mr Armstrong's Miss
Elaine: No Jane you shouldn't have forgotten it, now you'll have to get it later, now off you go.

Whilst there is a lot that we could discuss about this sequence, we confine our comments to the fact that there seem to be implicit understandings regarding who was allowed to go where and why. We find Elaine and the other staff present trading on an unstated rule which suggested that children's territory and time was expendable, and that the staff could legitimately make children follow elaborate rituals before they could enter into the staffroom. This rule permitted playing the apparently cruel games shown above.

Finally we looked at the ways in which teachers necessarily became involved in the translation of the professional themes into practical possibilities. Even if education on open-plan lines is all right in theory, it has to be translated nonetheless into the practical arrangements of day-to-day living and teaching.

Conclusions

We conclude by looking at some practical implications for teaching that have arisen from the analysis of the social organization of space and place in Cedars Junior. We also recommend some possible strategies for future research in the area. Let us first consider the question of future research in the area and what kind of research. We would like to stress again the need for and value of qualitative techniques involving the use of audio and video tape recordings, participant observation and the collection of field notes in documenting and analysing life in schools. This approach is gaining more and more popularity among professional researchers. Moreover teachers can become researchers and more importantly become their own informants. In other words, we would encourage teachers to look again at their own activities and thereby hopefully discover what it is they take-for-granted so that an improvement in the understanding of the learning situation may come about. One of the ways in which this can be done involves little extra effort on the part of teachers. It is to keep a diary recording events in school over a period of say one or two weeks. This diary could record for example the whereabouts of teachers and pupils during specified periods of the day, the kinds of activities that go on, their location, the incidence and causes of trouble or problems, etc. This diary can be examined later and as far as teaching in an open-plan school goes, can be scrutinized in order to see the extent to which the ethos and goal of open-plan are in fact being carried out in practice and the possibilities for the improvement of the activities in question. Once faced with ordinary routine accounts of what it is they do, teachers may thus be able to take a more considered look at the educational implications.

We now turn to some of the educational issues. From our observations and analysis, it seems that in Cedars Junior there is something of a 'professional contradiction'. As we have noted, however, the teachers do not see matters in this way. A school without walls has clearly been turned into a school where many walls and boundaries have been set up. What we have, then, is a situation where there is a professional theme regarding open-plan teaching, and an 'open' education ideology in general, to which a series of practical adaptations and responses have been made by the staff. These adaptations appear to oppose the professional themes. The retreat into the home-base, the search for privacy and enclosures, the setting up of barriers to interaction and the operation of a norm of disregard were all seen to be routine and *necessary* practices and activities for staff legitimately to get involved in. Yet at the same time, they were practices apparently in total opposition to the educational and professional goals we spoke of earlier. We have seen, however, how these practices are common sense solutions to the daily problems and troubles teachers face in Cedars Junior, and we have been concerned to establish their rationality for the actors involved.

Proponents of open-plan schooling would probably suggest that open-plan teaching need not be like this. Whilst they might have great respect for staff in Cedars Junior, they would argue that many of the teachers were still working within a traditional as opposed to a progressive framework and tending to interpret open-plan as being really unworkable, but prepared to make 'the best of a bad job'. As a result, their adaptations and responses seemed geared towards producing circumstances as like those prevailing in conventional classrooms as possible. Proponents of open-plan schooling might go on to agree that we have uncovered further evidence along with that provided by Bennett (1976) and Sharp and Green (1975) and others on the difficulties of putting progressive educational ideals into practice. To do so is difficult under favourable circumstances and the social situation of Cedars Junior, in a downtown inner city location, made it that much harder. Finally, they might conclude that for open-plan teaching to work on the spatial level, and hence on the learning level, a completely different orientation to that of the traditional school or classroom is required and that this point ought to be stressed again and more forcefully in the training of teachers. Moreover, once this different orientation has been adopted there is the further requirement that all teachers in an open-plan school operate as a team sharing the same general and common goals. Isolated teachers

The Primary School

committed to the ethos of open-plan teaching who have to work alongside colleagues searching to create the interactional equivalence of walls and classrooms will simply not produce good open-plan teaching. In short, they argue that to put progressive educational ideals into practice in the open-plan situation requires an extraordinary amount of cooperative organization, of a kind different to that which is needed in the more traditional set-up.

Whatever our feelings, inclinations and intuitions about such views, our task has been to describe and analyse what teachers in the setting of one particular open-plan school actually did. Once we turn to the question of what they *should* have done, there are major problems concerning what the ideal should look like. For example, Bennett el al. (1976) find in their survey that the term 'open-plan' itself had such a varied and disparate usage and meaning amongst local authority education committees, schools and individual teachers as to make it very nearly useless and consequently of little comparative value. In this respect, we may like finally to consider some remarks made by the head teacher of Cedars Junior concerning the organization of the school and teaching styles. He issued a guide to all members of staff, which said in part:

> The school is very open-plan and must be accepted as such. There is no point in any teacher working in the main school pretending that he/she is in a closed classroom. In the junior department the closed home base is timetabled for Juniors and teachers may use it as they wish – for small groups or for large. Each day will begin and end with 'Quiet-time', which must be strictly adhered to... . In our building a quiet beginning and ending are vitally important, the former to set the tone for the day and the latter to 'wind down' the day quietly... . In our building cooperative teaching is a must, i.e. the sharing of space and resources.

The above may be regarded as the 'official line' and makes claims about the organization of Cedars Junior which are straightforwardly consistent with the professional ethos of open-plan. We have seen, however, that teachers have both individually and collectively devized their own methods, for handling matters and doing their jobs, which bear only varied and tangential resemblance to the 'official line'. As researchers, it is not our task to put down and to criticize what teachers do from the standpoint of such official lines and ideology. Rather, it has been our concern in this chapter to develop an understanding, analysis and consideration of certain practical consequences of the social organization of space and place in one inner-city, open-plan primary school.

PART TWO

Familiar Teaching Routines in their Context: The Secondary School

Introduction

Although there are undoubtedly many common aspects of teaching to be found in the various stages of schooling and education there are also some very evident differences. In this Part we look at a few of the characteristic features of routine teaching in a secondary school.

One obvious distinction is that these schools are populated by adolescents. Teaching and talking to adolescents can be quite different from talking to young primary school children. Further, in secondary schools teachers generally manage pupils by the class. Story-time in an infant school is distinguishable from most of the rest of the day because it is a time when the teacher handles her pupils as a collectivity or single group, whereas in a secondary school talking to a group of 25–30 pupils is the expected way to teach. It is also routine in secondary schools for pupils to move around the school class by class from lesson to lesson. It frequently occurs, therefore, that here and there a pupil arrives late.

In Chapter 5, George Payne looks in detail at the talk produced by a teacher and a pupil when the latter arrives late for a lesson. He argues that although teachers deal with this occurrence so frequently that it is routinely dealt with unthinkingly, this example clearly shows that the management of a late arrival is a carefully orchestrated piece of social interaction. In the example studied, the teacher artfully presents to the pupil, through the organization of the talk, the occasion-relevant features of the situation as a typical lesson.

One feature of the situation as a typical secondary school lesson is the way the teacher handles the pupils as a single class. Having the late-comer as a full participating member of the group seems to be important to this teacher, possibly because it is one way in which the potential interruption can be minimized. However the author points out that getting a late-comer into a lesson quickly and effectively may be good for control but may not necessarily be good for the understanding of the lesson.

Introduction

Chapter 6 takes up the issue of how adults and adolescents talk to one another. Carolyn Baker's analysis is based on transcripts of conversations she had with adolescents in Australia and Canada. The topics of these conversations were 'growing up' and 'being their age'. Thus one interesting methodological point is that the parties to the talk are producing – in their talk – the very phenomenon they are most interested in, namely, the nature of talk about adolescence: how 'adults' view 'adolescents'.

Her analysis clearly shows that although adolescents are characteristically attributed the position of 'inbetweenness', they are usually able to gauge how far up or down the biographical continuum they are being placed by the way the adults talk to them. They can also make claims themselves for positions on this continuum. The transcriptions and analysis repay careful study in bringing out the subtle and delicate ways of seeking to claim and establish identities for which there are no clear-cut, easily available categories in everyday conversation.

In secondary schools, relationships between teachers and pupils are formulated through how they talk to one another. The identificational work involved in the daily talk can be particularly highlighted in counselling sessions, but Carolyn Baker suggests that we all – including teachers – have a lot to learn from listening to how we talk to adolescents at any time in school. She also provides a method for discovering some of the taken-for-granted practical usages of biographical identities by teachers in schools. Of course, these identities imply qualities and competences both in school and beyond.

5 Dealing with a late-comer
George Payne

I

A frequent experience for teachers is dealing with pupils who arrive late for lessons. Although the experience is probably more common in secondary schools where the day is typically broken up into a series of periods and where the pupil body moves around the school from one lesson to another, teachers in other school situations also handle the problem. To characterize the activity as a problem, however, may be misleading because the fact of the matter is that the experience is so common that it constitutes a normal unproblematic feature of doing normal teaching. Competent teachers manage the occasion of late-arriving pupils without great anxieties; they deal with it routinely, even unthinkingly.

We have on tape an example of a teacher dealing with a late-comer and from a detailed analysis of the talk of the episode it is clear that the teacher's apparently routine, unproblematic actions are tightly orchestrated and methodically organized. The general strategy the teacher uses is to bring the pupil speedily and effectively into the interaction already proceeding, through presenting to him in epitomized form the central features of the occasion into which he has entered.

II

In the lesson from which the materials are selected, the teacher is in full flow when a late-comer enters the classroom. As he comes in the talk is as follows:

118. T: .... Ethelwolf – father himself a famous warrior he himself fought a lot of the Danish invaders now where ave you been/
119. P: Sir ma bags broke ink (went) all over me books so I (had to dry them all out).
120. T: Oh and did it have to be in my lesson — um
121. P: Don't know sir (   )
122. T: Go on sit down — expect you've nowt— to do— show a lot of er

Dealing with a late-comer

     — answering a lot of the questions now — you've got a lo—
     you've go— five minutes work to catch up on haven't you —
     what were we talkin about last week. — um/
          (2.0)   ((General background noises))
123. P: E:r — Alfred the Great.
124. T: No that's what we're (just goin to) talk about now.
125. P: (   )
126. T: The Vikings lad the Vikings — an you'd better concentrate
127. P: Yeah (how uh — how they wus) going to invade Wessex (   )
128. T: That's it — yes — thats right — now then as we were sayin — his father Ethelwolf himself a famous warrior — King of Wessex — title that later Alfred himself was to get — King of Wessex — he had — Alfred — three elder brothers — now this is quite significant — because — well can anyone tell me why — why do you think its significant/
129. P: ⎰Sir (   )
130. T: ⎱ (   ) DON'T SHOUT OUT please

The following analysis is broadly organized around the sequence of the talk, that is to say it moves through the talk utterance by utterance. This procedure is adopted for several reasons. First it helps to convey a sense of the speed and effectiveness with which the teacher deals with the arrival of the pupil after the lesson has begun. Second, taking the talk utterance by utterance helps to demonstrate the progressive manner in which this work is accomplished. Further, because the teacher presents to the pupil the features of the lesson in epitomized form in this short episode, each of his utterances tends to do a lot of work, overlapping and cross-cutting the various aspects of the social organization of the occasion into which he is bringing the late arrival. Taking each utterance in turn helps to illuminate the intensified nature of this interactional accomplishment.

In his first utterance to the late-comer, the teacher says:

    T: .....now where ave you been/

This sentence comes at the end of an utterance which the teacher is directing to the class prior to the late-comer's arrival. There is no pause before it, the teacher carries straight on from what he is saying about Ethelwolf and then directs this utterance to the newly arrived pupil.

With this first utterance, the teacher is in effect telling the pupil that he is late and is asking him to account for that fact. It is an accountable matter for a pupil to arrive after a lesson has started and generally he is required to find some good reason or some excuse for coming late. Here, the teacher is not so much interested in where the pupil may have been, but in why he was not present when the lesson started. This hearing is provided for by the fact that the teacher does not make any reference to a particular period of time. He

91

simply asks the pupil where he has been. To ask someone where he has been without making reference to any particular time is to imply that the person being addressed knows perfectly well the period of time to which the speaker is referring. Here both the teacher and the pupil know that the latter should have been present at the beginning of the lesson with the rest of his class.

Further warrant for this finding is provided for in the pupil's response. In utterance 119 the pupil does not immediately say where he has been, but tells the teacher what has happened to him. From what can be deciphered from the barely audible talk, he tells what he has been doing, which happens to include an account of where he has been. In the second utterance in this episode the pupil says:

P: Sir ma bags broke ink (went) all over me books so I (had to dry them all out)

The pupil's response is difficult to hear because he says it in a very low voice. The quiet, subdued manner of his delivery may be making available his awareness that he is in trouble for being late.

In this utterance the pupil has artfully chosen an impersonal formulation to explain his late arrival. His bag broke; he did not break it. He does not say what he was doing when the bag broke, nor how it broke. He is providing for his lack of responsibility for the matter, and thus his lack of responsibility for being late. His bag has broken which was nothing to do with him; ink has gone on to his books, which again was nothing to do with him. He did, however, dry them out. Although he 'had to', he nevertheless did the responsible thing in trying to get them back into some good order. So not only is it the case that the reason for his being late is something he had no control over, but also while being away he has been behaving responsibly.

Thus in reply to the teacher's question regarding his whereabouts, the pupil has offered some reasons for not having been where he should have been and has formulated them in a way which exonerates him from any possible blame. By so doing, he provides some warrant for the finding that the teacher in his first utterance is, among other things, demanding from the pupil some good reason or excuse for coming to his lesson late. Here the pupil is trying to excuse himself by claiming that the reasons for his being late were essentially beyond his control.

In asking the pupil to account for his late arrival, the work the teacher's utterance is doing is thereby in part hearable through the formulation of the pupil's response to it. Both parties are observably orienting to the requirement of an excuse or good reason for arriving late. They are both making his late arrival accountable.

Through asking the pupil to find some good reason or some excuse for being late, the teacher can also be heard to be doing some identificational and relational work with this first utterance. The right to demand of others

Dealing with a late-comer

some explanation for their being late for such occasions as a rendez-vous, an appointment or a meeting may be variously enacted in different social situations because of the relationships operative between the members involved. Social peers may require for each other an explanation for being late, but subordinates in particular hierarchical social relationships may not be able to demand or even request that their superiors do likewise. Servants do not require their masters to account for being late, nor do ministers of monarchs. Routinely, pupils do not demand teachers give excuses or reasons for being late. It is not suggested that subordinates can never act toward their superiors in this way, but that it tends to be unusual for them to do so, whereas superiors seem always to have the right to require their subordinates to provide good reasons for being late. Teachers always have the right *vis-à-vis* pupils and especially so when the latter come late to a lesson.

Thus, in his first utterance to the late-comer the teacher is making available to the pupil the identificational and relational features of the occasion. He is providing for his own identity as the person is charge, the teacher, and for the identity of the pupil as one who is accountable to the teacher. At the same time, the pupil collaborates in the accomplishment of this identificational and relational work through offering his reasons or excuses for being late to the lesson.

Additional work the teacher does with his powerful first utterance is to indicate the general pattern of the allocation of the talk on this occasion. With this first utterance the teacher asks the pupil a question. He does not simply tell the pupil to go and sit down and get him into the lesson that way with minimal interruption to the teaching. Instead he stops teaching and provides for some continuation of this stoppage through asking the pupil the question he does. He wants to know where the pupil has been. Very probably, he wants to know why the pupil has been away from the beginning of his lesson in order to decide how to deal with him. Presumably how he deals with him will depend on his assessment of the worthiness of the reason for his being late. There are, then, good practical reasons for the teacher asking the pupil where he has been. If the pupil has arrived late for reasons the teacher may consider unworthy, he is likely to deal with him more severely; for being late to a lesson without 'good reason' is usually looked upon as bad behaviour in school. Late-comers can disrupt lessons in that they can stop the flow of the teaching, they distract the attention of the class, they can break up developmental sequences of argument or exposition, and so on. Thus to come late to a lesson without good reason is a serious offence in school. Here the teacher is beginning the interaction with the late-arrival by ascertaining his reason for being late.

Having been asked the question, the pupil has strong pressure on him to contribute to the talk, which itself constitutes the interruption to the teaching, through offering a response. The teacher can then go on to make of that

The Secondary School

response whatever use he wishes with regard to his practical projects in the occasion.

This pattern of talk is a feature of the occasion as a lesson. It is the teacher in a lesson who controls the talk, initiates the topics and asks the questions. In particular, by asking questions, the teacher provides for the pupils' participating in the lesson through the contributions their responses make to the interaction. Having the pupils participating in the lesson provides the teacher with resources for monitoring what is happening, how much they are learning, how effective his teaching is and so on.

Moving on from these first two utterances in this episode, it appears to be the case that although the late arrival has gone to some trouble in producing his response, the teacher does not readily accept his attempt to exonerate himself. In the next utterance (120), the teacher says:

T: Oh and did it have to be in my lesson — u:m.

In this utterance the teacher does not in any way indicate that the pupil's absence has been for a worthy cause. Rather, he responds to the pupil's effort to excuse himself with a measure or sarcasm as he 'puts him on the spot' in front of the class by asking him a second question which is practically unanswerable. Asking a question requires the pupil to produce a response, but the particular formulation the teacher selects makes it very difficult or virtually impossible for the pupil to produce an adequate one.

The teacher's question is practically unanswerable in that he has not asked the pupil if he himself has been responsible for the events which have befallen him, but instead has asked him if it *had* to be that way. Who in the world can say when things *have* to be? What individual is able to account for the workings of fate or some impersonal powers which mobilize events in the world? Only gods and those blessed with very special powers can say such things; ordinary pupils certainly cannot. Consequently, by asking the pupil if it had to be in his lesson that the bag broke, the teacher, through his sarcasm, is presenting him with a difficult interactional problem.

An indication of the measure of the pupil's difficulty is given in his response in utterance 121 when he says he does not know. He goes on to say something else which cannot be deciphered because it is said so quietly and because in the middle of it the teacher speaks again with utterance 122 overriding whatever it is the pupil might be saying – thereby indicating that he, the teacher, is not really concerned about whatever it is the pupil might have to say for himself. Showing himself not to be particularly concerned with what the pupil might have to say further warrants our finding that in asking the question in utterance 120, the teacher is primarily concerned to do something other than find out an answer to his question. Its unanswerable nature suggests that it is not an answer he wants. Rather, it demonstrates a concern to give the pupil a difficult time. The teacher is making it clear to the pupil

Dealing with a late-comer

and to the class – who are an audience to the interaction – that pupils should not come late to lessons. By coming late, this pupil has rather messed the teacher about. He has missed what has already been done with the rest of the class and thereby presents the teacher with the strong probability of some extra work. To be fully efficient the teacher would have to fill the late-comer in on what he has missed. Such extra work would not be necessary if everyone was on time. Having a show-down with this pupil in front of the class reminds them all of that fact and shows them what the teacher's feelings are on it.

Additionally the teacher is building upon and reinforcing the occasion-relevant identifications and relationships he provided for in his previous utterance to the late-comer. To go about the world asking unanswerable questions is to do some identification work. Persons who ask unanswerable questions can find themselves describable as bores, or they may be jesters, or mystics and possibly a host of other things. Here, the teacher with his question provides for an identification of himself as the member in control of this occasion to such a degree that he can ask others there more or less whatever he likes. He is letting it be known that he is responsible for the lesson and in charge of the occasion.

We note that this finding on the work he is doing with this utterance is further corroborated by describing the lesson as *his* lesson. It is not the class's lesson, it is not even the joint lesson of the class and the teacher, but the teacher's lesson alone. It 'belongs' to him. In describing it as 'his lesson' he reinforces the knowledge that he is in control of this occasion. During the period of the lesson the teacher has complete control over what will be done and over how it will be done. In this way, he can describe the setting as his lesson, his occasion, his time to do with these pupils whatever he sees fit. Here he simultaneously shows both his orientation to the occasion as one in which he is in charge, together with achieving some control over the late-comer himself. He has established his control over the pupil through getting him to act by asking the first question and then by asking him another immediately after. Although the second question requires the pupil's further action, at the same time it brings him to a standstill by its formulation as an unanswerable question. Not surprisingly, the pupil in utterance (121) mumbles in a very subdued manner, 'Don't know sir'.

With speed and art, then, the teacher has brought this late-comer under his interactional control. He has brought him into the relationship which is operative between him and the rest of the class. He has in that way begun to bring the pupil into the class, to make him a part of the class, to have him included in the cohort of pupils he is managing in this lesson.

An aspect of the social organization of the occasion as a lesson is the teacher's management of the pupils as a class or a cohort. This feature of a teacher's practical management of classroom lessons has been analysed more

The Secondary School

fully elsewhere by Payne and Hustler (1980). Their analysis focused particularly on the teacher's subtle management of the turn-taking practices in the talk of a typical, fairly formal, secondary school lesson. But they emphasize that a teacher in that situation can routinely and 'unthinkingly' provide for an organization of his pupils as a class or a cohort throughout the duration of a lesson. In the event under discussion here, the arrival of a late-comer is potentially threatening to any work the teacher has already accomplished in this respect.

The arrival of the individual presents the situation of a cohort of pupils with another pupil 'outside' it. The arrival of the 'outsider' could possibly re-invoke a sense of individuality among the pupils in the class. Their sense of themselves as a single collectivity which the teacher has worked at providing for, could be threatened and possibly disrupted by his arrival. Here though, the teacher has speedily and effectively provided for bringing the pupil into the relationship he has with the rest of the class and has thereby minimized the threat to any order he has previously established.

Moving on to utterance 122, here the teacher follows up this early work with some stronger provisions for getting the late-comer into the class as a participating member of the cohort. Utterance 122 is longer than the others so far considered in this episode, and with it the teacher does an enormous amount of work of different kinds. In this utterance the teacher says:

T: Go on sit down — expect you've nowt— to do— show a lot of er — answering a lot of the questions now — cos you've got a lo— you've go— five minutes work to catch up on haven't you — what were we talkin about last week — um/

Generally in this talk the teacher can be heard to be getting the late-comer into the cohort of pupils which constitute the class, while at the same time putting him through a further troublesome time in front of them. One fundamental problem for the late-comer is the fact that his late-arrival makes him noticeable. By coming into the lesson late, he has already attracted attention, and the teacher displays how this attention will be staying with him as he describes ways in which the pupil's actions are going to be particularly noticeable for some time yet.

Taking the various parts of this longer utterance separately, it can be noted that the teacher begins by telling the pupil to go and sit down, thereby getting him into the same physical or ecological arrangement as the rest of the class. Through telling the pupil to sit down however, the teacher also further confirms the relationship he has already established between them in the previous talk. He neither asks nor suggests that he sit down. Instead, he tells him to, implying that the pupil has no option or choice. In this occasion the teacher can tell the pupil what to do; the pupil has to do as he is told.

Dealing with a late-comer

The teacher follows up this work by indicating other features of the occasion through telling the pupil what is expected of him now that he has come into it. He informs him of the kind of activity he is expected to get involved in, in this occasion. Clearly the pupil is expected to become actively involved in the lesson although the teacher appears to have some difficulty formulating exactly what it is the pupil is expected to do. The teacher says the pupil is expected to '*do*' and then reformulates that as '*showing* a lot of...', and then reformulates that into, '*answering* a lot of the questions'. The pupil is in no way expected to be a passive observer of the interaction; he cannot just sit and listen to the others or listen to the teacher. He is expected to participate in the activities of the lesson.

We suggested earlier that a teacher routinely displays a concern to have pupils involved and participating in the lesson. Although he may use several techniques to accomplish this aim, the most frequently used organization of activities in the lesson is to ask the pupils questions. One major way pupils get to contribute to the talk of the lesson is through providing answers to a teacher's questions. The lesson from which this selected extract comes is typical in that much of the talk which constitutes it is organized around the teacher asking questions and the pupils supplying answers. Here the teacher is telling the late-comer that he is expected to answer a lot of questions.

In this way, the teacher is intensively making available to the pupil certain features of the occasion. While telling the pupil how noticeable he will be, the teacher also describes the pattern of the distribution of the talk of the lesson and the interactional devices employed to achieve its allocation. He describes the pattern of the talk for the pupil and tells him how to fit into it by indicating how he is to participate.

At the same time the teacher makes provision for the pupil to pay attention in the lesson. In order to be able to answer any questions that may come his way, he will have to know what is going on, and now that the teacher has specifically pointed out to him that he is expected to answer a lot of questions, any failures to answer are likely to be more than usually noticeable, especially if the reason is his lack of attention to what is being said.

Thus although the late-comer is being brought into the group by providing for his integral membership of the class, he is at the same time being individualized within that organization in that he is brought into the class in an intensified fashion. For him the generally expected behaviour of the class of pupils is being highlighted with the spotlight on him. By providing for his paying attention in this manner, the teacher is bringing him into the class very swiftly. Bringing him swiftly into the organization of the occasion minimizes the potential disruption his late arrival may produce.

It is also noticeable that within this short episode of interaction when he is dealing with the late-comer, the teacher asks several questions. Thus as well as describing an organization of the talk for the pupil he is also producing it.

The Secondary School

His first utterance to the pupil is a question, his second utterance to the pupil is a question, and his third, the one we are currently considering, also ends up with a question. Finally his sixth utterance in this episode, that is utterance 128, which is the first he directs to the class as a whole after the pupil arrives, also ends up with a question.

The teacher is at one and the same time both constituting and describing the organization of the talk. In this methodic work, he is making available to the pupil in an intensified manner an aspect of the social organization of the occasion into which he has just entered.

If we move on to the next part of the teacher's utterance 122, we note that he makes available to the pupil another feature of the occasion into which he has come. He says:

.... cos you've got a lo— you've go— five minutes work to catch up on haven't you...

Here the teacher is describing to the pupil the scheduled and phased nature of the occasion. Anyone knows that secondary school lessons are typically time-tabled for fixed periods of time, starting and finishing at publicly indicated times. In this part of the utterance those general features of the occasion are being presented to the late-comer, again in epitomized form.

The pupil has a lot of questions to answer and a lot of work to do because he has missed five minutes of the lesson. Now five minutes may not of itself sound like very long, but how long any period of time is considered to be depends on the various contexts of consideration. Within the context of this particular lesson of about 30 minutes during which, as can be seen from the transcript of the whole lesson, the teacher wants to get over some information about Alfred the Great to the whole class and wants them to write up that information in the form of an account of his rise to power, then five minutes may be considered to be a lot of time to miss. The five minutes cannot be added on to the end of the lesson, for lessons have to end on time if the timetabled day is not to be disrupted, so they will have to be made up for within the limited period of the time available.

Although within the period of five minutes the teacher is not likely to elicit many answers from the class and very probably there are several pupils who have not given the teacher any answers at all, many of his questions have been directed to all of them. So although the limited amount of time which has elapsed has enabled very few pupils to produce answers, through the general two-party organization of the talk, which his management of them as a class provides for, they have all had several of the teacher's questions directed at them. The late arrival has missed all of these questions. The two-party organization of the talk provides for his having missed a lot of work, in that he has missed all the work the pupils have been doing as a class. It is in that sense he has a lot to catch up.

Dealing with a late-comer

The constraint of only having a limited amount of time available may suggest to the teacher that he has not really got sufficient time to go over with the pupil all that he has missed. If he were to do that there might not be sufficient time to get through all that he wants to with the class. Further, the teacher's orientation to manage the pupils as a class may suggest to him that if he takes time to bring this late arrival up to date, the others will be hearing what they have already covered and consequently may feel that they are not required to pay attention to what the teacher is saying. The teacher is not likely to want to set up a situation which encourages the pupils not to be paying attention and thereby risk losing some control over them as a class. To keep close control involves engaging them all in similar activities for much of the time, and this involvement requires having their attention as a class. We suggest that this professional knowledge of the occasion provides for the teacher displaying a strong concern to bring the pupil into the occasion speedily, through getting him involved in the required activities in concentrated form rather than bringing him up to date with the actual information he has missed.

It is here perhaps that the teacher's concern to manage the occasion, to have control of it through managing the pupils as a cohort, overrides his concern to teach them. Having this pupil in the class as one of the class is more important just now than making sure he knows what he has missed. Perhaps it is more important in that getting the pupil into the class, as an involved and integral member of the group, is the most efficient way of ensuring that the potential disruption caused by the pupil's late arrival is kept to a minimum. Getting him 'into the class' may be the quickest way of assimilating him into the occasion, and speed is of the essence if his late arrival is not to take up too much of the lesson's allotted time. Dealing with him in this manner shows the pupil how the teacher is constrained in his organization of the lesson by the fixed period of time within which it has to be executed.

Through adding 'haven't you' to the last part of this section of the utterance the teacher can be heard to be pointing out to the pupil that he too should be very aware of the fact that lessons have this timed character. The 'haven't you' is not obviously hearable as a question requiring an answer; it is rather a rhetorical question. In effect, with his use of it here the teacher is pointing out to the pupil that he, the pupil, knows the nature of the occasion. Through pointing that out to him, he is then doing further work which brings the pupil into the occasion quickly. It is as if the teacher is saying 'now you know the nature of this situation as well as I do, so let's have you in it and part of it as both of us know you should be'.

Subsequently, the teacher does some work which, among other things, points to another aspect of the phased nature of the occasion. He says to the pupil:

.... what were we talking about last week — um/

Here the teacher is linking the lesson to the previous lesson they had together last week. As any pupil knows, although a typical secondary school day is fragmented into a collection of lessons or periods, each lesson is usually one of a series in that subject, tied together by overlapping or related topics which constitute a syllabus. In this utterance the teacher is providing for the pupil finding this lesson as the next one in a series of lessons he is having with this class of pupils.

As well as the linking work done by this part of his utterance, the teacher also, and at the same time, acomplishes other things. Importantly, he brings the late-comer right into the lesson by introducing him to its topic. In this episode, the teacher has already been doing the identification and relational work relevant to the occasion, by describing its features in terms of the pattern of distribution of the talk and its most frequently used device of a question-answer format. Now he introduces the topic of the lesson in such a way that the pupil is required to produce it for him. With all the other interactional work the teacher has accomplished, once the pupil knows what the lesson is about, he has been given a pretty full indication of the central features of the occasion and thereby has been provided with the resources for displaying his full membership in the occasion. As it happens, it appears to be the case that the pupil jumps the gun a little. In answer to the teacher's question about what they were talking about last week, the pupil in utterance 123 appears to offer this week's topic. After some hesitation he offers 'Alfred the Great'. In response, in utterance 124 the teacher says:

T: No that's what we're (just goin to) talk about now.

In jumping to this week's topic the pupil displays his recognition of the linking work the teacher has been doing and is possibly indicating his concern to get into this lesson as quickly as he can, given that he has arrived late. From the full transcript of the lesson it is clear that at the end of the last lesson the teacher told the pupils what they would be covering in the current one. Possibly that is what the pupil is remembering from the last lesson. Whatever the reason, the fact remains that the pupil appears to offer this week's topic which indicates that he is now well and truly a participating member of this current occasion.

In utterance 126 the teacher very briefly tells the late-comer what it was they were talking about last week and then tells him that 'he had better concentrate'. Up to now in this episode the teacher has been directing his talk at the late arriving pupil; it is not until utterance 128 that he 'continues' the lesson and talks to the class as a whole. Utterance 126 is the last of the utterances the teacher directs to the pupil individually. The topic for the lesson has in fact been introduced or announced even though it was produced as an incorrect answer to the teacher's question; nevertheless the pupil knows what it is, from what the teacher says in utterance (124): 'No that's what we're (just goin to) talk about now'.

By telling the pupil that he 'had better concentrate' (utterance 126) the teacher not only states his expectations but also does so in a somewhat threatening manner. In choosing this particular formulation, the teacher implies that the pupil will be concentrating in this lesson if he knows what is good for him. He has come late, the teacher has his eyes on him, he will be watched for some little time yet. He will have to be careful because anything he does now, which he ought not to, will be on top of what he has already done, i.e. arrived late. Besides doing these things the teacher has already indicated to him, the pupil will in addition be expected to concentrate on what is happening in the lesson and to be doing so observably. Concentrating will constitute part of the model behaviour now expected of him.

By way of continuing with the lesson, the teacher recaps a little on what he has been doing with the rest of the class, pausing frequently within his relatively extended utterance, presumably to ensure as far as possible that they are all listening and understanding what he is doing. But in his recapping he goes no further than picking up what he was saying when the later-comer arrived. What the pupil has missed has been formulated by the teacher as a period of time, i.e. he has missed five minutes rather than any particular information. The teacher picks up what he was saying when the pupil entered by repeating almost exactly the same words. In utterance 118 and in utterance 128 in this extract he says, 'father Ethelwolf himself a famous warrior'. To be exact the Ethelwolf in the first utterance comes in front of 'father', but that slight variation does not significantly alter the basic symmetry of the utterance which can be heard to provide for closing off the episode. What the teacher was saying before just as the late pupil was arriving, he is saying again now that the pupil has been brought into the occasion and has been made one of the class.

Thus the teacher's management of the late-comer amounts to the production of a 'side sequence' (Jefferson 1972) within the on-going activity of the lesson. The pupil's arrival is not so much a 'part' of the lesson but constitutes a break within it. His appearance in the occasion does not bring the lesson to an end but rather is artfully managed by the teacher to be seen by all as a minor interruption in the on-going flow of the lesson. While managing the late-arrival the teacher does not 'lose' the class and now, having dealt with him satisfactorily, he can continue with the lesson from the very point it was momentarily interrupted.

III

We hope that our analysis makes clear how the mundane activity of the teacher dealing with a late-comer constitutes a considerable accomplishment. For the teacher this accomplishment is a taken-for-granted unproblematic achievement. Yet it displays an immense amount of work. Our

The Secondary School

analysis has intentionally focused on the methodic characteristics of that achievement. In focusing upon the detail of the methodic procedures and practical reasoning made available in the organisation of the talk which constitutes the episode, the intention has been to explicate those seen-but-unnoticed features of interaction glossed by the description, 'dealing with a late-comer'. Producing these findings and making visible the work which goes unnoticed in the day to day routine of doing a day's teaching, has several practical implications.

It is notable that our taped episode presents an example of a well executed management of a latecomer. With regard to further research and the development of understanding of classroom management it would probably be very useful to compare this episode with an example of a mishandled or poorly managed late arrival. From the comparisons it is likely that a wealth of possible lines of analysis and investigation would be generated which could prove instructive to practising teachers and students alike.

Out of this particular example we may note that speed of action is important when bringing a late-arriving pupil into an already proceeding lesson. In not giving the pupil opportunities to go into long explanations of why he is late, the potential interruption is kept to a minimum. What works, however, may not be what is desirable. In this case, the teacher is clearly domineering and fairly heavily sarcastic. Given an opportunity to hear himself by playing back the recording, perhaps he would not like what he hears. Listening to episodes of this kind with other teachers can generate discussions on how late-comers are handled by others and on what are desirable strategies. If dealing with a late-comer involves indicating to him the features of the occasion into which he has come, some benefits might accrue from a carefully selected presentation of features. Teaching and learning may be encouraged by presenting some features rather than others.

Whatever interactional strategy is used, one broad implication arises out of the ways in which teachers deal with late-comers. It relates to a teacher's continuous concern with balancing his management and control of pupils with the teaching/learning which takes place in his lessons. Late-comers are potentially disruptive; should they be dealt with in a way which minimizes the disruption without regard for the understanding and learning they will experience in the lesson? Or should the teacher take time to ensure that a pupil arriving late is put fully into the picture and given all the necessary information to be able to participate on a basis of understanding? Lack of understanding now may be storing up potential disruption later in the lesson. Teachers are frequently having to make such decisions. Would their actions be better informed, more effective, desirable and balanced if they could hear, analyze and discuss a variety of examples of such episodes? We suggest that the chances are that they could benefit tremendously from listening to themselves and to others.

Dealing with a late-comer

The arrival of a late-comer is in some ways similar to the beginning of a lesson. It is a moment when the teacher can define the situation in terms of the relationships operative there and the activities he has in mind for those present. If a lesson is not going very well a late arrival can give a teacher an opportunity to do some of this definitional work for the benefit of the whole class and not simply for the pupil who has just appeared. He may want to take the opportunity to revise earlier definitional work and make a new start. For example, the arrival of a late-comer allows a teacher to emphasize control aspects of classroom management. Whatever direction the teacher may decide to take, a late arrival gives him an opportunity to do that work without having to stop and start again. Although interruptions can be a nuisance, they may also be turned to a teacher's advantage in the daily routine of classroom management. The likelihood is that there is more to dealing with a late-comer then meets an unreflective teacher's eye.

6 Adolescent-adult talk as a practical interpretive problem

Carolyn Baker

The phenomenon and the problem

When young adolescents are asked to comment on what it is like to be their age and how they experience growing up, one of the issues they raise in various ways and in different contexts is the way adults talk with them. They present this issue in terms of how they are spoken to by adults and how their own talk is heard by adults. Further, they offer their own competence to converse with adults as a criterion of their own maturity. Thus they raise the recognition by adults of their conversational competence – how they are treated as conversants (Speier, 1976) – as issues in their own adultness and in their relationships with adults.

When adolescents identify 'how to talk' and 'competence to talk' as phenomena in their world, they show their appreciation of conversation as a source of reality and identity affirmation or disconfirmation (Berger and Luckman, 1967). The interactional management of biographical difference between adolescent and adult, especially in conversation, is a matter for observation and comment by adolescents; they themselves recognize it as a phenomenon and identify it as a problem in their relationships with adults. We therefore pose it as an issue for consideration by teachers, since talking with adolescents constitutes in large part the doing of teaching, particularly in secondary schools. In such conversational contexts, notions of the social place and qualities of 'younger' and 'older' can be seen to be invoked and employed in the way the talking is done. In this chapter, we provide a method for observing this phenomenon in adolescent-adult talk, discuss the practical interpretive problem posed by adolescent-adult talk, and offer implications of our analysis for teaching.

We begin with some examples of conversation between an adolescent and an adult, drawing on some transcripted passages from interviews with adolescents in Canada and Australia on the topic of 'growing up' and 'being their age'. In these passages the phenomenon and the problem are raised as

Adolescent-adult talk

substantive issues. Each example presents a different aspect or formulation of our topic of adolescent-adult talk.

Example 1:

1 I   When you're with your friends d'you feel more grown up – than when you're with your teachers — like d'you feel more//
2 Uta //Some teachers they make you freely, really, like— what you *are*, a person (hh) you know and — you know they talk to you — at what you *are* – not as though you're, some, little-grade, y'know – 6 or 5 – there's a// difference there
3 I   //M hm
4 U   from between grade eights and grade 6-and-5's — but there're other teachers that— will think you're still – y'know a little kid – and they don't understand that – you *really can* cope with what they're gonna – say – but they say it different
5 I   Does that bother a lot of kids
6 U   I-think some kids it bothers them because they like ta – they know how they're *usually treated* you know — b— an' then-someone-comes-up-and-tries to treat them like they're grade 5 (hh).

Uta, grade 8

In conversation we provide for others indications of what we take to be our relative positions in the world. We also provide others with a sense of what qualities we are assigning to them, for example what we expect them to understand. Knowing how to design our talk for others may be seen as a practical interpretive problem involving the management of identity.

Example 2:

1 I   In what ways do you feel that you are particularly mature
2 Fay The way I can talk — it's – hard to put it but – I can *talk* – with grownups – and yet – I am only – y— *way* younger than them – and yet they take me for someone older — I don't like that *all* the time because if I'm taken for *too* old – then they start getting on at things I don't like – and – so – ((uncertainly)) I don't know.

Fay, 14

Conversational competence is taken (or mis-taken) as an indication of social maturity in our world. Social youngness and oldness may be interpreted (or misinterpreted) from how we talk. There is therefore the potential for error in how we hear the talk of another.

105

Example 3:

1	I	In your life so far – to this point what are the major kinds of things that have happened that have *shown* you – or m— y'know – *proven* to you that you're really growing up
2	Mark	(9.5) ( ) (5.0) ( ) Say the question again
3	?	hh//
4	I	//Can you remember any things that *happened* in your *past* that you thought were really *important* – as – *signs* that you were getting older
5	M	Oh yeah like now like when we go over to someone's house I can *talk* with the adults – rather than just sit there and listen to what *they* say — I even get my – words in, in having a discussion
6	I	Do you enjoy that
7	M	Yeah
8	I	You see that as a goal
9	M	Mhum
10	I	Uh I suppose there was a time when you couldn't do that
11	M	Yeah
12	I	How long have you felt comfortable talking with adults
13	M	– M 'bout – two years

Mark, 13

As members of our society, we work easily with the view that we gain competencies as we get older. The phenomenon of 'growing up' is evidenced in the everyday world through reference to differences and distances between then and now, and the acquisition of increasingly adult-like qualities is treated as a positive achievement (Speier, 1976). Adulthood is set up as the reference point for the adolescent, and is used as a criterion of progress.

Example 4:

1 I What are the worst things about being at the age you're at now
2 F Well when we have a family discussion – they all suggest things and when I suggest one they say you're just – you're young don't – y'know they don't let me have my words.

Frank, 13

We draw on our everyday knowledge of how conversational competence is associated with relative age to interpret (or pre-interpret) the quality of another's talk. At the same time we reveal our grounds for differential interpretation. By putting forward the age of a speaker as a criterion for hearing or expecting to hear talk in a particular way, we sustain the idea of an age-related distribution of conversational competence as a feature of the social world.

Adolescent-adult talk

Example 5:

1 I	Are there ways in which you consider yourself to be quite grown up
2 Chris	Well I think — um — I think I c'n – I can talk – in a conversation without – feeling out of place with adults
3 I	*Without* feeling – out of place
4 C	Ye//ah
5 I	//Mm
6 C	And – I think I act with a reasonable amount of maturity (hh) I hope so (hh) anyway — And ( ) I uh – I think I can – mix – *in* an adult group and – um – people my age with – reasonable – ease

((and later))

7 I	When you're with your friends – do you feel more grown up than when you're around adults
8 C	No (no)
9 I	D'you feel more grown up when you're around adults
10 C	Well it depends on how the adult – is – is um behaving towards you – you see – some adults can, make you *feel* younger – whilst other adults can make (you) feel *older*, by talking to you as an equal rather than an inferior.

Christine, 14

In our culture, we see adults as having available to them options for how to talk with younger persons. Their conversational behaviour has the potential to produce a sense of biographical identity in the adolescent, to move the adolescent conversationally up or down the biographical continuum, closer or further away from a sense of social equivalence with the adult. Similarly, adults can hear in the talk of adolescents claims for a relative social positioning. Such claims by the adolescent can be heard as appropriate or inappropriate given their respective identities as adult and non-adult. In short, both adolescents and adults have options for 'how to talk' and both can hear the social positioning that conversation carries.

Example 6:

1 I	Have you noticed any changes over the past year – in the way your— your parents respond to you//um
2 Bill	//Oh yeah they *respect* me a lot more they like— they didn't like if I said something they just let it pass by right – but now they pay attention to what I say like if I give a suggestion – they pay *much* more closer attention to it – than (what) say 'bout two years ago

107

The Secondary School

  3 I   What d'you think is th— y'know the *major factor* in that change – in the change o— of their attitude towards you

  4 B   Well that you've got a bit more s— that I've got a bit more sense and I'm not, as silly as I used to be – like, just not saying it for the – to get attention or somethin', that I really know what I'm talkin' about

((And later with reference to the school context:))

  5 I   D'you think that – y'know in growing up, y'know in, in becoming older and thinking older and so forth that this school is really helping you

  6 B   Oh yeah sure, like – they don't treat you as babies – like you— they respect you more like I was talkin' to Mister Barry the other day, an' like he can *talk* to you right – he doesn't like ((mimicked)) uh yeah I understand what you mean, y'know, as if he *doesn't* understand – but he c— like he c'n talk sorta like man to man

Bill, 13

We discover changes in the quality of someone's talk and take these to index changes in the person; conversely, discovering changes in the social characteristics of the person informs the hearing and interpretation of that person's talk. The changing qualities of persons and the changing qualities of their talk are taken to provide evidence of each other, and are used as documentation of the phenomena of growing up.

In these passages, the adolescents employ a variety of terms and phrases to identify how adult talk may define them: 'a person', 'as an equal', 'a little kid', 'just young', 'as babies', 'man to man'. These terms are left unexplicated in these excerpts. They are effective shorthand references to the phenomenon and the problem of who they are addressed as and heard as, of where adults place them in conversation relative to the adult. Where they are placed conversationally appears to be taken by them as indicating where they are placed socially: this connection between talking with adults and social identity is available in each of these passages and is expressed in different ways.

We also notice in these excerpts several instances where the notion that adolescents 'can talk' with adults is presented as evidence of growing up. It appears to be presented as an achievement, as evidence of increasing social competence, in the world we talk about.

So far, by taking this initial look at these excerpts and by making some interpretive comment on them, we have introduced 'adolescent-adult talk' as our topic, elaborating the adolescents' references to it as a phenomenon and a problem in their world. Following the adolescents' use of relative-place terms in capturing and communicating the sense of the phenomenon, we will continue our analysis by expanding on the notion of biographical placement and then return to examine these conversational passages again, in another light.

The achievement of relative place in conversation: the case of adolescence and adulthood

When we talk about the world we live in, we engage in the activity of giving it a particular character. Inevitably, we assign features and phenomena to it and make it out to work in a particular way. When we talk with someone else about the world, we take into account who that other is, what that person could be presumed to know, 'where' that other is in relation to ourself in the world we talk about. In taking these considerations into account in the design of our conversation, we place the other person somewhere in relation to ourselves. This placement is largely implicit in how we talk and might be indicated through what we choose to talk about, i.e. you are the sort of person to whom we talk about this kind of thing. For in conversation, both a sense of what the world is like – and of who we are – are achieved simultaneously.

In discussing the issue of social 'placement' in talk between adult and non-adult, we refer particularly to biographical placement. Members of any culture or social world share ideas concerning what persons at various points in life typically could be expected to know (their knowledge resources), and what their capacity for understanding and making sense of things should be (their interpretive competencies). This notion of a biographically referenced order in the world (Berger and Luckman, 1967), i.e. the notion of the biographical distribution of social qualities, is a basis for our meaningful use of such concepts as 'childhood', 'adolescence' and 'adulthood'. These concepts or categories indicate places relative to each other along recognizable overlapping continua of age, maturity and competence. We use our knowledge of this biographical order to assign or impute degrees of knowledge, maturity and competence to ourselves and to others, and we use our knowledge of these distributions of qualities in organizing 'how to talk' with others. Thus we speak differently to children from how we speak to other adults, drawing on our commonsense knowledge of a difference and a distance between them and us. As adults, we expect to be spoken to in ways which affirm – or, at least, do not challenge – this sense of where we are. In our own conversational practices, then, we maintain a sense of biographical order as a real feature of our world and assign each other to places in that order. We do so without necessarily using explicit biographical terms. We reveal to a listener our sense of who and where we are, and who and where they are, in the way we design our talk.

We have both commonsensically and analytically attributed particular features to the biographical 'places' we talk about. To adolescence we have attributed a particular problematic, that of 'inbetweenness'. In everyday life, and in the social scientific literature, adolescence is seen as a transitional period between childhood and adulthood, leaving relatively open what the qualities of persons in this period are taken or claimed to be. Practical interpretive problems may involve such issues as 'how to talk' with persons in this space or place and where in this space they are being put in the talk of other persons. We see this sense of 'how to talk' being raised as an interpretive problem in the transcripted passages.

In our interactional activity, particularly in conversation, we achieve a sense of distance or difference, or a sense of continuity and commonality, between 'adolescence' and 'adulthood' as places in the world. In the activity of socializing the young, we can variously invoke distance or closeness of knowledge and interpretation both as grounds for and accounts of our and their behaviour. Pre-adults can call such notions into play as well. In this sense, we negotiate and achieve what we take our relative places to be and the qualities we associate with those places.

In our everyday world, however, we conventionally assign to adults the competence and the right to locate the 'criteria of adulthood', and adults adjudicate on the non-adults' claim to be meeting those criteria. How adolescents talk, how their talk is heard, appears to be one of these criteria as we have seen from their statements in the passages already presented.

The interviews from which these passages are drawn may well have occasioned their selection of 'talking with adults' as a topic. For, at the same time that these passages contain comment about adolescent adult talk, they are instances *themselves* of adolescent-adult talk. They are conversations between a researcher who could commonsensically be understood to be an adult, and persons who could similarly be describable as adolescents, given their age. Further, and more importantly, the interviewer assigned the persons being interviewed to a place between childhood and adulthood, and they entered into the discourse in these terms. As well as invoking notions of an adolescence and an adulthood as real places in the world in the substance of their talk, the parties to the conversation do the work of assigning each other to these biographical categories. We can see them to be orienting to each other as adolescent and adult (as commonsensically understood) in the interview and on this basis we can use these categories for our analysis. On these grounds, therefore, we can reasonably proceed to examine their conversation as conversation between an 'adolescent' and an 'adult'.

Thus we will treat the interview conversations as instances of the phenomenon being discussed substantively, i.e. adolescent-adult talk. Seen in this light, the interview conversation becomes our primary resource for advancing this discussion. Our attention will turn, therefore, from an initial concern with the content of what is said to an examination of this conversation itself as illustrating and displaying its own subject matter. The talking about the phenomenon exhibits the phenomenon itself.

We turn to re-examine the interview passages in which the phenomenon and the problem were introduced as topics in order now to observe the phenomenon and the problem in the interview conversation. In doing so, we provide a method of observing features for which parallels could be found in the more familiar scenes in which adolescents and adults converse, and we also address the practical interpretive problem of 'how to talk'. Subsequently, we outline implications of our analysis for teacher-student talk and for schooling.

Some features of adolescent-adult talk

i THE DISPLAY AND DISCOVERY OF COMMON SENSE COMPETENCE
We have identified the issue of biographical placement as a phenomenon in adolescent-adult talk and have suggested that this notion of biographical placement is a way of collecting together the various referents to 'where' the adolescent is placed as a listener or participant in adult talk. We turn now to examine some of the instances of adolescent-adult talk previously presented in order to describe how the practical interpretive problem of 'how to talk' is managed by both adult and adolescent in these passages. The examples we have drawn on show a few of the many questions asked in the interview. Together they provide some indication of the stance adopted by the interviewer and the kinds of questions to which each person was asked to respond.

We will begin with reference to the passage in which Uta and the interviewer discuss 'feeling grown up':

Example 1:

1 I   When you're with your friends d'you feel more grown up – than when you're with your teachers — like d'you feel more//
2 Uta   //Some teachers they make you freely, really, like— what you *are*, a person (hh) you know and — you know they talk to you — at what you *are* – not as though you're, some, little-grade, y'know – 6 or 5 – there's a// difference there
3 I   //M hm
4 U   from between grade eights and grade 6-and-5s — but there're other teachers that— will think you're still – y'know a little kid – and they don't understand that – you *really can* cope with what they're gonna – say – but they say it different
5 I   Does that bother a lot of kids
6 U   I-think some kids it bothers them because they like ta – they

111

know how they're *usually treated* you know — b— an' then-
someone-comes-up-and-tries to treat them like they're grade 5
(hh)

Uta, grade 8

In this example we can find illustration of those features outlined in the previous section. First (as in each of the examples) the interviewer provides and places a problem-relevant-to-being-her-age into the discourse, in so doing suggesting what her world must be like (1). The interviewer presents possible social contexts for this 'feeling' problem, e.g. 'when you're with your friends', 'when you're with your teachers', thereby showing Uta how and where this 'feeling' could be located. Thus in the question itself, there is an interpretation of Uta's world, and of Uta as a member of it. In asking the questions, the interviewer is showing Uta how an 'adult' organizes an interview on 'adolescence', for example what she chooses to ask about. In both these respects, we can see the interviewer's work here as presenting an adult description of adolescence and calling on Uta to develop that description. Uta has no problem working with the domain of knowledge captured in the interviewer's questions; she can fill out and advance the sense of the problem as a problem for people her age (2). In these ways, she demonstrates her knowledge of the biographical order which these questions refer to and are embedded in.

The substantive content of Uta's comments will be recognizable by most readers, i.e. some teachers are not appropriate in their behaviour in that they fail to recognize how persons her age should be spoken to, or in this regard fail to recognize the differences between year groups in the school. Drawing on the vocabulary introduced previously, we could treat such teachers as placing students further down the biographical continuum than the students wish to be placed. Uta suggests that some teachers do not know not to 'say it different' (4), and that their saying it differently may be taken as an indication of who they think she 'still' is, 'a little kid', further down the continuum. Here we have Uta saying in her way what we said previously about formulating our talk for an other on the basis of where we think the other is, and what interpretive qualities append to being there. In talking on this basis, we effect the putting of the other somewhere, in this case, down. The mistake Uta refers to is the inappropriate distribution of competence by the teacher. The mistake is discoverable, as in this case, by the person whose claimed identity is being denied.

Uta claims to be in a substantially different category from 'grade 5' or 'little kids' (2). She uses these referents to point out just how improper such teacher behaviour is, relying on the interviewer to appreciate the magnitude of difference and distance between herself and grade 5's. Just what the teachers have done is not available to us; indeed the interviewer did not need to probe further because the sense of the problem has been accomplished quite competently by Uta in showing the comparison to be ridiculous. Uta's use of the future tense in 'what they're gonna say' reinforces her claim to be prepared, before the event, to 'cope' with an adult language and adult verbalizations (4).

In expressing in this way her social distance from 'little kids' and her ability to handle adult talk, she may be seen to be implying that she and the interviewer share in this interpretation. Thus there is an implicit description of a relationship between the parties to the talk in that Uta places herself and the interviewer together as observers and evaluators of the behaviour being discussed, as people who agree on the sense of error being revealed. Uta claims commonality of interpretation here and calls on the interviewer to share her recognition of herself as well beyond grade 5 level in coping with adult talk.

Uta's talk about 'some teachers' may be taken to affirm implicitly that the interviewer is not behaving inappropriately, i.e. is not talking down to her. Otherwise, she would be unlikely to be drawing the interviewer into mutual marvelling at the mistakes others can make. The problem is being diagnosed as a problem 'out there' in the world they are talking about. The interviewer's second question, 'Does that bother a lot of kids?' (5) helps in the achievement of this external location.

We can begin to recover what constitutes this conversation as outside the domain of 'adults talking down', i.e. what constitutes it as a setting in which Uta can talk in this way about how adults talk to her, although she is in fact offering these comments to an adult.

In asking these questions, with their assignment of adolescent-in-the-world to Uta, the interviewer is sustaining a sense of their relative places in the age-graded world about which they speak. Uta, like the other interviewees, appears to go along with this placement as both context and topic of this encounter. 'Being her age' is made a problem in the world outside the interview, talking with adults is made a problem there too. The interviewer's questions, then, render Uta's adolescence a problem, but also a phenomenon (a fact of life) in the real world. In the questioning, Uta's adolescence is treated not as a conversational problem but as a phenomenon, and in the questioning Uta herself is assigned the interactive and interpretive competence to treat it that way. Otherwise, the 'interview' is a charade.

Uta and the others are being asked to step outside their adolescence and report on it to an adult. In doing so, they step into and draw upon some common interpretive ground, namely the everyday, common sense knowledge that we share as members of the same social world. This common sense knowledge enables us to talk about 'being one's age' as easily as talking about the weather. This knowledge is what the interviewer is asking to be displayed.

For further illustration, we consider briefly the conversation with Bill:

Example 6:

1 I   Have you noticed any changes over the past year – in the way your— your parents respond to you//um
2 Bill   //Oh yeah they *respect* me a lot more they like— they didn't like if I said something they just let it pass by right – but now they pay attention to what I say like if I give a suggestion – they pay *much* more closer attention to it – than (what) say 'bout two years ago
3 I   What d'you think is th— y'know the *major factor* in that change – in the change o— of their attitude towards you
4 B   Well that you've got a bit more s— that I've got a bit more sense and I'm not, as silly as I used to be – like, just not saying it for the – to get attention or somethin', that I really know what I'm talkin' about

((And later with reference to the school context:))

5 I   D'you think that – y'know in growing up, y'know in, in becoming older and thinking older and so forth that this school is really helping you
6 B   Oh yeah sure, like – they don't treat you as babies – like you— they respect you more like I was talkin— to Mister Barry the other day, an' like he can *talk* to you right – he doesn't like ((mimicked)) uh yeah I understand what you mean, y'know, as if he *doesn't* understand – but he c— like he c'n talk sorta like man to man

Bill, 13

Here again, as with Uta, the questioner is achieving (i) the biographical placement of Bill in adolescence; (ii) an interpretation of what adolescence is like' (iii) the simultaneous placement of Bill as a person who can comment on being his age. The interviewer relies on Bill's common sense interpretive competence as a resource for doing this interview. In what the interview is about, i.e. substantively, these people are formulated as 'adolescents'; in the doing of the interview, i.e. methodologically, they are relied on to make sense of the questions and confirmed in their capacity to do so. Their 'adolescence' is not seen or made to get in the way of their provision of interpretations about it. By examining the form of the questions in our examples, we can see how they promote this casting of 'adolescence' as a phenomenon rather than as a problem for the interview itself.

In the passage with Bill, the interviewer's questions ('Have you noticed...' (1) and 'What is the major factor...' (3)) essentially require Bill to report as an outsider on any changes in his relationship with his parents. He has to step outside and the place he steps to is the common interpretive ground we have mentioned before. From there he describes his progress from being 'silly' and 'seeking attention' to having 'sense' and 'knowing what he is talking about', a description which he designs for an adult listener who can also appreciate these terms in the negative and positive lights in which he uses them.

These framings of the question ('Have you noticed', 'What is the major factor') also imply that Bill, the listener, is competent to be observer, interpreter and analyst of social behaviour. Indeed, he is asked to provide an account of the behaviour of adults. To be so asked suggests he has a capacity comparable with other members of the category, 'adult'. Thus, the questioning offers a topical equivalence of adolescence and adulthood, in that they are both made topics for discussion from the same 'outside' observational point.

The framing of the questions in such terms may be the feature of this questioning which appeals to the adultness of the adolescents, while the substantive content places them in adolescence. For another example, Fay is asked, 'In what ways do you feel that you are particularly mature?' This question is not simply a more complicated way of asking, 'Do you feel you are mature?' Such a formulation not only assumes a sense of 'in some ways' (i.e. not all ways), but also assumes that such ways are themselves identifiable by the adolescent. To be seen to be able to locate ways in which one is and is not 'particularly mature' assigns a general knowledge of the nature of maturity. Similarly, the questioning of Mark (example 3) and Christine (example 5) presupposes their knowledge of what kinds of things would evidence 'being grown up'. While they may not be fully grown up yet, they are assumed to know what it looks like. Thus the form of the question does the work of attributing to the individual everyday knowledge and the competence to work with it in such a setting. Again in the interview with Bill, the appropriateness of the interviewer's way of talking is indicated through his reference to the fact that he (Bill) can talk 'man to man', that he really knows what he is talking about, that people 'pay attention' to his talk. These notions would be difficult to advance as confidently if these same capacities and qualities were in fact being disconfirmed in the conversation. Bill also appears to have found room for claiming interpretive continuity with the interviewer as shown, for example, by his use of 'right' (2, 6) as an incorporative device.

It may well be that our formulation of others is most clearly revealed in the way we design our questions (or comments, or their other conversational equivalents). These questions provide an indication of the expected competence of the listener to answer and make visible, for example, our conceptions of what people at this age could be expected to understand and cope with conversationally. Such competence is necessarily assumed and relied on when adults converse with non-adults, although it is not necessarily recognized interactionally in explicit terms – a paradox in adult-child interaction located by MacKay, (1973). Given that 'questioning' is a major feature of formal teaching, then how we question can be examined for its formulation of the listener, as well as for the work also done in describing subject matter or displaying modes of thought. As we have shown here, these features would be simultaneous but separable.

ii INTERPRETIVE WORK

As we have shown, in the asking of questions and the providing of answers, identities are simultaneously claimed as well as assigned by speakers. We have shown how in answering questions, these adolescents may be seen to be claiming identities which, for example, establish a sense of their own maturity. The interviewer assumes her own adulthood in the doing of the interview and this is a tacit feature of the questioning. Both conversants do interpretive work in fashioning their talk for each other. This work constitutes resolving the practical interpretive problem of how to talk, i.e. how to formulate things appropriately for the other in this setting. We have seen how the interviewer has chosen to address and formulate the identity of the adolescents and we now look briefly at how the adolescents identify the interviewer and, in so doing, themselves.

In their answering work, the adolescents orient to their listener, designing their comments for that listener. In so doing, they assign to her qualities, competencies, and knowledge. At each point they resolve the practical interpretive problem of how to talk with her, of how to fashion responses to her questions. We will examine some of the transcripts to draw out this phenomenon in their talk.

We have already pointed out that in her interview Uta relies on her listener's everyday knowledge to make sense of what she is talking about (teachers talking down), appealing to the interviewer's appreciation of talking down as a problem for young people. Thus she casts the interviewer as a person sympathetic to her interpretation of the problem, thereby commenting on the interviewer's behaviour in the interview and simultaneously assigning to the interviewer the same interpretive stance she herself elaborates. In this interpretive work, each of the answers given by the adolescents is offered as a possible response to the question posed. Each answer will be taken to reflect something of the identity and qualities of the speaker, as well as suggesting something of the identity and qualities of the listener. Example 2, where Fay talks about her ability to talk with adults and how it can be misinterpreted, is compelling to read. It serves as a warning to the interviewer and also as a comment on the potential for the problem she talks about to obtain in this setting. Fay's comments around being 'only way younger than' adults asserts her sense of distance from that adulthood which is characterized by engagement with 'things I don't like', namely, adult topics. She shows a method for alerting adults to the potential inappropriateness of their talk by recalling her youngness and appealing to their common sense knowledge of what that implies. In Example 5, Christine points to talking and mixing with adults as evidence of being 'quite grown up'. In qualifying her statements with 'I think' and 'I hope so', she suggests the inappropriateness or the difficulty of making a definite claim, at least in this setting. Her recognition of this inappropriateness may itself be seen as a display of her interpretive competence, her knowledge about how such claims would be heard by an adult. It serves as a nod in the direction of her listener, who would know about criteria of maturity and would be in a position to comment on how well Christine converses. Thus as they describe their listener, these speakers describe themselves as persons who can do these descriptions. In Example 6, Bill characterizes himself from his parents' position (2, 4) showing how adults might organize an account of their 'changing attitudes'. At the same time, his description is designed to display his knowledge of what this listener would appreciate as signs of respect and reasons for respect. In all of these conversations, a version of adulthood is being invoked not only in what is said about it, but in what is being assumed about the interviewer's own knowledge as an adult, and about how she would interpret phenomena as a mature member of the social world.

The adolescents draw on the knowledge of how their listener would be thinking, and offer it in their answers. In this way, they achieve a formulation of their listener, producing an ongoing commentary on what that listener would understand, take as valid evidence, appreciate, deem plausible, etc. In the resolution of the practical interpretive problem of how to design answers for this listener, they offer versions of the listener, making appeals to the listener's concurrence with those versions.

Hammersley (1977) has analysed classroom talk to show that in answering teachers' questions in lessons, pupils have to solve problems of relevance, validity and elaborateness (what to say, what evidence to call on, how much to say, when to say it). They also have to take into account the identity of the other for an answer to be seen as competent and appropriate. Mehan (1979) has made use of a distinction between 'form' and 'content'. To be seen as competent members of a classroom, students must provide evidence of academic knowledge (content) in a situationally and interactively appropriate way (form). We could say they need to draw on their knowledge of the teacher's model of good teaching and good learning as and when it becomes revealed in his questioning and other classroom talk. To the extent that teachers and pupils identify the teacher as also an adult, pupils may be seen also to require some knowledge of adulthood and how adults think in order to talk to them. In engaging in educational activity at all, they must continually display what they know about adulthood, as well as what they know

The Secondary School

about how teachers think. We have shown how such reference to the adult's knowledge occurs in these interviews, and how these references may be viewed as attempts to establish a continuity of interpretation. We suggest that this conversational option is open to them in the nature of this particular setting, in which the interviewer does not seek to correct their interpretations or to recall herself as an arbiter of that correctness.

Thus we see that identities are claimed and assigned in the organization of the conversation such that a sense of who-we-are-and-what-our-qualities-are is negotiated in the course of talking. The practical interpretive problem of 'how to talk' involves hearing and responding to the claims of the other as well as organizing our own talk in order to produce a sense of our own and an interpretation of the other's identity. A social relationship is achieved through conversation, and is continuously indexed by conversation.

'How to talk' is not necessarily or usually a 'problem' in the sense that we need to stop and work out how to do it on each occasion. The interpretive work being identified here is undertaken routinely and unproblematically most of the time. We use our taken-for-granted knowledge of biographical difference and our notions of who we and our listeners are as unexamined resources for designing our conversation.

As we are told by the adolescents, however, and as we know ourselves, this process can become problematic in our social relations. We have shown here some ways of thinking about where the problem may lie and have suggested that it is in the formulating work, which is often implicit in everyday conversation, that identity confirmation or disconfirmation may occur.

In discussing the topics of 'growing up' or 'being their age' with adolescents, we have substantive as well as interactional references to biographical difference and relationship available to us. We have suggested that the features we have examined obtain in adolescent-adult talk about other topics as well. To illustrate this point and to examine an instance in which participants discover and then resolve a problem of inappropriate person formulation in their conversation, we draw on one additional interview passage. In Example 7, the interviewer turns the conversation to the topic of a boy's occupational future and it might be seen to capture the sense of a conversation in the practice of vocational guidance.

Example 7:

1 I D'you have any ideas about-the-kind-of work you do *not* wanna do - when you grow up
2 F Uh — no - I don't know what I *don't* wanna be (I've) never thought of that — garbage, cleaner I guess (hh) - garbage man
3 I How - um — your - ambition right now is is to be an electrician?
4 F ( )
5 I But how solid or how - definite is that kind of - ambition

6 F Not really that solid but – my *dad* actually wants me to be an electrician – but I want to be a carpenter
7 I D'you find that – choosing what you wanna be ha— is really important for you to do now
8 F I think so 'cos – my option is what I'm going to be — I gotta pick now – for what I might be when I'm older
9 I So do you feel some pressure about, deciding what you want to be
10 F Yeah — right now
11 I But then you *did* say that you didn't have much difficulty choosing your options
12 F No because that's what I *am* gonna be — y'know to be an electrician, but I don't wanna but – there's no difficult 'cos that's what I put down
13 I Why do you feel that you're going to be – an electrician
14 F It's good pay — and — I don't know, I like — it's not a, smart job and you don't have to be too brilliant
15 I H, d'you, h, is this something that you really desire – or is it something that you simply think is gonna happen
16 F Something I think is gonna happen — like I do— I don't actually not *wanna* be and I don't actually *wanna* be
17 I You just think the cards are gonna fall that way for//you
18 F //Yeah

Frank, 13

In this conversation, the biographical placement of Frank is effected through locating Frank's 'being grown up' in the future (1) and through casting Frank at this point as a school student, which in our culture is another form of biographical placement. The line of questioning being pursued can be seen as reflective of an understanding on the part of the interviewer that making occupational choices is an activity or a problem related to his biographical position (1, 3), just as 'feeling grown up' and 'changes in the way your parents respond to you' were presented earlier as elaborations of the model of the adolescent which was being used by the interviewer. Again, then, problems are being assigned to the adolescent in the questioning, thereby producing a biographical formulation of the listener. In everyday conversation, such problems may be self-assigned, as when adolescents, seeking guidance from adults, initiate the conversation in which both participants supply interpretations of the problem.

Here, the interviewer displays some assumptions concerning how subject choices at school and occupational intention should be linked or seen as linkable by the student (7, 9, 11). This interpretive activity on her part presents a version of how option-choosing should be done, and it proposes that Frank be describable, and describe himself, in these terms. The interviewer assumes that 'ambition', 'deciding', 'choosing' and 'really desire' are viable terms for a discussion of schooling with any student, including Frank.

Frank's work in this passage achieves a modification of the viability of the interviewer's interpretations as applied to himself, showing that for him, this vocabulary and the version of occupational achievement it documents, does not quite apply. He corrects the formulation of himself as the choosing-deciding-really-desiring adolescent which is embedded in the line of questioning. In so doing, he provides both a different version of how it works for him (12, 16) and a claim for an alternative identity. At the same time, Frank shows that he is aware of the interviewer's version by supplying an additional component which can account for the apparent logical problem located by the interviewer (11); *viz* he states that he already knows where he is headed (12). The apparent disjunction that she raises between feeling pressure to decide on an occupation and not having difficulty choosing options (9, 11) is thereby resolved. Frank shows his competence as a conversant with an adult by his recognition of the source of her problem and by supplying this additional information as a solution. Here we have an example of how a 'wrong' formulation of the adolescent by the adult is located and, for the purpose of getting on with the interview, mutually resolved (17, 18). As in previous passages, we see here that the adult reveals a version of who it is she is talking with (an adolescent, a student) and attributes qualities to him as a member of that category. Just as in the case of Uta some teachers get it wrong, the interviewer here got it wrong. The person being spoken to can identify the error as he can hear and interpret the formulation in the question. It requires considerable time, and work by Frank, to make the interviewer hear his version (1–18) and his claim to be someone different from the model in the questioning.

Of course, not only in questioning, but in telling, in commenting, and in answering, do we provide social-biographical formulations of the other. Indeed we have shown that the activities of telling, commenting and responding are part of this questioning in our example. Every sequence of questioning carries an interpretation of the world and the other person. This point is as true for classroom questions as for interview questions.

We have shown how formulations of adolescents are embedded in how we question, how we talk. We put into practice in this way, as members of society, our taken-for-granted knowledge of a distribution of interpretive competence, showing them what we take their qualities as thinkers-in-the-world to be in how we frame our communications with them. We have suggested that it is not the substantive topic itself, but the definition of the other as conveyed in how we ask them to deal with topics, which is central to their sense of where we put them relative to ourselves on a continuum of interpretive competence. In teaching, this point is reflected in how we present ourselves and them as potential knowers of the knowledge we teach and through how we ask them to treat the knowledge we teach. We have suggested that it is possible to break the tie-up between youngness and interpretive incompetence, to invoke their adultness as conversants and to be seen to be doing so. We have shown that this assignment of interpretive competence to others, and particularly the young, is part of socialization itself in that through this process, persons come to know what their capacities are, or are seen as being.

Discussion

In preceding sections we have shown that notions of biographical place are made available in conversation between adolescents and adults and that the reciprocal assigning of social qualities is achieved through 'how we talk'. We have identified this phenomenon of biographical formulation as a discoverable feature of adolescent-adult talk and have suggested that the social relationship which is held to obtain between the adolescent and the adult is displayed in the talk itself. We suggest that the adolescent can find in the design of an adult's talk what identities are being assumed and assigned, although they are found pre-reflectively and not with the explicit use of the methodology illustrated here. We have shown a possible method for elaborating or filling out the sense of what is captured in the adolescents' use of phrases such as 'man to man', 'as equals', 'as babies'. We have treated these phrases as the adolescent's own glosses for the phenomenon we have explored and as pointers to our use of the biographical dimension as a way of elaborating this phenomenon.

The immediate implications of this analysis for teacher-student talk include the possibility of using a similar method for hearing, in our own conversational practices with adolescents, evidence of the features we have described and also a method for discovering our own everyday practical use of notions of a biographical distribution of qualities and competencies. We have also raised the problem of hearing adolescents' uses as well and, particularly, their biographical formulations of themselves as these are embedded in their talk. Given that students do not typically claim or exercise the right to tell teachers outright 'how to talk' to them, to correct them in this regard, and that students of adolescent age particularly may be sensitive to this dimension of teacher behaviour, self-reflection on our own conversational practices as teachers could be useful. Similarly, we have indicated a way of listening for the social positioning and identity claims carried in adolescents' talk.

Some of the passages we began with may be heard as capturing the sense of 'categories of offence' committed by adults which adolescents claim offend their dignity and standing (Marsh, Rosser and Harré, 1978, pp. 35-6). Other passages may be heard as indicating commendation for the proper and affirmatory conduct of adults towards adolescents. From either side we have reference to the same issue of social identity which we have elaborated here through the notion of biographical placement in talk and shown to be a feature of the talk we have examined. If 'how we talk' is a practice through which the social identities of students are confirmed or disconfirmed, it may be useful to think of it as a potential source of consensus or conflict in our relations with adolescents.

If we see identity as a problem and, particularly, if we see identity as a problem for adolescents, then our conversational behaviour with young people can be located as an activity central to ongoing identity work in the classroom. Indeed teaching is largely an activity of talking, listening to talk, and interpreting that talk. Some implications of this view of teaching are offered as we make some concluding points.

One category of teacher activity which this analysis directly informs is the conversation which occurs between a teacher and a student in counselling settings and in settings in which various kinds of problems are discussed. Conversation constitutes such activities, and outcomes turn on how the talking and hearing goes. Beyond this basic reliance on conversation, the individual student's identity, or qualities, or behaviour, or problems, or future become the topic(s) in such settings. These one-to-one situations most closely parallel the interview situation we have drawn on here. In such situations, the adult's biographical formulation of the adolescent and the adult's self-formulation are likely to be made more explicit or more immediately available since such settings are typically understood as offering guidance, correction, information or support to the younger by the older. In the practice of counselling, the biographical relationship between the parties, e.g. the adultness of one and the non-adultness of the other, is likely to be invoked as premises or terms of the talk itself. We know that such activity is sometimes resisted and sometimes embraced by the recipient. The implicit as well as explicit identity work that occurs in the talk in such settings constitutes part of the grounds of how the 'guiding', 'informing', 'correcting', or 'supporting' is received. We have a sense of this work in Bill's report on the conversational behaviour of Mr Barry, who is the school counsellor.

We can move beyond this immediate parallel to offer some observations on the use of notions of biographical place and of the biographical distribution of competence in schools and classrooms.

In the interviews, the adolescence of the respondents is not made a problem in relation to doing the interview, although it is treated as a substantive topic in the world being talked about. Indeed, the activity of the interview is not directed at the problem of the respondents 'being their age'. Rather, they understand the questioning-answering to be for description, not diagnosis.

In the activities of schooling, the pre-adulthood of students is treated as a problem to whose solution teaching practices are directed. In the sense that schooling is expressly for the transmission of knowledge about the world from one generation to the next, the adults in the school are implicitly or explicitly understood to be working towards an increase of adult knowledge and adult competence in non-adults. In school, the adultness of the adults and the non-adultness of the non-adults may be seen as premises of the activity of schooling and, indeed, may be invoked as grounds for justifying and legitimating teaching as an activity. In this same vein, 'adultness' may be made equivalent to having common sense competence, non-adultness to having only pre-competence in this area. For example, teachers may use age comparisons which link proper or good behaviour to being older and inappropriate behaviour to being younger. Their legislation of definitions of adult behavioural competence is a means of displaying their own authority as adult (Hammersley, 1976, pp. 110–111). Not knowing how to 'act one's age' may be invoked as grounds for withholding privileges or for punishing, thus underlining a relationship between age-appropriate behaviour and social rewards. Teacher talk of this sort may of course be intended for individuals, groups, or whole classes (Payne & Hustler, 1980) as the hearers. Unlike the conversations we have analysed, such talk is public. Teachers may treat its public nature as a resource in itself, e.g. for purposes of social control. At the same time, such talk makes publicly available a teacher's display of 'where' he puts the whole class, the group, or the individual. In this way, appeals to the biographical distribution of 'common sense' competence may be employed as a resource for social control in schools. We note, however, that appeals to such a distribution of member-competence may be especially problematic where they are heard as misinformed. In this case, they may be taken as evidence of that very lack of competence in the speaker which the speaker is assigning to others. We have a sense of this outcome in Uta's comments.

Similarly, invoking particular versions of adulthood may be problematic. Criteria of adult competence and versions of how 'adulthood' is achieved as revealed in official practices and in the interpretive activity of teachers may appear to be non-viable or arbitrary to students who have access to alternative versions. For example, setting up criteria of adulthood such as good and respectful behaviour, or appreciation of the value of education, or competence with school knowledge, may ring false to students. Such students may 'know' adulthood to consist of other things and to be achieved in other ways, e.g. to be a matter of being out of school and working (Willis, 1977). To them, teacher formulations of adulthood and, indeed, adolescence may be heard as arbitary, implausible or foreign; as evidence of cultural difference or indifference.

If we treat 'adultness' as a social convention rather than a state or a thing independent of our everyday means of discovering and identifying it, we find that what is taken to constitute adulthood – the criteria and requirements for being an adult – is assembled through the interpretive work we have discussed. Teachers engage in this work of displaying to adolescents what adult competence (being grown up) consists of, what its observable and unobservable features are. As adults themselves, they claim the competence to recognize the evidence when they see it. Over time, adolescents are shown how to do this work themselves by adults who see their use of conceptions and criteria of adulthood as unproblematic. As we have seen, such usage can be potentially very problematic, especially where particular legislations of what constitutes adulthood may be challenged and where that same adulthood is invoked as grounds for the legitimacy of authority as a teacher. If we claim our own adulthood as grounds for our legitimacy as teachers, that claim is open to demonstration and possibly testing (Hammersley, 1976; Werthman, 1971).

Making adulthood a difficult achievement by sustaining the sense of a difference and a distance between them and us can be a device in the maintenance of a biographical distribution of competence and is a potentially problematic feature of practices of social control in the school. The notion of a biographical distribution of competence, however, can be seen to be involved in descriptions of and premises of schooling itself. We elaborate briefly on this notion.

The central problematic of schooling may be seen as the discovery, assignment and enhancement of knowledge and competence. Schools are, of course, especially reflective of the age-gradedness of competence. In the school context, we can meaningfully use notions of third grade work, fifth year standards etc. Thus a biographical distribution of competence is embedded in the organization of schooling. In the activities of teaching and learning, the interpretive competencies of students, their competencies as thinkers and knowers, become explicitly treated as topics and problems as well as being relied on as a resource for the very organization of teaching. That is, part of teaching activity involves commenting on and evaluating students' abilities to talk, interpret and understand as competent members in a school world. The problematic nature of these abilities in the process of schooling (and in parenting) is indicated when the demonstration of their presence is taken as a criterion of competence. The fact that these competencies are 'discovered' and made remarkable (as in the adolescents' own comments) shows they are presumed absent until proven present, i.e. they have to be found.

MacKay (1973) has argued that using a theory of 'childhood as deficiency' precludes the recognition of the competencies children must have, and are relied on to have, in order to communicate with adults. The use of biographical categories as theoretical terms can obscure the visibility of competence (as with children), or presuppose the presence of competence (as with adults). With 'adolescents' we may well apply one or the other category to find the absence or presence of qualities we commonsensically append to those categories. Consequently, 'adolescents' can be constituted by us on variable grounds: we can selectively invoke either theoretical category – 'child' or 'adult' – in our interactional and interpretive work with them. Of course, so can they. In this possibility lies our option for how to talk and how to hear, and their problem of how they are talked with and to, how they are heard.

In our analysis we have examined the adolescents' talk and have looked for evidence of their common sense knowledge and interpretive competence in how they design their responses in the interview. We have produced evidence and have shown a method for finding it in other conversational settings where adolescents and adults interact. Looking for and finding this competence (making recognition of it in our talk with adolescence) is a practice in the assignment of biographical place. Similarly, not looking for or finding it is also such a practice. If the discovery of knowledge and competence in the young is a central feature of the practice of teaching, the problem of where and how we look, and what we look for, becomes a practical pedagogical problem.

In the everyday world, we typically use notions of childhood, adolescence and adulthood quite unproblematically. These notions carry presuppositions of kinds of competence or incompetence; and we put them into play and on display in our talk as teacher, or parent, or 'adult'. These notions and the manner of their use are themselves part of our teaching methodology and as such we can examine the work we do with them in accomplishing teaching, and in socializing the young.

PART THREE

Some Practical and Theoretical Issues

Introduction

A book on classroom research can be of little practical use unless it gives potential investigators some clear guidelines on how to proceed. In Part Three clear guidelines are provided and an example of a teacher trying out the methodology for the first time is presented. In addition a fuller, more theoretical discussion of the nature of research generated by an ethnomethodological approach is included.

In Chapter 7, Digby Anderson argues that teachers should do the kind of research they are in a position to do. They have more access to classroom data than outside researchers ever will, and producing tape recordings of their lessons and episodes of classroom interaction provides records of data independent of memory or theorizing.

He outlines suggestions for making taping as easy as possible and lists several possible ways for teachers to make use of their tapes. Importantly, inappropriate approaches to the data are indicated. Thus quantitative and content analysis should be avoided as initial descriptions. Rather transcripts should be examined to see how teachers and pupils technically accomplish lessons and parts of lessons, and these examinations are best conducted by groups of teachers.

Several extracts from transcripts are provided for practice at analysis before readers collect their own material. Suggestions are offered on how teachers may move up into semi-technical issues and on how they may make strategic use of their data with outside agents such as curriculum innovators, advisers and parents.

In Chapter 8, a teacher who has never before used the approach advocated in this book presents us with the results of her first attempt. Carol Cummings produced her analysis largely on her own rather than with a group of teachers. She saw it as a kind of confidence-testing practice run. Having been pleasantly surprised by the experience she now feels that even more can be generated out of her materials through group discussions. 'Out-

Introduction

siders' may help her to see additional 'unnoticed' technicalities in her routine teaching. The part of her routine teaching day in an infant school she decided to tape was the beginning. That is, the period of time before assembly when children are arriving, often with their parents, and the register is being taken. It is a part of the day which might be seen as prior to the teaching 'proper' and one which seems inherently chaotic and very loosely organized. Further it is a period of indeterminate length; it ends when the head teacher is ready.

Yet from a close inspection of the transcript a strong sense of organization and structure emerges, as well as an awareness that a great deal of teaching is going on. The author exposes some taken-for-granted ways in which the organization and order are created and points to some previously unnoticed interactional strategies for having pupils participating. Given the 'natural unity' of the episode in the teaching she studied, the whole transcript has been included for others to examine.

In Chapter 9, Wes Sharrock and Bob Anderson discuss some of the theoretical assumptions which lie beneath the research policy presented in this book. They provide a wider theoretical and philosophical context for the detailed investigations made in the other chapters. It is their argument that there are inherent tendencies in sociology and other social sciences which militate against focusing on the substance of social activities. What is required before we can generalize about instances and relationships between them is an understanding of the instances themselves. The business of any one classroom is not something that should be abstracted out. Our first priority must therefore be the specific and detailed study of instances. At present, generalizations can only be vapid and premature.

Through a discussion of phasing and a use of illustrative examples from lecturing in higher education, the authors argue that what matters about an occasion is its 'business', i.e. what is going on in it. Here the authors widen still further the approach advocated in this book by suggesting that although verbatim transcripts may help to display the nature of an occasion, other evidence such as students' lecture notes or assignments may sometimes better tell us 'what has been going on'. In short, transcripts are a useful tool, but should not become a dogma.

In conclusion it is suggested that as things are from an analytic viewpoint we understand very little about the nature of classrooms and what happens there day by day.

7 The teacher as classroom researcher: a modest method for a new opportunity

Digby Anderson

A whole generation of teachers has now suffered the attentions of sociologists of education, psychologists of education, historians of education, philosophers of education, curriculum innovators, and educational technologists. If a discipline of education exists, it consists largely of their theories, concepts, fashions and ideologies rather than of the products of teachers. Now we are hearing calls for teachers to play a more central part in the creation of education wisdom in particular there are exhortations for teachers to assume a researcher role and for more school-based research (Nixon, ed., 1981).

These exhortations raise all sorts of practical questions about whether teachers have the time and resources to co-operate in or do research. They also raise the question of what sort of research teachers should do – what sort of wisdom they should create. In one way the practical problems dictate the answers to the second question – teachers should do the sort of research they are in a position to do. It is obvious that teachers have, as a body, enormous experience of classrooms. If experience is knowledge, then they are in a position to create a wisdom about classrooms, what happens in them and what could happen in them. Teachers have what researchers call 'access' to 'classroom data', much more access than researchers ever have. One idea behind the notion of teacher-as-researcher is that teachers should reveal this knowledge of the classroom to others and should build up a sophisticated knowledge of classroom teaching and learning from a combination of their diverse sources of data. Such knowledge would, we are told, be of much use to new teachers and to those who design materials for classrooms. It would be 'practical' knowledge from the 'chalk face' and of far more use than the elaborate theories of sociologists, philosophers, psychologists, curriculum innovators, historians and educational technologists.

This hopeful scenario neglects one difficulty. It assumes that teachers and theoreticians are two different sorts of people with different sorts of knowledge, practical and theoretical knowledge respectively. Further, if we could persuade practical teachers to talk about their practical knowledge, then they would give practical advice. Unfortunately at least two other outcomes are possible. First and most depressing, they may start talking like sociologists and philosophers!. It may be that when we ask someone to *talk* about their practical knowledge, they de-practicalize it, they arrange it. They tidy it. They systematize it. They hypothesize it. To put it briefly, theoreticians do not have a monopoly of theorizing. It is this insight which explains the possibility that, for example, in-service training may make teachers unfit to teach (Anderson 1980).

A second outcome is that the teacher, asked to talk about the classroom, will not be able to do so in the way necessary to build up a reasonable knowledge of the classroom. Practitioners when asked to talk about practice certainly talk. That is not the problem. Teachers tell stories, 'You know Andrew H, well last week he was late... .' They categorise lessons in terms of topic, 'I did *Macbeth*, Act II, Scene 1'. They abstract problems, 'When I asked Darren to read, he refused and... .' They talk of conditions, 'It was freezing in the labs'. They produce these very selective descriptions in response to selected and practical questions or in the course of conversations. Further, they give longer accounts of sequences of lessons. Such accounts are highly structured by the circumstances and form in which they are given. Curiously they share a defect with the academic theories – they are talk about something which the hearer cannot see. What we need in the first instance is *data* from classrooms, not reflections and theories. Then, when we do get the theories and reflections, they will be of far more use if they are about data that the hearer can see.

When we have a record of the classroom then we can make use of teachers' reflections, or rather we can see whether the reflections are any use. And one form of record we could have is a tape. In this chapter we argue that audiotapes form a possible *base* for teacher research and that without them or something like them teacher reflections are of little or unknown use. Such tapes are a control on speculation and on memory. They produce a record independent of memory or theorizing to which we can ask practitioners and theorists to address themselves. They require the development of a vocabulary to refer to the events of classroom life and they also encourage attention to detail.

In summary, if we are to ask teachers to build a knowledge of classrooms then they will have to acquire a data base. Memory is not enough. If we are to profit from teachers' detailed classroom knowledge we must encourage its expression to be tuned to the details that a tape reveals. To get the best out of teacher researchers of the classroom, a record of the classroom independent of the teachers' reflections is needed. There is no reason why teachers should not produce such data. They are well placed to do so and the rest of this chapter suggests how a small group of teachers could tape, transcribe and

Practical and Theoretical Issues

analyse what goes on in their classrooms. The notion of teacher-as-researcher and the more general concept of professionalism requires that the teacher should not only know about practice, but also be able to talk explicitly and in a detailed way about it. The methods described in this chapter are a modest way to develop the capacity for detailed and explicit professional dialogue and shared knowledge about the classroom.

The method – taping and transcribing

The following suggestions are designed to make taping as easy as possible: Use one recorder only. Bring it into the classroom on several occasions before the recording date. Try it out before that date. Set it going before the beginning of the lesson and do not switch it off till after the lesson even if you think you only want an excerpt. Make short notes after the lesson on room arrangement, any crucial visual matters, etc. Do this on the tape itself. As you practise more, you will learn what information is helpful. Certainly you should make some notes to help with speaker identification. Acquire any necessary permissions but treat the taping and the taped lesson as a normal occurrence. Do not use video-tape until you are well practised with audio. Do not tape classes where the taping might produce educational problems. Do not tape classes where there is likely to be much simultaneous talk.

Once you have a tape recording, you can produce different transcripts of varying detail. It is difficult to work from tapes alone so you should generally transcribe at least roughly. You should also produce some detailed transcripts. If you are working in a group comparing lessons, you might each try to produce, say, three transcripts of differing ratios, e.g. take four hours to transcribe in a rough way a half hour lesson, then one hour to re-transcribe a five minute section, then one hour to re-transcribe two minutes of the five minute section. In a group of five that will give you five lessons each transcribed at three different ratios. That data will be enough to work on for at least 15 fortnightly meetings. On page ix of this book you will find a transcript notation guide. If you use that and look at some of the transcripts in the book you will see what things can be noted in transcription. Incidentally transcription in itself has a beneficial side effect in increasing sensitivity to detail.

The method – analysing the transcripts and tapes

Your tapes and transcripts can be used in two main ways. First you can use them as a test of other people's research or proposals. You now have a fairly detailed record of a lesson and you may want to see how the elaborate academic theories and your fellow-teachers' reflections mentioned earlier square with your data.

But the main use will be in doing your research. You may of course, in one sense of the word, do anything you wish with the transcripts. These transcripts provide for you a partial reconstruction of the lesson. You can look at that reconstruction, unlike the lesson, for as long as you wish. You may look at it, unlike the lesson, as parts through your knowledge of the whole. These are very basic advantages of transcripts. These advantages can be used to do all sorts of things. You could, for example, look through the studies which researchers have done on classroom tapes and transcripts and note the sorts of questions they have used them to answer. If your interests also focus on these questions then you might use these researchers' work as an initial model on which to work. Barnes (1971; 1977) uses tapes to discuss pedagogic methods, in particular group work and questioning and to demonstrate aspects of the 'hidden curriculum' – its assumptions, knowledge and lesson control. Writers such as Young (1977) tend to use transcripts more illustratively as instances of wider educational and socioeconomic issues. Again, you may wish to look at tapes to consider pupils' and teachers' codes. Like Labov (1970), you may use them to inspect the difficulties that pupils have with standard English or the difficulties that teachers have with pupils' non-standard English. And even a cursory reading of one or two texts on classroom language will give you a list of possible enquiries and models. You may wish to see how others use transcripts to evaluate their teaching (Simpson 1966) or to assess topic coverage and classification in lessons (Gallagher et al. 1970) or you may wish to use them for micro-teaching (Trott 1977) or for studies of classroom interaction (Stubbs 1976; Stubbs and Delamont 1976). You may wish to disregard these and simply use the transcripts as data to ground your discussion of your own teaching problems, curriculum innovations, probationers' work etc. However, we suggest that you resist the temptation to do certain things at least initially.

What not to do
One thing that some researchers do with transcripts is some sort of quantitative analysis. They count, for instance, the number of closed questions on a sample of tapes. As a result of operations like this they suggest, say, that nine out of ten teachers' questions in general only require the pupil to find the 'right' answer, and maybe see that as some sort of trouble. You cannot do that. First you have not got enough transcripts to make such counts generalizable. What you find may be idiosyncratic to the lesson you have taped. Even if you could do such an analysis there are good reasons for suggesting that you do not do so immediately. For once you look at your transcript you will see that spotting a question, let alone a closed question or some such feature, is not a straightforward matter. Lots of utterances that are not in the syntactic form of a question get treated as if they were.

4.13 TA Sleeping tablets are taken quite often in a wrong dosage and cause trouble but there's another one that's more common.

Practical and Theoretical Issues

4.14 P   LSD
4.15 TA   No dear not LSD that is one of the ones that we hear about in newspapers a good deal but fortunately not many take it. There's one – we've mentioned it several times – there's *one very common little white tablet* which — I think all of you will have at your house
4.16 P   Are these for headaches
5.1 TA   Yes they are for headaches
5.2 P   Em again
5.3 TA   Not anadin
5.4 P   Disprin
5.5 TA   Eh well disprin or aspirin or junior aspirin

and

8.7 T   Fish — so — main part of your meal – meat or fish of cheese — and you get your carbohydrates in the way of potatoes — good — another food group (3.0) Emma
8.8 P16 (Food to protect us) — oh we've done that
8.9 T   Well — we've done that (haven't we in —) it's alright don't worry — another food group
8.10 P17 Vitamins
8.11 T   Vitamins — good — and the same way we break vitamins up we don't just say that if you ate an orange you would get — every vitamin from an orange — and you use the letters of the alphabet — one being Vitamin A — does anybody know (1.0) how vitamin A is used in your body

and lots that are in the form of a question are not treated as if they were questions

14.4 T   Calories - which we no longer use — have you done in physics yet the new unit of energy — we don't use calories any more — you don't go on a calorie controlled diet anymore — we're now in the Common Market we go on a?

Things, then, are not always what they appear to be. Their syntactic form is only one aspect to be inspected to see whether or not they call for e.g. an answer. Most important, attention has to be paid to the intonation and to what has been said before, i.e. to their sequential context. This inspection of context involves us in tracking back to see what introduced the utterance, what sort of sequence it is part of. For example, the reason why a lot of non-syntactic questions get heard as questions is that they continue a past question. 4.13 is preceded by

4.11 TA What's the commonest drug that is taken eh wrongly ((cough))
4.12 P Sleeping tablets

Elliptical comments on answers already given can imply answers required.

2.4 P They'd be sweating sir
2.5 C They'd be sweating. Well you might see that — yes. Even more obvious than that ((duplicating machine starting again))
2.6 P Heavy breathing

And our knowledge of the bidding system in classrooms can help us to make quite precise questions out of 'scraps' of talk

5.6 T ...and where will we find protein (1.0) which sorts of foods would you eat — to get protein — would get it in — a Mars Bar — a packet of crisps — Maxine
5.7 P6 Eggs
5.8 T Eggs good — anything else — Alison
5.9 P7 Milk and cheese
5.10 T Milk and cheese good C - the dairy products (1.0) Max — er Melanie
5.11 P5 Fish

The interesting aspect of these excerpts is not that we, and the pupils, can readily recognize what, mostly, the teachers are doing in them (asking questions) and what they require pupils to do. It is that our and their recognition is not simply based on the form of the question, but on the part it plays in a sequence and in a classroom system. Quite plainly two utterances of the same form can do different work and two utterances of different form can do similar work. Therefore it is no use simply adding up all the utterances that have a certain form. What has to be done first is to find out which utterances do what work and that involves inspecting them in their sequence, not in isolation (cf Turner 1970).

There is therefore a job to be done before anything like counting instances is started and that is some sort of qualitative analysis, an analysis which aims to find out what is happening in this sequence of the lesson and what the various utterances in the lesson do. These reasons for initially avoiding instance counting apply equally to another form of analysis you should at least initially avoid; content analysis. Content analysis is one of the pre-coded analyses. At least the simpler of these start with a shopping list of items or things you might expect to find in a lesson and fit the events of the lessons, particularly the topics that teachers 'cover', into the list.

On a tape there is a sequence in which the 'teacher' is remarking on work done on an earlier occasion. He chose to make these remarks in a dialogue, in a series of questions. The sequence has already been prefaced by remarks

Practical and Theoretical Issues

about food groups and is a continuation of a discussion about such groups. The teacher gives examples in the form of stories. One story is about a scientist, McCrendy, who conducted experiments on dogs. These dogs died having been given only distilled water to drink – the exemplary point being the need for minerals (which distilled water does not have). During the sequence he says

3.11 T   Because you can't survive without water — nothing can — so — let's try and answer the question as it was written – why was distilled water used — what's the difference between distilled water and water that comes out of — that tap over there or the bath tap at home
3.12 P13 No bacteria
3.13 T   Sorry?
3.14 P14 No bacteria
3.15 T   No bacteria in it — yes probably — and no what else (1.0) No ((pupil's name))

What is this sequence about? Is it 'about' McCrendy, a story, distilled water, a 'wrong' answer, minerals, food groups, dogs, bacteria or a certain form of dialogue? Of course it is about all of these, but even so that is an unsatisfactory answer. For to portray faithfully the sequence involves us not in counting what is mentioned, but in describing how topics and dialogues are interrelated and organized in sequence. In a sense the relationship between items gives them their character as items. Simply because 'bacteria' was mentioned explicitly three times does not mean that the sequence is 'about' bacteria more than about dogs. The teacher talks of bacteria in the context of acknowledging an offered answer and re-requesting another, i.e. 'minerals'. He talks about dogs as part of a story which exemplifies needs for minerals. A faithful description of the sequence is not concerned then with isolating what is mentioned, but with finding the relationship between the things mentioned and between what is mentioned and the organization of the dialogue.

All this is not an easy point to grasp, but it is crucial if our analyses are not to trivialize lessons. It is not that lists of contents of lessons cannot be made. They can. But consider some sorts of ways of doing this. You could simply argue that such a lesson as shown above contained the topic, bacteria, because it was mentioned three times. That is trivializing and misleading. We need to know how 'bacteria' got mentioned, what was happening around the time that 'bacteria' got mentioned. We need to know the context of 'bacteria'. We could avoid the trivializing literalism of the first method by simply using our intuition and saying perhaps that the sequence is not about bacteria. It is about a teacher trying to get pupils to give him the answer he wants. This at least has the merit that it unifies the stretch of talk by giving it a common purpose or strategy. It is, however, also unsatisfactory for several reasons. Inferences need to be accounted for if they are to be of any use. We need to know what is in the transcript that encourages us to think that 'the teacher is trying to get the right answer'. For it is the case that commentators with different perspectives infer different things about what is happening in a lesson, particularly if they do not have to account for their inferences. The important thing is to distinguish between inferences which are and inferences which are not supported by transcribed data. Unaccounted inferences are not helpful and are rather wasteful ways of looking at transcripts. The whole point of using a transcript is to ground observations about the lesson. Not only are unaccounted inferences wasteful, but in their eagerness to look at motive and results, they ignore the important area of how actions get done in the classroom. Even if a teacher is 'trying to get the pupil to give him the answer he wants', there are a legion of ways to do it. 'How does this teacher do it?' is the important question. Thus content and quantity analyses are premature. They should be postponed until a qualitative analysis has been done.

What to do

We summarize what has just been said by suggesting that if you wish to make inferences about what is happening in the classroom, these should be backed up not by isolated examples or illustrations but by working through a sequence showing how it develops. You should back your judgements of what a teacher is doing by explanation of how he is doing it. Let us call these explanations *technical*. Your assessments of lessons should be supported by technical examinations of the transcript. They may appear tedious but the technicalities you will be examining are after all the technicalities of your trade. You do them already intuitively. The object of working with transcripts together as a group is to bring into the open what you do intuitively so that you and others can look at it. Since this technical examination of how a lesson gets done is necessary to support any transcript-based judgement about what it does and whether it should be done, there is a strong case for starting with it. It is thus suggested that before any judgemental, coding, counting work is done, before lessons, styles, topics, and motives are assessed, teachers should spend time trying to build up an understanding of how particular lessons are technically accomplished.

There are two initial stages to this process. First you should choose a section of the lesson, most obviously one transcribed in detail, and quickly go through it making a rough assessment of what each utterance is doing to the preceding one or ones and what it is suggesting that the next one or ones do. Thus at the simplest level an utterance might be an answer to the preceding question and itself ask a question. Your assessment of what an utterance does, e.g. invite, disclaim, reply, evaluate, close off, preface, tie back to

Practical and Theoretical Issues

earlier talk, set up contrast, initiate a story etc., should be based not only on what you hear the utterance to be doing but on the way the lesson participants hear it. Obviously you cannot know for certain how they heard it, but you can see in the transcript, how they declared or revealed themselves to have heard it, for you have their replies. Questions for instance are questions not only because you hear them as questions, but because they receive answers or, if they do not, this non-receipt is remarked on or causes a question-repeat or some other course of interaction compatible with a question having been asked.

When you have made a rough assessment of utterance activities, then you can go through the section again refining and re-refining your assessment of the sequence of interactions in it. If you do so in a group, you can try to reach agreement about the sequence. You will find that when time runs out you are considerably happier about some bits of the section than others. That does not matter. But if you think you have 'understood' the whole interaction, try a simple test to show just how little you have actually appreciated: use your description of the interaction as an instruction and see what sequence of utterances could be built out of your description. You will quickly find that you have described only minimal features of the interaction.

For example, consider:

4.9 C ....why did they (cavemen) have to use their bodies more than we do
4.10 P They had to hunt for food
4.11 C They had to hunt for food — so what I have to hunt for food in Sainsburys ((laughter))
4.12 P They had to hunt eh live creatures
4.13 C They had to hunt live creatures which meant
4.14 P Running
4.15 C A lot of running — they didn't have machines to catch them or guns or things like that. They may have had bows and arrows but OK — a lot more physical in that way looking for food. What else did they do

You might start by noting that 4.9, 4.11 and 4.13 seem to be treated by the pupils as if they were questions, for the pupils give their answers at 4.10, 4.12 and 4.14. Then you could see that a description which makes 4.11 a question can only produce for the whole of 4.11 'a question'. So you might refine and add to your description a little. 4.11 receipts an answer then asks a question, 4.9 has set up a contrast between them (cavemen) and us: 'I' is one of us, thus the 'I have to hunt for food' shows that 4.10 is an inadequate answer. The question in 4.11 is thus built into the question so far and does not simply re-offer the question, but does so with more 'clues' through its remarks on the last answer. Even this is inadequate to reconstitute the utterance, so you continue refining. You do not ever reach an end of such a process but you do discover some things very quickly. First, to find what 4.11 is doing you have to explore the systematic links that exist between utterances in sequence. Secondly you become aware of the range of technical issues involved in accomplishing a lesson – deciding precisely when to talk, accepting bids to answer, not knowing what someone will say but finding an immediate response to it, and tying your utterances to what has just been said.

The second part of the initial procedure is as follows. In the first part, that is your refined analysis of a stretch or section, you will have started with simple links between utterances, simple interactions such as questions and answers and then have seen, by turning descriptions into instructions, that utterances link in a more complicated way than that. Put differently, starting with a simple notion that teacher says something and pupil replies to it you will have moved on to see (a) that the reply itself influences subsequent talk, (b) that 'reply' is really a loose term for a whole variety of ways in which utterances link to each other. It is a term rather like 'interaction' in that there are obviously different ways of interacting. As a by-product of your refining you will have produced a list of these different ways of verbal interaction – question, answer, closed question, ways of closing a question, answers to closed questions which reopen them, instructions to continue/stop talking, reformulation of what past speaker has said, invitation to comment, ways of disagreeing, assessment of past speaker's utterance, projection of what other speakers will say, etc.

You should collect these items and give them names – simple names such as 'continuers' or 'projectors' – whatever you like. You should also note that these are essentially components of interaction: they are things which get done together by teacher and pupils and like all things there is more than one way of doing them. As we have noted, questions can be asked by syntactic question forms, by intonation, by putting an utterance in a 'questioning position', etc. Thus what you collect are not lots of utterances, but a smaller group of actions. Armed with this short list of things which get done by words in interaction rather than the thousands of words themselves, you can now further add to and refine your collection by looking at other stretches in the lesson.

Once you have a list of lesson actions, you can then move to see which ones are basic to other ones and how different actions interrelate in different sequential stretches. On this basis you can then start to make data based remarks about different lessons and stretches of lessons. Here are some very simple and gross remarks:

1 Lessons contain lots of topics, activities and interactional features. They are not easily reducible to a theme or overall goal or objective. People in

our lessons talk about kings and queens and sums and vitamins. They also talk about each other and themselves. They explain, they question, they answer. They also tell stories, interrupt, digress, re-start, and anticipate what others will say. They cover the subject but they also exchange greetings, discuss whose turn it is to talk, check on absentees, tie topics to 'last week', give out and collect in materials. While it is difficult to assign time to activities, it should not be assumed that lessons consist largely of teacher-explanation and questions and answers on official topics with a little other business. The effect of these activities is that there is a series of layers of what is happening at any given moment, so that talk is about this by him in reply to her at this particular moment, in this sequence, and so on.

2 Lessons are orderly and collaborative. Teacher and pupil fit their utterances together to follow not only questions with answers, but all utterances in a natural flow. This is remarkable because utterances also are improvised, that is, you do not know what someone is going to say until they have said it. Lessons, then, have an order of improvisation and you may choose to consider what sorts of problems this presents to the lesson planner. This improvised collaboration is observable. Speakers do show their understanding of what each other is doing. They show it by transforming what the last person has said, by using the same words, by using pronouns which refer to the same words, and so on. This is an advantage for you because you as analyst can look at the transcript and by seeing what people do to the utterances of others, how they reply to them, you can provide a plausible description of how they understand them.

3 Such order as exists in the interaction seems to exist not only as a result of grammatical structures and the dictionary meaning of words, because a lot of the utterances are not formed in conventional grammatical structures. Grammatical structures stretch across more than one utterance and many of the utterances contain very unusual lexical items. Order and understanding seem to be as much a product of operations which people perform on the utterances of others as of conventional grammatical structures. These operations attempt to make sense of utterances while looking at surrounding items, at what the person might be reasonably expected to say, at what they said last time, at what they could have said instead, and so on.

4 Lessons are busy. All that we have described – the improvised yet orderly organization of a lesson, the making of meaning out of short elliptical phrases, it all happens extremely fast. Look for example at the very small gaps that exist between the talk of different people and, if you wish, consider and visualize the teacher's task as making decisions at each of these transitions between utterances. At each time that someone stops talking,

The Teacher as Researcher

the teacher has to decide on a large number of things, what is he to say, when is he to say it, who is he to select to speak next, what is he to instruct them to do, and so on.

Your first task then is to build up a basic understanding of how the lesson gets done, refining your descriptions of interaction in short stretches and collecting actions from these and seeing how they work in other stretches. On this basis you can make some tentative working generalizations and are ready to look at some of the other uses of transcribed data.

Uses: semi-technical
You have just done a small technical analysis with the data of how the lesson gets done and it is sensible to move very slowly up from technical materials. You cannot move straight from a consideration of how utterances are joined to each other to a consideration of the future of education. Start then with some semi-technical issues, with issues perhaps that might confront someone new to teaching, a probationer, with issues that can be seen to be related to teaching technique. You might look at the reformulation of questions, at the ways open to a teacher to reformulate his question when it does not get the 'required' answer or at the ways he can introduce a questioning sequence. You should have a collection of these different ways. Look for example at this introduction and these reformulations:

6.3 T Rhodesia — yes — ( ) — Cecil Rhodes was um — a British imperialist — won't go into that — he enjoyed himself in Africa — he wasn't too popular with some people there — however he — did give his name to — (one of the topics in the news) — what was Rudyard Kipling's idea (1.0)
6.4 P ( )
6.5 T What — what *did* he do — what was his idea where did he look for the idea ( )
6.6 P ( )
6.7 T What was Rudyard Kipling's (idea) (3.0) (Christopher)
6.8 P ( )
6.9 T (Well you *would* — if you were to refer to it) — Andrew?
6.10 P2 That western man had a duty to — civilize the rest of the world

You might look at the discussion-initiators teachers use. (Here they do not seem to work).

5.14 TB Yes — they want to show off. Eh does this affect boys or girls more what do you think
5.15 P Boys
5.16 TB Boys do you think so — do all of you
5.17 P's Yes (unison)

141

5.18 TB Have you met boys who think that they're grown up to smoke
5.19 P's Yes ((unison))
5.20 TB Don't you think that some girls do as well
5.12 P's Yes ((unison))

You might look at topic closing.

12.8 TV Do you think parents give different advice to boys and girls – your dad says if someone hits you you hit him back, is that what you said; your dad says don't get involved in the fight if (   ) worth anything. Do you think that's because you're a girl and a boy that you got different advice or... .
12.9 P (Sharon's mum gives the same advice)
12.10 P Yes
12.11 TV Gives the same advice
           ((pupils chattering))
12.12 P Yes
12.13 P It's not worth it
13.1 TV (Its a different) attitude to solve arguments. We could carry on with that but let's just leave it for a minute and have em a boy's situation. Take the girls one from that. Which are the boys — now David would you like to eh read out the situation you've got there

You might look at bidding systems

17.8 TV All the time. You'd agree with that. What do you mean by two-faced
17.9 P If you get // (they say people) they who talk to you they are your friend and that next minute they go to someone else and eh say things about ye
17.10 P Well its
17.11 P Is it the reason that
17.12 TV I'd better have Diane because she has her hand up. Diane then Aden ((laugh)) (   ) you've had your hand up so long
17.13 P Let Aden go
17.14 TV OK Aden first then Diane
17.15 P (I forgot what I was going to say)
           ((Laughter))
18.1 TV Oh Diane's remembered
18.2 P Em my friend is always talking about me (Chris told me)
18.3 TV How does that make you feel — upset
18.4 P (   )
18.5 TV What did you do about it, did you go and kick them in or whatever the boys

The Teacher as Researcher

18.6   P   No
18.7   TV   I didn't think you would. Have you remembered what you were going to say
18.8   P   Yeh I 'av em
18.9   TV   Not really
               ((Laughter))
18.10   (What about)
18.11   P   Yes

You might look at examples

2.6   T   You're going to find it much — more harder to do — physical activity aren't you if you've got too much fat on you (1.0) alright? (3.0) what about um (1.0) can we imagine first of all — some of us — are quite — skinny — and we might be able — we might think well it — it's no good *me* thinking about being overweight (1.0) because I — I've not got any — but if we think about — looking at it logically if we think about carrying say two pounds of — two *stones* of potatoes around with us every day and I said to you right — come on then Sarah you've got to run up and down the flight of steps to the music room — three times carrying this — weight of potatoes — half way through she'd begin to get tired and she'd say — can I put it down I can't cope with that — but if you've got that in fat — if you've got that weight — if you've got that extra two stone in weight in*side* of you — you can't stop halfway and say oh let's get rid of it now for the next ten minutes — you don't just get rid of it like that so we've got to educate ourselves into *not* being overweight — so that we don't have to think about — you know — how

3.1   T   we're going to get rid of it — (have to) educate ourselves right from the beginning — it's like — I explained to the other group — you've got — a good set of teeth (1.0) it's no good waiting till they're all decayed and all dropped out and then say well now I'll start cleaning me teeth — you start cleaning them when you *so* big — not when you get thirteen or fourteen or — twenty five or whatever — you start cleaning your teeth when you're little — educate them so that they — *stay* healthy rather than (   ) right? — prevention is better than cure quite often

You might look at teacher assessments

5.6   T   ....where will we find protein (1.0) which sorts of foods would you eat — to get protein — would get it in — a Mars Bar — packet of crisps - Maxine

Practical and Theoretical Issues

5.7	P6	Eggs
5.8	T	Eggs good — anything else — Alison
5.9	P7	Milk and cheese
5.10	T	Milk and cheese good — the dairy products (1.0) Max — er Melanie
5.11	P5	Fish
6.1	T	Fish — // Sarah
6.2	P8	Meat

You might look at corrections

2.9	T	Why's the blood important
2.10	P8	(To keep awake)
2.11	T	((Laughs)) ( ) ((children laugh)) ((name))
2.12	P9	Keeps you warm
2.13	T	Your blood keeps you warm yes it does to a certain extent but far more important than that
2.14	P10	( )fuel — you know — food

You might look at story organization

11.9	T	The *rich* and the wealthy — if you go to London today and you're — standing around the Dorchester Hotel and you watch the big posh cars turning up and you see the women getting out in their big posh — big animal coats — which incidentally look much better on animals ((laughter)) — and men in their evening dresses — usually corpulent — (I mean) fat rather than slim — with their cigars — and they go into the Dorchester and they have a whale of an evening and they come staggering out — full of (expensive) drink and good food — and then we travel across London to Charing Cross Station and look under the bridge and the arches there — and dingy ill-lit side streets —
12.1	T	and you see the other side of the picture which is London's homeless — men wrapped in newspapers to try and keep (out) the warm — in fact there's a song by Roger Whittaker ((laugh — pupil)) what's the song by Roger Whittaker

You might look at selectivity in summarizing

6.2	P	Well, I was best friends with another girl and the other girl always wanted to be with another girl, you know, more or less fighting over her all the time
6.3	TV	Yes I think that's an example here isn't it
6.4	P	In the end eh I had to go with somebody else
6.5	TV	Did you, you in the end lost did you
6.6	P	Yeh

6.7 TV Right — Maxine
6.8 P Well at the other school there was me, Tracy and Michelle and we never squabbled or anything
6.9 TV Em so you had a three that wasn't a crowd // Three that go on well

These excerpts should be long enough for you to do a little practice and tentative work on before you collect your own materials. When you look at them you will be aware that we have named the various activities such as 'bidding systems'. What names you choose to use is something for you to decide, but you will find that you need as a group to work out names in order to refer to the new technical things that you have discovered in lessons. This working out of the terminology to describe what happens in lessons is itself an important resource in making explicit your understandings. You will also be aware, looking at the various activities that have just been listed, that in order to make things clear it is sometimes necessary to suggest that one utterance does one task. Of course, this is rarely if ever so and you may wish to work through the utterances noted above and look at how the work of doing something like, for example, closing is related to other interactional tasks.

Episodes

By episodes we mean various units of lessons, such as closing sections or starting sections, or prefaces, or questioning sequences, or teacher monologues, or areas in a lesson where things somehow break down. When you think that you can recognize such instances, one thing you can do is to codify in some senses different types of them. You can look at different ways that lessons start, you can look at different ways that lessons break down and different ways that order gets re-established. You have now got the basis for some data-based comparative analysis of each other's classrooms, perhaps of different teacher styles. Try also not to look at these episodes in isolation, but to look at how they come out of the surrounding sequences and the overall organization of the lesson. One fascinating task is to take a whole lesson and go through, as it were, backwards, trying to see how the various things that got said came to be said, that is, how the lesson got to go where it went. Another way of selecting episodes is simply to take those which are of interest to you for some other reason. Someone may wish to discuss a particular bit of a particular lesson which they felt to be unsatisfactory, or which went particularly well, or which was particularly unusual for some reason or another.

A next stage up, and a most difficult one, is to start a discussion of educational themes in terms of your data. You might wish to take a theme like opportunity or equality in the classroom, or a theme like encouragement or indoctrination or making topics relevant or revision or assessing pupils.

Practical and Theoretical Issues

Now the tendency with such themes is to use data illustratively, that is to talk about the theme in a theoretical and often vague way, occasionally bringing in some data in order to illustrate it. Try not to do this. Instead treat your data as something upon which to ground your themes. Treat it perhaps as a lawyer might treat his evidence; he knows there is another lawyer presenting the other side of the case, who may well have access to the same information and do something different with it. Your job is not just to show that the sense you make of the data is plausible, but to show that it is more plausible than someone else's. You have to show, then, how your version is embedded in the sequence and how by looking at people's responses you can see them responding to what you described as happening and so on. Try to approach this particular operation with a very open mind as to the definition of the themes you are talking about. Themes such as indoctrination seem to have been defined in the educational books as though they were matters of topic.

A very short look at your data will show you the way that talk is arranged; the way rights to talk are distributed and the way questions are asked have a great influence on the sort of answers that people might arrive at. Indoctrination is not a pure matter of topic and neither are such other matters as assessment or relevance. One obvious theme to try and relate your data to is that suggested by a particular curriculum or syllabus or lesson plan. Take a document describing one of these and try to see how it relates to the sorts of activities which you recognize as going on from the data in your lesson. See what provision it makes for its theme to be converted into the interactional cut and thrust of the lesson. Consideration of themes will probably lead to at least two other tasks. Once you have a reasonable number of recordings and once your group has been going some time, you will be able to attempt some long term analyses, that is to say you will be able to look at development over a period of time, perhaps a few weeks, perhaps comparisons between one year and another, perhaps comparisons of lessons before and after various changes were made in curriculum or organization. You will also be able to use your data and your analyses of data strategically. By strategic use, we mean the use of data and analyses in discussion with 'outside' agents such as curriculum innovators, advisers, parents and so on. You now at last have some evidence of what you do and of what the children do in your classes and this should be used, especially when people suggest to you vague and various changes to make in classrooms.

Conclusion

It is important that we should not leave the topic of teacher research without a comment about professionalism. We have suggested that detailed explicit knowledge about practice is a characteristic of professionalism. One optimistic scenario of teachers-as-researchers might see cell groups of

The Teacher as Researcher

teachers all over the country recording and analysing lessons, producing together a bank from which probationers, student-teachers, researchers and other teachers could draw examples of different sorts of lessons and different analyses of lessons. That bank could be the basis for research to synthesise and tabulate different teaching and learning techniques as they are done in practice.

If teaching really is a profession, it should be capable of creating a knowledge of practice. Here we have suggested a method for helping to create such a body of knowledge. The method can be considered in that sense as a way of testing the claims of professionalism. It may be, of course, that the development of banks of material and analyses of lessons do not lead to better teaching. Perhaps teaching is not best learned, or not learned at all by explicit and systematic knowledge, but by imitation and informal socialization. On the other hand, it could be that claims of this nature get the greater part of their support through the kind of knowledge currently provided by sociologists, psychologists, historians, philosophers, curriculum innovators and technologists who comment upon educational practice. Knowledge of practice created by the practitioners may be able to demonstrate the superficiality of such claims. The point here is that teachers have to produce that knowledge themselves and thereby stake their own claim for professionalism. No one can do it for them.

8 A first try: starting the day

Carol Cummings

Introduction

Self-evaluation can be frightening. Some teachers will honestly feel that they have, through lengthy experience, 'found *the* answers'. The less confident might perceive the whole notion as a threat, and those who vary approach and method in an attempt to follow ever-changing trends might see self-evaluation as yet another 'solution'.

It obviously requires some degree of courage and an honest desire to look more closely at what happens in one's classroom, to overcome the initial trepidation. The threat is probably greatest to those who feel most confident in their teaching; honest evaluation of what has *actually* taken place may provide some surprises and disappointments – it may shake confidence. However, it cannot be denied that for any teacher it may also provide a basis for change and pointers towards greater effectiveness.

For those who might view the approach to self-evaluation being advocated in this book as a 'latest trend' to follow, a word of warning. This type of self-evaluation may be valuable and enlightening, but following it does not bring easy solutions. It requires no initial changes of approach, but may point the way to modifications that the individual teacher hopes will remedy perceived shortcomings. It cannot be seen as a universal panacea, it leaves the evaluation and any consequent changes to the individual. Perhaps, then, such changes might better suit the individual than blanket changes in philosophy or practice evolved 'up there' and 'imposed' on the chalk-face practitioner.

It is probably true that the majority of teachers look at what they are doing, judge their effectiveness, and plan future strategies based on their evaluation of past successes and failures anyway. But they generally do this work almost subconsciously, often haphazardly and most frequently unsystematically. Digby Anderson (see chapter 7) does no more than suggest an alternative and, perhaps, more systematic and efficient method of carrying out self-

Starting the Day

evaluation. It was with these thoughts that I, an infant teacher, decided to tape-record the early part of a typical school day.

As any infant teacher will know, especially if, like me, they plan their work around the 'integrated day' (whatever that phrase is taken to mean!), there are likely to be only two times in the day when one finds all the children with the teacher, and when taping is likely to be comparatively uninterrupted and free from excessive background noise. That doesn't mean to say these are the only times teaching activities can be taped but they do present possibly the easiest place to start. These times are story-time and the start of the day. I chose to look at the start of the day because I felt that it was a relatively unstructured get-together and because I wanted to look, in more depth, at the way I used the time, at what I felt the children might be gaining, at how they handle and manage the occasion and at how I could make the time more effective. (See pp. 157–169 for my transcription.)

Why do I, in common with most teachers of young children, reserve the first part of the day for general, usually child-initiated talk? I think that infant teachers are perhaps more aware of home/school links than teachers in other kinds of schools, particularly as many schools, in common with my own, encourage parents to bring their children into the classroom, and because the children have not yet been taught to keep home and school apart. Later in their school careers, one gets the impression that 'out-of-school' talk is discouraged in the classroom as irrelevant to the business of 'learning'. In common with most infant teachers, I base the children's learning on their own experiences, on the things they seem to find relevant, and find the early morning an appropriate time to discover those things.

Recording

I found the actual recording to present no real problems as I have often used a tape-recorder in the classroom to record children's conversation, and very few children noticed the recorder after the first few moments. More difficult, though, was my own slight self-consciousness. I felt, during the session, that I was, perhaps, being 'the good infant teacher' to a greater extent that usual. I was probably a little more solicitous, answered children's questions a little more thoroughly and expanded the talk more than I might on a 'bad' day, but with the same sort of zealousness as I might if there were a stranger present. This self-awareness, though, was spasmodic; at times I completely forgot about the presence of the 'black box'; at others I was acutely aware, although I had previously promised myself that a complete disaster could, and would be erased. When I listened to the tape, I found no such utter disasters, although the reader is at liberty to disagree! Nevertheless, 'disasters' could be fruitful events to have on tape. Perhaps one would learn more from them, but it would have needed more than my meagre supply of courage and confidence to display them publicly at this stage in my career as self-evaluator.

The most time-consuming part of the exercise is the transcription, and one could be tempted to pass on this onerous task to others. It would be a mistake. I feel that I gained as many useful insights into what actually happened during the slow and repetitive task of transcription as during subsequent evaluation. The first impressions were very telling and answered many of my initial questions such as how many of the children took part in the session, which children dominated the talk, did I talk too much and did my questions lead the children to gain new or deeper understanding, knowledge or skills.

Having read transcripts of other people's recordings, one thing became increasingly clear as I made my own. Useful as the transcripts of others may be, using a transcript without the benefit of knowing the situation, the children and the ethos of the session does seem to have less potential for fruitful analysis. I was there, I can remember much of the background and circumstances of the session, the personalities of the children and my own reactions to them. The tape *added to* my perception, rather than *providing* a perception of an unknown situation. Nevertheless, the dangers inherent in such 'knowledge' must also be acknowledged. The fact that I was there makes the assumption of a position of 'anthropological strangeness' doubly difficult to achieve. Not only do I 'know' what 'everybody' knows about classrooms, and teachers and children, but I also have more explicit knowledge about these particular children, this particular teacher and the circumstances within which this episode occurred. The methodology employed here presents the reader with the opportunity to draw different conclusions, to place different emphases and to use the materials presented as they wish. For myself, it required great effort to attempt to 'see' the transcript without the 'knowledge' I had, and led me to think about the nature, validity and reliability of that knowledge. One assumes that one 'knows' both oneself and the children. Our 'knowledge' of children is based both on hearsay and personal observation. But usually one only observes what is presented for observation (and how often do overheard playground remarks show us a different 'side' to the children we know so well!); rarely does one question, as a 'stranger', occurrences that have become commonplace and routine. Thus, although familiarity with the situation can heighten awareness and deepen perception, an attempt to divorce oneself from the situation, to assume an attitude of 'unknowingness' facilitates the discovery of some of the seen, but unnoticed, features of the interaction.

Some early observations
As I transcribed the tape, my first impression was of a very disjointed session with many more interruptions than I was conscious of at the time. Perhaps

these are so routine and so expected that they are dealt with, in most cases, without interrupting the 'real' work of the session. I also noticed how easily the conversation seemed to 'jump' from interaction between myself and one child or small group of children and another such individual or group, whilst the majority of children either listened, chattered amongst themselves or read a book. Perhaps when we are the only adult, and therefore, generally the focus to which the children come, we only remember those parts of a session when we are personally involved; it would be interesting to have placed another recorder closer to those children farthest away, to catch their conversation.

In a session theoretically based on the need for *children* to talk, show their 'treasures' and generally guide the conversation, I was surprised at how much I talked, although, on reading through the transcript, most of the talk *was* child-initiated.

The session seemed to be very much a question/answer one, with me feigning ignorance in order to draw out from the children the knowledge and ideas they possessed, interspersed with information-giving and 'mothering' on my part. Although the child questioned generally seemed able to provide an adequate (in my opinion!) answer to my questioning, I suppose that this conversation might benefit others, although I had not really thought about why I use this approach. As with many things in the classroom, it seems to be appropriate and is based, I suppose, on some sort of belief in the child's need to display his knowledge and his desire to share his experiences with others.

Such 'discussion' interactions seem to be regularly interspersed with 'control' episodes – it is apparent, through explicit instructions and the almost inviolate 'teacher speaks, child speaks' sequencing of the conversation that children accept the teacher's right to speak, and that their right to speak is governed by the teacher's will. Explicit control appears throughout the transcript although, as all the children were not expected to sit and listen throughout the session, it might be less in evidence than in a more formal situation where all children are expected to listen quietly. Nevertheless, some administrative jobs, such as registration, are an integral part of such a session, and for this and other times when I thought all the children could gain by listening, they were called to order. It is noticeable that the teacher feels entitled to do this and that the children unquestioningly accept that entitlement. Parents and children accept the authority of the teacher in the classroom. Those children who came with messages for other children and those parents who arrived in the classroom with their children after the start of the session felt the 'rightness' of speaking to me first.

How, one wonders, does this come about? The classroom is continually referred to as 'our' classroom, implying a sharing relationship, but the children obviously accept the inequality inherent in the situation. Although this is not something that I had previously considered in any explicit sense, I

Practical and Theoretical Issues

suppose within the notion of 'class control' lies a sense of differential status. In common with many recently qualified teachers, I would have named class control and organization as my overriding concerns in my early years and, indeed, great emphasis was placed on the need for such control as a prerequisite for teaching/learning during training. Perhaps the concept of the teacher authority can be seen to be more deeply rooted than that. One remembers one's own school days with the authoritarian teacher only too well – teachers are seen to hold authority over children and even the youngest child entering school has, more than likely, been briefed to 'be good and do what teacher says'. And, although we may not like to think of ourselves as 'controllers', perhaps such degree of order as emerges from the tape would not have come about if all concerned did not accept this notion.

The device, previously unnoticed, of 'feigning ignorance' is interesting too in this context. It can be seen as a manipulative (and almost dishonest!) method of drawing information and conversation from children. I can think of a few instances when one might employ such strategies with co-equals (in an attempt to 'trip someone up', or in an interview situation), but even then the parties involved are not really interacting on a basis of equality. Here, the teacher is 'playing tricks' on the children, some of whom may be aware of the nature of such 'ignorance' in a way that produces the specialized kind of talk that occurs in classrooms. The implication that emerges is one of inequality, with the teacher controlling and manipulating the talk towards specific ends. The children do not have such power, either in this situation or over conversation generally, seem largely unaware of the device and so are not, in this sense, practising adult conversation, but are perhaps learning a little more about the strategies adults employ.

First reconsiderations
Looking more closely at the transcript, the session seems to fall into two distinct parts: pre- and post- registration. Despite the fact that it was not a 'planned' part of the day and the length of the session was indeterminate (the assembly bell is rung when the headteacher is ready and such a session can last from 15 to 35 minutes), a strong sense of organization and structure seems to emerge.

The pre-registration period seems to be a more informal and personal time than post-registration and children offer topics to the teacher which seem to be, in a sense, 'stored' for future use with the whole class. So, for example, the 'teeth topic' recurs, as do all the other topics raised by the children on a more personal basis in the early part of the session; they seem, in some ways, to be 'filed' and later brought out to be shared with the rest of the class and used for some more explicit teaching purposes.

Not only do the topics recur, but so also do the syntactic formats. In the 'chopsticks topic', for instance, the teacher 'rehearses' the initial utterances

Starting the Day

with the child (33–38), which are later almost exactly replicated in the more 'formal' part of the session (266–315), but the topic is then covered in more depth, with a more directly 'educative' feel to the interaction which involves more children. Perhaps this 'rehearsal' technique may be seen to put the children at their ease when the topic is later reinvoked on a less personal (and therefore more intimidating) basis. Thus when the topics of the chopsticks ('like a knife and fork'), the Bollin shop ('a what shop') and Buckingham Palace ('Guards?') recur, the children have some familiarity with the format that the initial utterances are likely to take.

From these initial observations and early reconsiderations a host of possibilities are raised for further analysis, but for now let us look at two of the episodes in further detail to see in what ways they are similar, and how their emergence in different parts of the session contributes to their difference.

A child offers the information that (80) 'My tooth started bleeding last night'. This is but one of a number of simultaneous offerings, but is the one which is taken up by the teacher. Why? Perhaps because it was the most audible, perhaps because another child also showed a wobbly tooth, perhaps because it was more in tune with the class topic of the time which centred on personal growth.

The initial 'teeth' sequence was comparatively long (80–97); most of the others were shorter. Was this because there were no external interruptions until 98, or because the children themselves seemed to want to dwell on the topic longer? Could it have been that the teacher thought the topic worthy of fairly lengthy discussion? The significance of children losing their first teeth was certainly impressed on me as a student; perhaps this was at the back of my mind and I felt that the children needed to be allowed to express their attitudes and feelings to avoid any sense of distress. Bearing this in mind, utterance 85 is interesting. Here the teacher involves other children (Have you got one too?), perhaps to reassure, and then confirms the wobbliness. It is the 'Very good' at the end that seems interesting. Why should one praise a child for something that is completely beyond his control, and why is it 'Very good' to have wobbly teeth? It may be partly reassurance, but I would suggest that the praise may also be underlining the increasing maturity of the child, in some sort of 'older is better' way.

The episode then moves on to an 'extension' phase. The children are invited to proffer suggestions as to why they lose their milk teeth and the first such suggestion (88), 'because we eat too much sweets', is dismissed with no real explanation. The negative teacher-response effectively cuts off this argument and the teacher then takes the initiative in suggesting another possibility (91), 'Do you get new ones instead?', leading the children to a simple affirmative response, which then requires the teacher to ask the initial question again in an almost identical format, which is repeated this time (95) stressing the word 'think'. This could, perhaps, have been

Practical and Theoretical Issues

intended as mild censure. The children had not been thinking hard enough and were, therefore, asked to think harder, and come up with the 'right' answer. The response, though (96), is equally inadequate and is, therefore, questioned by the teacher with the intention of asking the children to question the child's response (97), with the implication that it is not acceptable. This first session on the topic of teeth is ended by a parent bringing a child into the classroom.

The register had arrived immediately before this episode, and now the number of children is checked and discussion follows concerning the whereabouts of a particular child. Utterances 98–100 could be described as a 'control' episode and the atmosphere of the session changes from highly informal to more teacher controlled. There is some degree of social training – 'Talk one at a time' – where the children are requested to follow the normal turn-taking procedures of conversation. Specific children are addressed, but the first child so named seems to be treated as a representative of the whole group. 'Lee, put your book away' might, on first sight, seem to be highly specific, but, I would suggest, exhibits a widely-used technique for controlling children. Despite the naming of an individual child, all children are included and expected to follow the injunction. This interactional strategy is commonly used by teachers, although it is often reversed; in other words, one can either start with the specific and then make the information more general, or turn the technique around and ask the group to do something, followed up by a specific reinforcement.

After the attention of the children has been gained and biscuit money and hiccups dealt with, the teacher reinvokes the topic of teeth (111). The teacher feigns ignorance (as on other occasions in the transcript) to gain a response from the children. It would have been possible to have merely given the information, but the technique enables the teacher to draw out the correct response from the class. One wonders why this is preferred? Might it be that teachers feel that children need to make their own attempts to find out; to display their knowledge (or ignorance), or that children learn best from other children who, perhaps, talk their own language? In 115 the teacher can be seen to pick on the 'right' response and then to deepen the reasoning to find the causal factors involved in the loss of milk teeth. It takes a lot of cajoling and, finally, the naming of a child who is more likely to know than others to draw out the desired answer, but this is still not enough for the teacher. The topic could have been left at any stage, but the teacher obviously feels it worthwhile to continue and uses the same method to gain a further insight into the topic (117). The teacher's reaction (119) to the child's response (118) seems noteworthy. The praise is quite forceful, perhaps because the teacher has put in quite a lot of work to get to the desired answer, and the utterance continues with the teacher reinforcing what has evolved in the previous utterances.

Starting the Day

It is at this stage that a child interrupts to display her understanding of what she has heard, followed by others, and the teacher then feigns ignorance again, perhaps to demonstrate to the children (although falsely) that she has learnt something new too, or perhaps to lighten some of the intensity that has built up and bring the discussion, which is becoming a little uncontrolled, to a halt. One more child has a stab at creating time to express his own knowledge (123) but the teacher indicates that the topic is exhausted for this session, and calls the children to order (124), using registration as a device to finish the topic and as a control mechanism to regain authority.

Discussion and conclusions
Analysis of this small extract of a small part of the day was very enlightening. It highlights some of the techniques used to draw information from the children. Most of the questions require more than single-word, yes/no answers, and allow the children to display both knowledge and ignorance. Unintelligible responses seem to be ignored (94, 127), perhaps teaching the children that what they say must be intelligible to gain a response. Despite the child-oriented nature of the session, the teacher is firmly in control and re-introduces the topic when she feels it to be appropriate. What could merely be a time-filling exercise does seem, however, to advance the children's understanding in a less directive way then during the rest of the day.

The episodes with the feather (1-9 and 179-188) and with the whistle (188-211) demonstrate another teaching/learning technique; that of allowing the children time, later in the day, to find out for themselves – to touch and play with other children's 'treasures', but directed towards specific aspects of those objects. These aspects are those which the teacher considers the children would not necessarily discover for themselves and which she feels at least some of the children might find interesting.

This exercise in analysing tape-recorded classroom data has proved fascinating. It has highlighted techniques which were used unconsciously and has shown their effectiveness in achieving the classroom ethos in which I like to work. There are, nevertheless, certain disquieting aspects of the session. On reflection I feel that not enough children spoke, and particularly not the more passive children, who could perhaps have been given more encouragement and opportunity. I also feel that we tended to 'flit' from one topic to another, although on analysing the progression from one to another, and the content within each topic, in some ways control and orderliness were maintained, and perhaps the depth was great enough for such young children, whose thinking and activity is demonstrably of this butterfly nature. Indeed, at times, some of what was said may well have been unintelligible, especially to the youngest children. The chopsticks incident, on reflection, is particularly unsatisfactory, as these children obviously had no real concept of Italy or China, and an attempt was made to salvage this break-down by referring to the children's only point of contact with these two countries, namely their food. For children who had eaten neither spaghetti nor rice, however, this whole topic must have proved a mystery. It is a recurring problem when teaching young children to try to imagine how limited some of their experience is and to tailor talk to their level, whilst still attempting to widen experience and deepen understanding.

I was struck by the competence of the children to communicate their ideas in an intelligible and, mostly, grammatically correct way, and by their cognizance of the rules of talk. For the most part, unless a general response was invited, they took turns, and interruptions were remarkably few. The morning routine seems to have been accomplished and interruptions dealt with, without 'wasting' too much 'teaching' time; and this time, 'children's time', although controlled by the teacher, does seem to have been largely child-initiated and centred around their interests.

Thus, an apparently unstructured and potentially chaotic part of the school day, which is basically an open-ended session of indeterminate length, with many interruptions and various procedures to be got through, has emerged as structured and fairly tightly organized. This orderliness would seem to come about through pupils and teacher managing the situation with a previously unremarked adequacy. The situation emerges as the kind of occasion which enables young children to handle complex conversational arrangements and to demonstrate their growing verbal competence.

Classroom teachers often feel themselves to be under scrutiny. When that scrutiny is seen to take on an aspect of criticism and censure, paranoia and self-doubt or, conversely, self-justification and a closing of ranks tend to negate the usefulness of the efforts of HMIs and educational researchers. Teachers feel that they have to 'do' teaching, that *they* face the daily problems and that academics, in their ivory towers, politicians with a view to votes, and HMIs with their exalted and distant view of the 'chalk-face' rarely provide answers to the problems that beset the practitioner in the classroom. But negativism solves no problems and rejection pushes forward no frontiers.

Perhaps, then, it is up to teachers themselves to look to their own methods and, through self-evaluation and teacher-group discussions, to produce 'answers' to the problems *we* perceive. Perhaps we can help not only ourselves, but can gently push teacher-trainers towards producing new entrants to the profession with the sort of skills and the 'more realistic' expectations, both of children and themselves, that many teachers can be heard to grumble newly qualified colleagues lack.

I set off on this voyage of discovery with extreme trepidation. After all, one can never have such supreme confidence in one's ability and methodology that a deeper look will not be disturbing. At the outset, I worried about what

Starting the Day

might emerge from the tape which memory would otherwise have expunged, and which I might regret. However, as I began to look more closely at the transcript, feelings of personal involvement began to fade; I began to look at the tape as impersonal, and at the interaction as involving 'the teacher', often losing sight of the fact that 'the teacher' was me.

The emerging structure of the session and the competence of the children were surprises which I do not think I could have discovered without this analysis. Neither would I have perceived the strategies employed by both the children and myself to widen and deepen both interactional competence and the acquisition of knowledge.

I am not sure if any tangible changes will follow this exercise; I am certainly more self-aware, and more aware of the children's reactions in similar situations. I have not found any 'answers', but perhaps have a deeper understanding of the way in which a daily part of my job and the children's school experience comes about; of how we interact to produce that experience, and of how such a session both demonstrates and, hopefully, deepens the children's linguistic and social competence. With the tape and my observations on it, I have something concrete, something tangible to use as a resource in discussions with other teachers who have to manage the same part of the day. I am optimistic that together we could produce some constructive strategies for more effective teaching.

I found the experience interesting and enlightening and well worthwhile. We, as teachers, *can* do our own research, and can use such research to understand and, perhaps, answer our own problems. After all, we *do* the teaching, we must be in the most favourable position to look to that teaching in an attempt to understand what we do and to improve our ways of doing it.

Transcription

This is a transcription of 23 minutes of classroom talk at the beginning of the day as children arrive, often with mothers, in the classroom.

1	C	Me cousin found this when we went for the day.
2	T	Where?
3	C	Um near Dunham Park.
4	T	Oh – who's your cousin?
5	C	Claire.
6	T	How old's Claire?
7	C	Seven.
8	T	Very good. Does she live near Dunham Park?
9	C	No.
		((approximately 1 minute untranscribable background chatter whilst T attends to child from another class))
10	C	Mrs Cummings

11	T	Yes.
12	C	Watch this.
		((laughter))
13	T	Oh. Where did that come from?
14	C	A (bollin) shop.
15	T	A what shop.
16	C	A bollin shop.
17	T	What's that?
18	C	Um — uh – you – you can buy strawberries there.
19	T	Oh. Do you go and pick your own strawberries there?
	C	((shakes head))
20	T	No. Oh. Let me finish doing this writing.
21	C	( )
22	T	Right — are you ready to do a job for me? Can you go and take that ((a piece of paper)) to Mrs A or Mrs F — please //
23	C	// Can I go with her?
24	T	Yes.
25	T	Now then, what have you got here? Buckingham Palace by Rebecca ((reading from paper with child's drawing)) Who are these then?
26	C	Guards.
27	T	Aren't they *lovely*. Are they the guards at the palace gate.
	C	((nods))
28	T	Very nice.
29	C	Can I go and take it to Mrs H ((head))
30	T	Not at the moment lovely because I think she's quite busy, we've got some visitors today.
31	C	( )
32	T	From America.
		((C holds up chopsticks))
33	C	Look at my chopsticks.
34	T	What are chopsticks then.
35	C	Chopsticks. Watch this.
36	T	What are they?
37	C	To eat with.
38	T	You eat with them? Well they don't look much like a kn— knife and fork to (hh) me.
		((Interruption of another teacher with changed plans for the day))
		((Ch crying))
39	T	Now what's the matter?
40	C	I bumped my knee
41	T	Well that was a very silly thing to do — Where did you bump?

Starting the Day

42	C	( )
		((Mother comes in asking for permission for child to come to school on his bike))
43	C	((Showing badge)) ....hospital //
44	T	// What's that now //
45	C	// mummy's hospital
46	T	((Reading)) new born infancy care unit – is that where your mummy works?
	C	((nods))
47	T	Is it? With all those new babies?
	C	((Nods))
48	T	Oh, does she?
49	C	At Park Hospital.
50	T	Well *that* doesn't say Park Hospital. That says St Mary's Hospital.
51	C	Well it *is* ( )
52	T	That's not the same hospital as Park Hospital because St Mary's is in Manchester.
		((to another child with earrings))
53	T	I see you've got your crosses on again — in your ears. I think they're lovely, those. ( ) aren't they.
54	C	( )
55	T	Now then ... let's see.
		((Child comes in from another class with party invitations))
56	T	Have you got one for me?
57	C	I forgot – ((big smile))
58	T	Have you forgotten mine?
	C	((nods and giggles))
59	T	// Ja:yne ((laughter))
		((Parent comes in to tell T about taking a child to dentist in the afternoon. Child looks reluctant to let mother go))
60	T	Morning. A nice smile. Special smile. Special smile today ((cajoling))
61	M	If she's falling asleep this afternoon, she went hiking yesterday so she's rather ( )
62	T	This afternoon?
	M	((laughter))
63	T	Right. So long as we know it's not till this afternoon we'd better work *very* hard this morning ( ) ((to child)) Try to keep awake this morning — then you're allowed to sleep this afternoon.
64	T	C'mon. See you later ((referring to mother — taking role of child)) Sit down now.

159

65	C	((older sister)) David won't be coming to school today. He's got a tummy pain.
66	T	Oh right. Thank you for letting me know, Jenny.
67	CC	( )
68	T	Right boys and girls. Are you going to sit down? — ((Ch looks like crying)) *Don't* start now mummy's gone — ((Ch smiles shyly)) Right. Better? — What are we going to do with you when all the new little ones start? You'll make them think they've got to cry — and that won't do at all.
69	C	My friend's coming to this school —
70	T	When?
71	C	September.
72	T	Really – who's your friend?
73	C	Karen — and Paula //
74	T	// Yes (to another child) Where do you know Karen and Paula from?
75	C	From my play school.
76	T	Oh smashing. Have you told them all about it?
	C	((Shakes head))
77	T	*No?* ((Child brings in registers))
78	T	Thank you.
79	CC	( )
80	C	My tooth started bleeding last night //
81	C	//I've got one there.
82	T	Did it? Is it going to be wobbly?
83	C	(I've got one there)//
84	C	// Yes.
85	T	Have you got one too? Oh yes it's wobbly too. Very good.
86	C	( )
87	T	Why do you think you teeth fall out?
88	C	Because we eat too much sweets.
89	T	Not *those* teeth, do they?
90	C	My daddy's got ( )//
91	T	// Do you get new ones instead?
92	CC	( )
93	T	Yes. Why do you think those baby teeth come out?
94	CC	( )
95	T	Why do you *think* they come out?
96	C	Because they're bad.
97	T	Are they bad, though? ((Parent comes in about asthma inhaler for child))

Starting the Day

98	T	Hello Darren. Are you better? ((C nods)) Good. Don't forget not to go ((for inhaler)). Don't go at lunchtime for it. Right.
99	T	((Counts children on carpet)) 1, 2, 3, 4, 5, 6, 7, 8, 9, 10, 11, 12, 13, 14, 15, 16, 17, 18, 19, 20.
100	C	( )
101	T	He *should* be. Yes I wonder if he's ( ) Where was he. Where's he been ((referring to a child who's been on holiday and should be returning to school today))
102	CC	France // France // France // Abersoch.
103	T	He's been to France on his holidays. He's not been to Abersoch.
104	C	I'm going to France //
105	C	// I've been on a boat //
106	C	// He went in his holidays — and he went he's — he's been on a boat.
107	T	Boys and girls d'you think we — boys and girls could you close your books up. D'you think we could just talk *one* at a time. Just *one* at a time — Lee, put your book away. Put them away. Put the books *away*. Sara Jane *wake* up — Put it away Lee — Kim is that your biscuit money. Well where does it — // No.
108	C	// ( ) change.
109	T	Well put it in — there's your change. Put it in your pocket.
	C	((hiccup))
110	T	Oh — hiccups — Oh.
111	T	Now I want to know about these teeth because Rebecca here says — that — your teeth go wobbly and come out because they're bad because you've had too many sweets. Is that right?
112	CC	No. No. No. Yes. No.
113	T	Lee.
114	C	Because there are new teeth growing.
115	T	Because there are *new* teeth growing. I wonder why you don't have your new teeth when you're very small then. Why don't you have the — the new teeth when you're very small. Why do you have two lots of teeth — Jonathan.
116	C	( ) (because — can grow — little teeth) ( )
117	T	Yes, that's right. When you get bigger your little teeth *do* get more wobbly but — why do you have to have two lots of teeth. Why don't you just start and grow your big teeth — straight away — Nicholas.

161

118	C	Because you haven't got a big mouth.
119	T	*Good boy.* Good thinking. Your mouth wouldn't be big enough would it for those *big* teeth. Wouldn't be big enough for *my* teeth – when you were very little //
120	C	// Little babies grow bigger and then – and then – then we're big and then they come out //
121	C	(//)
122	T	Do they. I didn't know that was what happened.
123	C	( ) baby teeth.

((Child comes in with register.))

124	T	Right, let's do the register. Mark sit down please. Timothy isn't here. Perhaps he's not – perhaps he'll be here tomorrow.

((T goes through with register and children answer names))

125	C	Nigel's always late.

((Child holds up something she's brought to school))

126	T	Well put them down. We'll look at them in a minute.
127	C	( )

((T carries on with register))

128	C	Who's missing. Kelly, Timothy.
129	C	David.
130	T	Oh – and David, Yes. He's just coming.
131	C	( ) Mrs Cummings.
132	T	Pardon.
133	C	( )
134	T	Yes I did too. Should be back but he might not get back till late.
135	C	I'm going to France with Jonathan Lamb.
136	T	I know, you *told* me. Aren't you lucky.

((T counts members for dinner))

137	T	Oh well, we'll send down what we've got. Er – Stuart – oh Lee isn't it. Can you take it on your own, Lee.
138	C	Yes.
139	T	Can you manage it ((dinner money box and register)).
140	T	((counts dinner money envelopes)) Shouldn't there be another one — Who has dinners? //
141	C	// David.
142	C	// Alan
143	T	No, David doesn't have dinners.
144	C	He has sandwiches.
145	C	Nigel. //
146	C	// Nigel.
147	T	Oh it's Nigel. Have I put Nigel here and he's not. Hold that

Starting the Day

		a minute — go and get a pencil from over there for me will you.
148	T	( )
149	T	Here we are. Thank you.
150	C	Mrs Cummings, can we show — um -
151	T	Yes - we can - indeed. Come on. I still want to know where you got it from — Now then, I wonder what it could be ((laughter)) Don't show them yet (exciting) I wonder what it could be.
152	C	I know.
153	C	(A puppet)
154	T	Katrina.
155	C	( )
156	T.	Could be.
157	C	A ( ) doll.
158	T	How d'you think you'll get to see it.
159	C	Pull it down.
160	T	What down.
161	T	Go on.
162	C	((Pulls down stick to reveal pop-up doll)) *Oh* ((Laughter))
163	T	Isn't it beautiful.
164	C	I've got one //
165	T	// Now I still want to know *where* you got it from. Tell me again.
166	C	Shop.
167	T	A shop. Can you remember what sort of shop - Because you told me once before and I didn't understand. Try again.
168	C	( )
169	T	( ) shop. Is that the name of the shop.
170	Parent	It's called the Bollin Craft Shop // ( )
171	T	Oh // Oh, I see. Very ( ) isn't she //
172	C	(going round)
173	C	dances
174	T	She dances doesn't she. ((T makes doll dance)) *Oh* ((laughter)) Isn't she beautiful //
175	C	// I've got one.
176	T	Have you //
177	C	( ) //
178	T	// Look what happens to her - pigtails — There you are. Are

163

Practical and Theoretical Issues

		you going to keep the paper bag to keep her safe — Now what's this Laura?
179	C	Feather.
180	T	Feather. Where did you find your feather.
181	C	(Dunham Park)
182	T	Oh. Is it from one of the ducks there – d'you think. Where did you find it?
183	C	On the ( )
184	T	*Could* it be a duck feather d'you think.
185	CC	No.
186	T	No. Very clever things feathers you know. Push them the right way they all stick together – can open them out, but if you push them back again – push them back again they all — stick together again. Re:ally very clever. It's lovely that. If you put it on the half hexagon table in the other room – for people to look at – and to feel – and to be – *gentle* with 'cos it feels beautiful and silky — //
187	C	( )
188	T	Did she really. Oh — I can't imagine that. Go on, off you go. Now what's this. It's very small. Couldn't you find a bigger one.
	C	((shakes head))
		((child shows huge whistle))
189	T	No. Why did you buy such a small whistle.
190	C	Got it from a party.
191	T	Whose party?
192	C	Er – can't remember now.
193	T	Have you had it a long time?
	C	((shakes head))
194	T	D'you think it's a very small whistle?
195	CC	No.
196	T	It's *huge* isn't it?
197	C	I know it //
198	C	(Blow it)
199	T	That'll be a good idea. Go on.
	C	((blows whistle))
		((laughter))
200	T	Go on ((blows again))
201	T	Oh it's not got a very big noise. I wonder if you can – find out — during the day — What makes it make the noise. You'll have to blow it and somebody else'll have to look down that little hole —
202	C	( )

Starting the Day

203	T	Don't think so Paul.
204	C	Ball //
205	T	Don't think so //
206	C	Ball //
207	T	There's a little ball in there. But have you seen what the little ball does when you blow it?
208	CC	No.
209	T	Well you'll have to have a try during the day. Go and put it on the half hexagon table.
210	C	( )
211	T	Don't *tell* them, then. They've to find out for themselves. What have you got there Kim – What's that.
212	C	( )
213	T	It's from Jane. What is it?
214	C	( )
215	T	Just a minute. I want to know if Kim knows what it is because it says – *Kim* on it. What is it Kim — what *is* it?
	C	((nods head))
216	T	It's not a nod of your head is it? What's inside here — what's inside – what's this?
217	C	( )
218	T	Pardon.
219	C	Going to Jayne's party.
220	T	You're going to Jayne's party – what's this called then — what's it called when somebody asks to you their party — what's it called — Paula.
221	C	A invit— invitation.
222	T	An *invitation*, yes. Jayne is *inviting* you to her party – on the seventeenth — I think it's on Friday – after school. Can you read what it says. Come here.
		((Child brings invitation to T))
223	T	((reading)) Dear
224	T+C	Kim.
225	T	Here's an invitation — at 1 Delamere Road. Date seventeenth of the seventh – that July //
		((Child brings letter into classroom))
226	T	Thank you. Oh for Adrian in class 6 – 1981 time 4 o'clock till 6 o'clock from Jayne please – let – me – know – if – you – are – coming. Very good.
		((Child enters late with mother and dinner money))
227	Mother	Sorry we're late but I had to ( )
228	T	Could you take it up to the other end because it's gone ( ) //

165

229	Mother	Where shall I take it to.
230	T	Up to the – to the office to Mrs Spencer please. OK Thank you. Thank you.
231	T	There you are ((handing invitation back)) Have you – have you got a *coat* with you today?
	C	((nods))
232	T	Well go and pop it in your coat pocket. And that's for Adrian — Er Carolyn come and get this lovey.
233	C	( )
234	T	Oh you have. Just — sit down with it for a minute Carolyn cause Rebecca's got something to show ( ) here little box. She's been working very hard this weekend haven't you. I wonder who can tell us what this might be a picture of
235	CC	Castle.
236	T	No.
237	C	It's Buckingham Palace.
238	T	Buckingham Palace – and — What's this?
239	CC	Guard
240	T	The Guardsman.
241	C	Been there.
242	T	And what have you written up here then Rebecca.
243	C	Buckingham Palace.
244	T	Buckingham Palace by Rebecca Robinson. Have you see a picture of Buckingham Palace — When are you going to see pictures of Buckingham Palace – When do you think you'll see them — Who can think when they're going to see pictures of Buckingham Palace. Lee
245	C	When it's the Wedding.
246	T	When it's the Wedding. Where will you see the pictures then.
247	CC	On tele // On the tele.
248	T	On the television for the Royal Wedding won't you //
249	C	I've been there.
250	T	Tell me what Lady Diana's going to go to her Wedding in.
251	C	Coach //
252	C	Silver – silver coach.
253	T	I think it's a *golden* coach actually.
254	C	It's silver.
255	T	Is it. Well you'll have to watch and see. She not going in an *ordinary* car is she.
256	C	Mrs Cummings.

257	T	Yes.
258	C	I might be in France then.
259	T	Might you. I expect they'll have it on the tele even in France.
260	C	( ) Prince Charles in the middle
261	T	You're going to –
262	C	Wear when I go – wearing Prince Charles tee shirt in the middle of France.
263	T	Oh you'll have to. Yes. And I think you'd better take a flag //
264	C	And my – and my brother's got one the same as me.
265	T	Has he. Good. Well everybody'll know where you come from won't they. Yes love.
266	C	They haven't seen my chopsticks.
267	T	They haven't. Right Rebecca. You pop and sit down with that thank you. Now, Lee's brought these sticks. Say's they're chopsticks.
268	C	They *are* — chopsticks.
269	T	Told *me* they were to eat with and I said they don't look like a knife and they *don't* look like a fork and they *don't* look like a spoon so I don't know how you can eat with *those*.
270	CC	I know // I do // I know.
271	T	Do you. Well – just a minute just a minute lets – let Lee show you how d'you eat with them. Can you do it —
272	C	I don't know.
273	T	You don't know. It's not easy is it.
274	C	( )
275	T	You have – yes.
276	C	( )
277	T	For spaghetti. Well. I don't think it's quite spaghetti 'cos where does spaghetti come from — where do they eat lots and lots of spaghetti — Elizabeth.
278	C	Italy.
279	T	Italy. Are chopsticks from Italy.
280	C	Yes.
281	T	Are they.
282	C	Yes. I've seen //
283	T	// Is that Italian writing up here.
284	C	I can't read it.
285	T	You can't read it. No. That *is* writing. D'you know where chopsticks are used.
286	C	No.
287	C	China.
288	T	*China*. Yes, that's a long way from Italy and that's Chinese

		writing up there — Ve:ry hard to understand.
289	C	( ) brought them back.
290	T	Who did.
291	C	(Jim big)
292	T	Who's (Jim big)
293	C	One of my daddy's cousins.
294	T	And where did he come from.
295	C	(Australia)
296	T	Well that doesn't sound like England does it.
297	C	No.
298	T	Or even Italy. You'll have to find out *where* he comes from and find out all about it //
299	C	( ) a big bag of sweets.
300	T	Did you.
301	C	Yes special ones.
302	C	Yea — No.
303	T	No.
304	C	( )
305	T	Who's been to eat Chinese food – in a Chinese restaurant —
	C	((puts hand up))
306	T	Now then Kelly, d'you have spaghetti in Chinese restaurants — can you remember — because I'm still not clear what you eat with these and *I* don't think it's spaghetti — Daniel.
307	C	You have rice with them.
308	T	You *do* have rice – yes. Is it rice you meant?
	C	((nods))
309	T	Yes. D'you //
310	C	// I don't like that rice.
311	T	You don't like that rice but it's usually rice and meat and things and they're *very* hard to use. You have to keep them like that and try and move them together to pi— very hard to pick up little bits of rice with *those*.
312	C	I've got chopsticks at home.
313	T	Have you?
314	CC	And I have ( )
315	T	They're very smart. Thank you for bringing them. They're lovely. And Nicholas brought us something – also something lovely. What have you brought us Nicholas.
316	C	(Flowers)
317	T	What sort of flowers?
318	C	Roses.

Starting the Day

319	T	Roses. Where're the roses from.
320	C	In my garden.
321	T	Have you got lots and lots in your garden.
322	C	((nods)) I've got loads of them.
323	T	They smell very delicate those roses.
324	C	*I've* got loads of them.
325	T	Um. Some roses have a very *strong* smell. Nicholas' roses you really have to smell very hard — they're a very *delicate* smell – now what are these, these aren't roses.
326	C	Cos they – they were – they were — I went walking into Derbyshire on Saturday — and we went — we went to see Michael and went to — wanted a walk ( )
327	T	Mark and Da— and Nigel stop it //
328	C	// And we found those grasses.
329	T	These *grasses*, that's what they *are* a:ll sorts of beautiful grasses — they're lovely — unfortunately I don't know very much about grasses, I think these look like wild oats, these very fuzzy ones — they feel lovely, very sort of spiky and rough feeling — ((Bell for assembly rings)) So we'll put them in a vase later on — and you can feel them yourselves — what *are* the little bobbles on um – on the grasses – now you should know by now – are they the flowers?
330	C	No.
331	T	What are they — Elizabeth.
323	C	Seeds.
333	T	They're the *seeds* aren't they. When will they start to fall off the grasses.
334	C	Autumn.
335	T	*Autumn*-time yes when they are – what's the word. When they are r—
336	C	Ripe.
337	T	Ripe. Very good. When they're ripe in the Autumn-time they'll fall off – and they'll stay — on the ground or under the ground till the –
338	CC	Spring.
339	T	Spring. Good. And then what do they do?
340	CC	Grow // They start growing.
341	T	They start to grow – Now, boys and girls, that was the bell for assembly so can you stand up *very* very quietly and go and make a line by *that* door. ((Children line up to leave the classroom))

9 Talking and teaching: reflective comments on in-classroom activities

Wes Sharrock and Bob Anderson

Introduction and conclusions
One complaint which is often made against sociologists is that they tell you what you already know. There is substance to such a complaint, though it might be a little more precisely worded to indicate that they tell you what they know as though they were telling you something that was news. Telling people things they already know is not always a redundant pursuit, for there are times when it is important (and difficult) to keep attention focused upon the well-known, for that can all too easily be left out of account when abstract or theoretical thinking is being done.

What we have to say here, if there is any truth to it, will be no great news to teachers who will be wholly familiar with the kinds of things we pay attention to, but we will be trying to show the importance of taking note of these things in any proposed sociological rendition of life-in-the-classroom. Though what we have to say is said in response to and in continuance of the internecine disputes over the nature of sociology itself, we will contrive to suppress or simplify technical sociological issues and will make the argument as accessible as we can to the working teacher.

The aim of this book is to give the teacher sociological resources for independent thinking about the organization of activities in the classroom which, in the typical case, is the environment of the working day. We will not attempt to contribute to it by providing another exercise in the close examination of detailed organization of some activities, but rather by trying to place such detailed investigations within a larger picture, within the context of the basic effort to understand the organization of activities and the order of social settings.

Whilst the introduction of the audio and video recorder has proven a significant step forward in social research, we should not confuse ends and means; we should bear in mind that whilst the question of what we are to look at is by no means a trivial one, it is a little less important than the question of how we are to look at whatever we do look at. Indeed, there are critical ways in which the decision as to how we are to look at things determines what we shall be seeing when we look.

It is perhaps an unusually early moment at which to give our conclusions, but we will nonetheless offer them now, using the remainder of the chapter to get back to them.

We will endorse the view that what goes on in classrooms is (often, in large part) talking and that, therefore, to understand teaching we must look at talking. There are senses in which an understanding of teaching would be entirely coincident with an understanding of the organization of talking, but to see how teaching and talking do relate, it is always important to be clear about what is understood to be 'the organization of talking'. There are ways of representing the organization of talking which will represent the things that go on in classrooms well enough, but which will in other respects comprehensively miss the point of the activities so represented.

Sources of trouble, sources of order

There are tendencies inherent in (at least certain modes of) sociological reasoning which lead researchers to pay attention to almost everything that goes on in a social setting except the relevant business of the setting. Though there is a wide variety of sociological specialisms, including the 'sociology of education' along with 'the sociology of science', 'the sociology of work', 'the sociology of medicine' and so on, it might be more accurate if they were to be renamed to characterize more faithfully their actual content. Hence, the sociology of medicine could more accurately be called 'the sociology of almost everything about health provision excluding the nature of medical "treatment" ' and, in a matching fashion, the 'sociology of science' could be called 'the sociology of almost everything about science, except the work of making scientific investigations and discoveries'.

This point is no longer quite so true as it was a very few years ago, for some people, under the pressure of views like our own and from other considerations, are recognizing the importance of taking serious and central note of the need to look at the actual business in which the parties to the setting are actively engaged.

Acknowledging such a need and fulfilling it are alas, two quite different things and it is easy enough to slip over into doing something very different even when we set out to fulfil it. To fulfil it here, we shall be doing no more than recommending that attention be paid to in-classroom talk as involving the oral exposition and inculcation of a subject. In plainer words, regard classroom talk as a matter of talking through a subject in such a way that it can be learned.

As we have pointed out, to say that teaching involves talking will be no news to teachers, but as we also remarked, in thinking theoretically about a familiar activity it is only too possible to exclude obvious and vitally relevant matters from consideration.

We do not, then, say that teachers are unaware of the oral nature of much of their practice, but we do advise them that they will not find it easy to take account of it in applying sociology to their own classrooms and they will not find many (if any) resources in sociology for enabling them to do so. In talking of the need to develop ways of seeing what goes on in classrooms, for example, talking history, talking sociology, talking biology, then we are talking about the need to do something which will have to be undertaken almost from scratch.

There are, we said, inherent tendencies in sociology which militate against the treatment of the 'substance' or 'business' of social activities. Some sociologists will even differentiate explicitly between 'form' and 'content' and elect to attend to form rather than content! Of these inherent tendencies, we think there are two main and related ones, namely generality and abstraction.

Here we touch upon what are, within sociology, very deep issues indeed. It is simply taken for granted that sociology is or is to become a generalizing discipline. Though there is much discussion as to what that means and amounts to, in practice its current implication is for people to tend to case their descriptions in very generalized terms. Having studied a classroom, a few classrooms, even a substantial number of classrooms, the researcher feels required to cast his report in terms of comments about '*the* language of teaching' (Edwards and Furlong, 1975), or '*the* work context of teaching' (Denscombe, 1980), or '*the* organization of pupil participation' (Hammersley, 1974). Thus the operative aim of much research is to see instances of the activity under scrutiny as being typical or representative of the whole category that they instance. Consequently, *a* classroom comes to stand in for *the* classroom.

Our objection to this approach is not at all the usual one, namely, that a few instances studied in some detail are not a sufficient basis for generalization to the type or category. No – because this usual and standard criticism requires the assumption that the aim of generalizing is the right one and that the issue for discussion concerns means of obtaining it. For us, ends come into question. For the presumption of the need for generalizing involves the desire to talk about classrooms-in-general before we can seriously claim to have understood what goes on in any one of them.

We do not accept the stock reply that to understand a classroom *is* to understand it in general terms, i.e. to see it as the product of the same factors or forces which produce order and organization not in one, but in the generality of classrooms. We do not think that this is the right way at all and would say that generalization is a matter of understanding the relationship between instances, and to do so requires an understanding of the instances themselves. We need do no more to counter the stock reply than resort simply to pointing to the consequences of a premature wish for generality. The desire to generalize has the inevitable consequence of directing the attention of researchers to the organization of classrooms only insofar as they resemble one other. It creates an interest in those elements of classroom organization that are the same from classroom to classroom, regardless of the diversity of things that might otherwise be seen to be going on in them.

The employment of abstraction is the problematic accompaniment of the urge to generalize. The argument goes that science must abstract, that we all do abstract and that we cannot avoid doing so. Accordingly, to understand the organization of classrooms we must abstract, we must leave out of account what is being taught. Whether the pupils are being taught music or chemistry or English or history, we must look at the general dynamics of the organization of classrooms as collective and co-ordinated occasions; or at the formal properties of teacher-pupil relations and the power asymmetries that obtain; or at the sequencing of question-answer alternations in talk.

We suggest, however, that whilst abstraction may be an inevitable feature of scientific work, it is a strategic one, whereas the question of what we can leave out is pivotal. And what we can leave out depends upon what we are trying to do. We think that we are looking for something rather different from those sociologists who may seem in many respects to occupy something like the same position as us. We are interested in the question of how actions are done, how activities are organized or, more accurately, how they organize themselves. We are not interested in seeing what standard of typical patterns the same sorts of activities 'fall into', but on the contrary want to see how activities are accomplished without caring whether they do or do not show the same forms of arrangement as other activities.

Consequently, we are not looking for those sorts of patterns which become visible only through comparing many different occasions or undergoing a sophisticated sociological training. We want to attend to those matters which are visible in the midst of the activity which manifests them. We attend to such matters because we want to emphasize those things which are practically indispensible to the staging of an occasion as that occasion.

Thus our emphasis shifts away from questions about the way one occasion resembles others of the same sort in favour of questions which ask about the way a specific occasion is put together. In short, we move to questions about the occasion's specificity, about the way 'this one' is put together. We recognize that such a characterization of our approach seems repetitive and could be thoroughly opaque so we will shortly attempt a more lucid formulation of these contentions by providing illustrations for them.

From this point of view, the 'business' of occasions is not something which can be abstracted out. On the contrary, its treatment becomes something which is analytically inescapable. From our point of view, the practical

Practical and Theoretical Issues

organization of the classroom is inextricable from its 'subject matter'.

For some sociological analysts, it is wholly legitimate to disregard the question of how teachers and pupils talk history or biology or whatever. If their interest is in questions like the share-out of talk in the classroom between teacher and pupils, or the sorts of distribution of types of utterances (interrogative, imperative, etc.) amongst different types of parties to a classroom, then it does not really matter about the content of the talk. If, however, such investigations are intended to contribute to understanding the operation of social life and settings, then the selection of such topics leaves quite unclarified the nature of the relationship between the patterns of distribution which they reveal and the workaday business of taking 4x through the administrative reforms of King John in period 3 on Tuesday.

From our standpoint, we cannot afford to abstract out such matters for it is precisely the issue of what is to be said/talked about which is the issue for practical organization.

For those who must conduct classes, the question of what is to be talked about and how, word by word, it is to be talked about is the very stuff of the work. The working teacher cannot dispense with the content of the talk and utter a sequence of interrogatives and imperatives. To continue with the example from history, he must ask for the names of kings, the dates of battles, the summary content of court rolls, the enumerated content of legislation and so forth. What can be mere detail for the sociologist interested in distributional aspects of talk cannot be so treated by the speakers and hearers in the setting, for they must 'enact' that 'mere detail', they must produce it in and as the business that they do.

A cautionary point – we are not saying that the parties to classroom activity cannot dismiss things as mere detail, for assuredly they can and do. If they do so, however, then it is incumbent upon us not to take this dismissal as a standard of our own judgement of what does and does not deserve attention. Instead, we must treat it as the occasion for considering, for example, the way in which exposition of a subject can involve dispensing with details on that occasion.

Contrastive orientations to phasing

Let us try to clarify the character of our argument by exemplifying the contrast we are trying to make through the consideration of how 'phasing' in a lesson, seminar, or lecture might be treated. Though the points we are making can be applied equally to the organization of the lesson, seminar, or lecture, the problems and practices we shall choose to illustrate our comments will tend to relate most specifically to the environment which is most familiar to us, that of higher education.

We must take our argument most carefully at this point because we can seem to be producing a glowing contradiction, i.e., criticizing generalized accounts of teaching on the one hand, but providing an equally generalized, even over-generalized, version on the other. Let us make it quite clear, then, that the following remarks make no kind of pretensions to being, or even preparing to be, some generalized, systematic account of how teaching is organized. They are addressed to some issues of principle which bear upon research methodology and they are generalized remarks only in this sense. At no point is any mention of 'teaching' to be taken to imply that the kind of practice we are talking about is a standard or widespread one. We are talking purely of some things than can and do happen in the world of teaching, things that must be allowed for in any putatively general account of that activity. Thus, comments on 'teaching' are not presented as the products of careful study of instances of that phenomenon but as suggestions as to how we might begin the inspection of such instances.

We are taking it that the elemental problem is to understand not what patterns activities fall into, but how they are 'put together' into whatever patterns they might make: it is the assembling, not the final shape of the assembly, that is of interest. This contrast applies to the treatment of phasing.

It is clear enough that activities in classrooms often have an episodic character, that the kinds of activities being engaged in over time differ quite considerably and that progress through them is made by 'finishing' with one kind and 'initiating' another. Thus, we can see that the typical class moves from arriving-and-settling-in at the beginning through to clearing-up-and-preparing-to-leave at the end.

What are we to make of this episodic character to events? One thing that can be and has been (Hargreaves et al., 1975) made of it is an effort to identify a standard and ordered sequence of phases for the typical classroom and an associated set of procedures for moving from one stage to the next. Of course, we know only too well that in actual classrooms the episodic arrangements are endlessly voiced, that the duration, constituent activities, character and interrelationship of discernible episodes are all greatly diversified. If we wish to achieve an identification of generally followed phases without necessitating an inordinate amount of detailed study of an enormous range of classroom activities, then the way to do so is to make the stages simple and very abstract, to characterise them in such general terms that they will readily be applicable to any classroom. For example, we can readily identify broad stages like 'entry', 'settling in' 'down to business', 'finishing up', 'leaving'. In the same way, we can identify practices for moving from one phase to the next. These practices too can be done, for example, abstractly and generally, e.g. by using 'changing place and position' and 'making announcements of phase transition'. Such broad categories would encompass the multitudinous range of doings from 'sit down' through 'I want all of you to come over here' and 'get your books out' to 'now its story time' or 'you can go now'.

It is not *too* difficult, then, in a rough way to contrive an order of phases to a lesson, but how does it contribute to our understanding of the way activities are organized, or done? By studying diverse classroom activities, we can contrive categorizations which are sufficiently abstract to classify the activities in them all. By comparing and contrasting aspects of these different locations one with another, we can build up a composite picture of them all, but by doing so we beg the question, of how they achieve the order that we find them to have. How came this order-of-phases? Is it the product of some 'logic of social interaction' or what? How do the phases we as sociological analysts identify relate to those that the participants can discriminate? How do they 'follow through' this order-of-phases? Do they (somehow) simply fall into it or fall in with it, or do they aim to produce it? And if they aim to produce it, how do they ensure its accomplishment? These questions are surely compellingly relevant to any claim to understand how ordinary in-classroom activities work. Indeed, before setting out to identify general properties of classroom activity, we need to have given a lot of thought to what we are doing it for.

In the analytical mentality of the researcher, one of the things that an effort to discriminate phases and episodes requires is their precise definition, the identification of exact points of transition. The approach requires an orientation to activities in a way designed to pick out and bound as sharply as possible the discriminable episodes. Yet, we note that one thing which is widely noticeable about classroom activity is that the parties to it are engaged not in discriminating episodes (as a cognitive or perceptual matter), but in segregating them (as an organizational or managerial matter). Therefore, the extent to which the researcher can identify distinct phases will depend upon the extent to which the parties have kept them separate. It is easy to talk about the ordered phases of 'settling in' and 'getting down to business', but casual observation shows that the extent to which 'settling in' takes place before 'getting down to business' depends on the extent to which people insist on getting settled in first. Thus, a start can be deferred whilst waiting for all parties to arrive and until everyone present has subsided into silence. Equally well, a start can be made even as people are arriving and settling in or starts and restarts can be made in response to the appearance of late arrivals. Sometimes, indeed, a start can be made and then abandoned in favour of some other item of business. The extent to which episodes are ordered, and segregated, then, can depend upon the extent to which someone insists that they be so shaped. Thus the teacher can insist, 'no start until you are all ready'.

Similarly, it is possible for parties to orient to and achieve imperceptible transitions between episodes, to move things from one phase to another in such a way that the realization that a transition has been made will occur

Talking and Teaching

only retrospectively, being noticed only when in the midst of the new phase. The visibility of the organization of in-classroom activity in its course is something that is deeply implicated with their organization. It is a practically relevant matter for teaching and lecturing whether people should be clearly aware that they are stopping doing one thing and starting to do another, different one, or whether they should be started off doing one thing and led into doing something quite different without being aware what is happening to them.

We are not, however, suggesting that phases 'just happen', that classroom activities 'turn out' to have an episodic structure. On the contrary, they turn out to have such a structure because it has been projected from the outset.

Although what goes on in the classroom does have a moment-to-moment organization, it is not organized on that basis alone, for the moment-to-moment organization represents (can represent) the realization of a prior design, the fulfilment of an intended succession of phases. For some parties to the occasion, then, the future development of the occasion will have been anticipated. It will not, however, have been idly anticipated in the sense that it was expected and it did happen. Rather, it will have been actively anticipated in the sense that it will have been projected and action taken to bring it about as projected.

The projection of an anticipated course of development implies, for understanding what is going on at any point in time, attention being paid to the way in which present activities possess the potential for future development. We have to attend to the way in which the arrangement of matters now is being undertaken in order to provide for the possibility that later (in fifteen minutes, say, or 'after we have finished what we are doing now') the parties will be 'in position' to make the projected transition from this episode to that. Thus, present activities can be examined as 'preparation' or 'groundwork' for the achievement of a required transition: just what do we have to do now to ensure, for example, that there will be time to clear away before the bell goes and the next class comes in? Just how do we make a start so that we not only visibly 'get down to business' in such a way that first remarks will identify the topic being initiated, but also ensure that the mode of address to this topic will produce coherent subsequent talk that will lead into the next topic as its natural successor? For example, it is possible that as a lecture begins, and specific remarks are made, the lecturer has no idea how specifically the transitions will be made. Instead the talk is genuinely improvised, and, having begun, ways will be found to bring about the promised organization. Indeed, laying things out at the beginning, by giving a promised arrangement, is a way of keeping the business to an anticipated course. To write things up on the board in anticipation of doing them is a way of ensuring that they will get done. To list things to be talked of is a way of reminding ourselves later, when we have talked on some of them, which other intended objects of discussion we have promised. In fact, promising is a way of construing future possibilities of development by setting up commitments to do the promised activity.

An important aspect of phasing is pacing. We would certainly not want to be taken as arguing that those who project a course of development for a class have a definite and precisely timed preconception of the course to be taken. Matters can be more or less definitely anticipated and subsequent development can be tied more or less firmly to a strict scheduling. The pacing of phasing may follow a strict schedule so that the approach of the scheduled termination of a phase may also terminate that activity without regard for its stage of completion. Alternatively, an activity may be brought to a 'natural' closure by means of the expeditious and truncated treatment of matters outstanding. Adherence to the schedule can be given priority, but need not be. Nor need any strict scheduling be attached to a projected arrangement in the first place. We can pace ourselves so that matters will be treated, however long that proves to take. Therefore, the completion of a task in hand will be guaranteed, though all will have to wait to see how long that will take, to see what will have to be said to comprise exhaustive talk adequate-for-our-purposes to some topic. Thus, announcements of projected phasings can take the form of contingency plans of the sort, 'I'll try to finish talking about that this week but if not I'll carry over into the next class. On the other hand, if I do get to the end then I'll start on...'.

Providing the organization

In the previous section, we have been trying in part to make a contract between (1) the idea that it is the researcher's job to find an organization in activities which is standard and related to the requirements of sociological theory, and (2) the idea that we might look to find the organization that is, so to speak, put there to be found.

The organization in (2) is not put there to be found by sociologists; it is the organization that is put there to be found by participants in the activity being organized. It is the organization that is put there to be found by the students, colleagues, administrators and all those who have legitimate interests in and rights to know 'what goes on in classrooms'. In fact, so far we have been taking it for granted that talk in classrooms can be seen as carrying out the tasks of teachers and students or pupils and we have been leading up to the point that it is someone's task to give the occasion organization.

Returning to the main theme, then, we can say that the task of giving an organization to events in a classroom often falls to the teacher though it need not necessarily do so. How the class is to be run, what it is to do, who is to do what – these are matters which can be collectively decided, and negotiating a division of labour in organizing the occasion (or the course) can be one feature of the occasion (or course) itself. Further, the word 'negotiate' has been

Talking and Teaching

somewhat abused in recent years in sociology in the form of a generalized conception of social order as negotiation, but in the arrangement of some classes it can and does find quite liberal application. For the arrangements of a class can be made in the form of a deal of the sort, 'if you'll do this, then I'll do that', and 'if you'll do this I won't do what I could, i.e. if you'll talk up I won't set assignments for you to do'.

Of course, the task of giving the occasion organization does usually fall to the teacher and the work involved is not achieved simply through the making of talk in the classroom alone, but through the production of artefacts such as the provision of course outlines, organized reading lists, essay lists and the adoption of a textbook's organization as the model for the course to follow. In these ways, parties to the classroom activities can be informed about the purpose and content of the course, the topics to be treated and their sequential or phased order of treatment.

Again, we do not want to be understood to be proposing that it is invariably the case that the teacher decides these matters. We are well aware that the negotiation of a division of labour for a course can involve such matters as electing a theme and deciding an order of topics. Even where teachers retain control of the course organization, they can attempt to 'farm out' the work of discovering thematic unity, developing arguments or cumulating information in course activity. For example, the provision of required readings as a basis for the organization of classes can give students the task of making out the connections between texts and between topics. Tussles can and do take place over the discoverability of projected course contents, with students complaining that they cannot see the plan, direction, unity, development or payoff in the things they are presently doing. Thus teachers often have 'time out' from projected organizational arrangements in order to review and debate these very arrangements with a view to proposing and accomplishing some reconstruction of them.

Such observations of classroom organization are sometimes criticized on the grounds that we cannot understand what goes on in a classroom without reference to the 'context' within which activities are set. Often, this argument is about whether we need to 'relate' what goes on in the classroom to the organization of the school as an organization, or to the organization of the society as a whole, especially its history and class structure.

It is all too easy to exchange views about the importance of 'context' without ever achieving any sort of clarity as to what is to be counted as relevant for inclusion in 'context'. Here, we cannot pursue the very complicated question of the role of 'context' very far save in one of its most cogent aspects, namely, the question of whether in understanding in-classroom activities we can do so without reference to 'a wider social setting'. One argument about the importance of 'context' supposes that there is a determinate, all-inclusive context, that of the society as a whole, and that no action or

179

Practical and Theoretical Issues

activity can be understood unless it is set against this 'context'.

In sociology, there is much controversy about this. One issue, which many people think is the most important, concerns scale. Roughly, sociologists are divided between those who look at societies as a whole and those who look at face-to-face transactions. Still others seek a compromise and try to show that the way to resolve controversy (if it can be resolved) is to treat both approaches as complementary. Without denying the legitimacy of looking at life in the classroom with all the accompanying fine details of conduct, these conciliators suggest that we need to understand how the classroom 'fits into' the society as a whole.

We have already suggested that the key methodological question is never only 'what do we look at?', but always and importantly is also 'how are we to look?'. Clearly, then, in our view, scale cannot be the significant question. Here we disagree with most students of in-classroom activities who are likely to share the assumption that the consideration of scale is crucial. In their view, such a consideration does reflect a real difference in what is done, because they tend to see their contribution to the sociology of education as that of turning attention away from the study of 'the education system as a whole' and towards the examination of 'what really goes on in classrooms'.

We do not see any point in taking militant positions *vis-à-vis* the issue of whether we should or should not confine our attention to what goes on in the classroom, especially since we are trying to raise questions as to what (from a sociological point of view) does 'go on' in classrooms. Further, we do not see all answers as cumulative and interconnected and the question as to whether we can or cannot understand what goes on in the classroom without reference to the 'wider social context' seems only to raise other questions: what aspects of life in the classroom do we seek to understand? Do we require reference to 'external' considerations to understand them?

As we have already noted, questions about the organization of actions are often begged and never more evidently so than in sociologists' discussions about the relationship between in-classroom activities and the 'wider environment'. For their arguments presuppose that they have a clear understanding of how activities actually do relate together and that they do understand the way in which local events such as classroom activities build up into that most complex system of activity, the society as a whole. We do not simply doubt, but go so far as to deny, that such an understanding has been attained. The argument is that our task is precisely that of understanding how one action relates to another, how one activity relates to another.

In the first instance, this task does not query the relationship between two specific actions, A and B, but raises the question of the kinds of relationships that are to be looked for. Thus, many think of the kind of relationship between activities to be looked at in causal terms, i.e. does one action bring about another? Others like the idea that actions can be looked at as part of a strategy to see what kind of calculated connection action A may have to B as a way of achieving a goal. On our part, we are trying to suggest yet another way of looking for connections, namely that actions are to be looked at as constituents of courses of action, to see how they relate to each other in carrying out the courses of action they make up. This way of making our point may be too abstract and some exemplification will be useful.

In a classroom it may be that there is something which can be pointed to as 'the business' of that class, i.e. what it has been organized to do. For example, in a lecture it is the case that, sometimes, the lecture 'makes one point' and that what the lecture has to say is said briefly, in so many words, at a late point in the lecture's course. Nonetheless, a great deal of talking may be done in that lecture prior to the making of that point. How does that talking relate to the making of the lecturer's point? It can, of course, relate in a great many ways, but it could be, for example, that the previous talk provides 'scene setting' for the making of that point, laying the groundwork for the business of that class by giving the students background to the point to be made, by giving them technical information to let them understand the point when it is made, by providing context for the point to be made so that its significance will be seen when it is made, by 'setting up' the argument so that the point will come as a surprising conclusion and so forth. The work of the lecture may, then, be preparatory to, elucidatory of, facilitating progress toward and explicating the sense and significance of its own conclusion. We are suggesting, then, that it is in terms of their 'organizational contribution' that we can look at the diverse activities in the classroom, to see – as we illustrate with the example of the lecture – what role they play in getting the work of the classroom done.

Understood in such terms, what is 'going on' in the classroom consists in its business-like organization and a bare transcription of the talk, however faithfully it might depict every sound made in the classroom, would not, for those involved in the classroom, count as an adequate record of what was said and done. A page of student notes, however sparse, listing 'main points made' might be, for them, a better, more relevant, more useful record, identifying not 'what was said' but, instead, 'what the lecturer was getting at with what was said...'.

For students to show that they understand what took place it would not do for them to produce a good record of the talk in a lecture for they are required to attend to that talk not as specific utterances but as the presentation of a subject matter. Consequently, they are required to see what is said as, for example, exhibiting a subject's principles, steps in a developing argument. They are required to see in the talk things that will never be explicitly said, to identify hints, allusions and elliptical references, to see the connection between what is said here and now and what has been said in previous meetings of the same course or in different courses than this. That they under-

Practical and Theoretical Issues

stand what was said is not shown by reciting the words that were used; they show they follow the sense and course of remarks by reformulating them, by saying things in their own words, by seeing what is said as something that can equivalently be said in quite other words. For teachers, reading student assignments and examinations is a way of finding out what has been 'going on' in the classroom, how the things that were being said were being understood, what arguments, themes, conclusions, etc. were being extracted from the talk, etc. It is not usual for such readings to yield surprises.

The oral exposition of a subject

Throughout, we have been trying to return attention to the 'official business' of the classroom, to play up the extent to which talk of and thought about events in the classroom are inextricably involved with what ought to be going on in classrooms.

It has often come to be conceived as a mark of sociological artfulness to show that what goes on in any social setting is almost anything except its official business. Just as in courtrooms the waiting, rather than the trial, can be seen to take up the time and effort, so in classrooms the struggle-for-control rather than the teaching can be seen to be what is important. We do not wish to deny this importance. After all, it is a matter which will be the material for common room/staff room gossip and speculation for any teaching organization. At the same time, however, we would wish to give recognition to the fact that the struggle-for-control is usually undertaken in the service of getting some teaching done and that keeping control and getting through the requisite subject matter are tasks which can be done concurrently.

We are suggesting that there is no need to suppose, because teaching is sometimes a struggle-for-control, that it is generally so. Therefore, we need not see all that goes on in any classroom as instrumental in maintaining control and need not think of all occasions where someone is not overtly maintaining control as being ones in which they must, therefore, covertly be doing so. Rather, we should ask: when does control arise as a problem for teachers? And when it does, how then is it resolved?

We would rather see this question asked because it does not then tempt us to exercise ingenuity in contriving ways of seeing how talk about the imagery in *Othello* is 'really' an exercise in social control. We want to propose that it be seen instead as talk which is really an exercise in identifying the imagery in *Othello*. Of course, we know that the 'official business' of the classroom does not occupy all the time, and does not always take place, in class. Knowing these things does not mean, however, that the analysis of that 'official business' when it is done should be slighted.

Although, a lot of the time, the talk in the economics class is not of marginal utility or other recognizably relevant matters, a lot of the time it *is* about such matters. As a discipline, we sociologists are a long way from understanding how lists, anecdotes, diagrams, sketches, equations, assertions, interrogations, allusions to writings, monologues, demonstrations, picture shows with commentaries, discussion of handouts, walking the streets and talking about what is seen – how these comprise 'teaching sociology' or 'chemistry' or 'economics' or whatever. Drawing pictures, making lists, reading out quotations, putting things in numerical form, summarizing arguments, these sorts of things are the practices of our society and we do not think that anyone can yet claim to understand how such practices work (other than in a practical sense). Nor does anyone know how, heterogeneously combined, they can serve to comprise 'a basic course in statistics', 'advanced chromodynamics' or 'an introduction to physics for those without maths' and in the course provide, for example, a 'rigorous and systematic exposition of principles', 'a guide for beginners' or 'a basis for independent practice'.

Some more conclusions

We always find it cheering to end with the recognition that as yet we, as *analysts*, understand very little about the things we study. After all, this recognition means that more or less everything remains to be done. At the same time, we stress that *members* routinely accomplish their everyday business without undue problems. We hope that we have fulfilled our promise of making some inroads into the study of this taken-for-granted accomplishment in classrooms. That is to say, into the practical management of 'doing teaching'.

Prospect: what happens next?

Where do we go from here? It is important to us that the collective effort represented in the research reported in this book is not allowed to dissipate. For we hope to have provided a practical basis for teachers and others interested in education to set about their own research into everyday classroom activities. To do so requires neither expensive equipment nor extensive training. To make a start, all that is needed is a tape-recorder and a preparedness to approach the familiar as strange. Of course, there may be initial problems of not being able to record just what you want, but this sort of obstacle should not prevent you making a start somewhere. After all, given the kind of approach we have been advocating throughout this book, it might subsequently turn out that wherever you happen to begin seems useful and interesting once you have taken the plunge. In our experience, apparently unpromising situations can often provide useful insights into the all-too-familiar, taken-for-granted world of teacher-pupil classroom practices.

In this respect, we have seen how a teacher new to this approach – Carol Cummings – had anxieties about how she would cope and what she might find. As we can see from her chapter, however, the great advantage of being your own researcher is that early on it is possible to avoid areas which you find personally troublesome or threatening. Of course, we are not suggesting that such avoidance should necessarily be continued indefinitely. For to do so might have the effect ultimately of stultifying thought or, at least, ending up in very conservative postures which avoid all challenge.

A radical drive is implicit in most research which is to be worth anything at all. We do research to further our knowledge, to increase our understanding of the social world. Such knowledge and understanding, however, is available for use and application. We can try to apply it, though of course, there can be no guarantees that such applications will always be successful in improving our everyday interactions in schools. But insofar as they induce us to think more penetratingly and systematically about what we do from day to day in education, the promise over time is good. It is even better when this thinking can be done in conjunction with, together with, our peers and colleagues who are also engaged in similar endeavours for the improvement of pupil learning and understanding.

Much of the work of the Schools Council is formed around these beliefs and ambitions. More specifically, as far as we are concerned, we cite the Schools Council current Programme 2, 'Helping Individual Teachers Become More Effective'. This programme is intended to encourage teachers to study their own classroom activities with a view to increasing their knowledge for the development of improved practices of teaching, and for enhancing pupil understanding. It seems to us that the nature of the research presented in this book lends itself readily to goals of this kind.

Clearly, there is a wide variety of possible research strategies which can be deployed to meet these goals and this observation is borne out by the reported variety of activities already being undertaken by teachers all over the country. Many of these activities come under the rubric of 'action research' and are reported in Nixon, ed. (1981). We see our own approach as being broadly within this enterprise. Although it is certainly less eclectic, offering a specific methodology and techniques, we hope it can provide the whole area with some rigour and penetration.

In this book, we have presented in considerable detail a number of illustrative empirical case studies of a particular research strategy. This strategy has an integrity of its own and also, we believe, a high potential for practical application. We are only too aware that in the past, critics of ethnomethodology have criticized the whole approach for its apparent concern with the 'trivial' and also for not telling us enough about the social world. For example, such critics allege that ethnomethodology cannot give us the 'objective' evidence provided by such techniques as wide-ranging and large samples, surveys and statistical analyses. Here we refer the still sceptical reader once more to the chapter by Wes Sharrock and Bob Anderson. These authors argue cogently that we really have to put aside pseudo-scientific paraphernalia if we are to get on with the task of understanding the very nature of classroom life, as it is lived and experienced by those members of society whose activities help to produce it day in and day out. Furthermore, virtually everything that can be seen to occur in this classroom life can be dubbed as 'trivial' if by that is meant lots and lots of mundane and detailed routine activities. But the school day is made up of such details. That is what we want to study and better understand.

Since setting out to bring this book together, we have recognized its obvious links and relevance to Schools Council Programme Number 2, as described above. Consequently, we have established an organizational link by encouraging the formation of a group of teachers interested in researching the teacher-pupil interaction in their own classrooms. These teachers are

Prospect

trying out the kind of ethnomethodological approach that we have been demonstrating in this book, and they are evaluating their findings in the context of the Schools Council Programme. At the time of writing, the work of the group is still in its early days, but already analyses of various teaching situations and familiar routines are being accumulated.

Finally, we would like to repeat the invitation we originally made in the Introduction of this book. We would very much like to hear from any teachers who are contemplating trying, or have tried, to apply the research strategy we are advocating. Moreover, the teachers in our research group would greatly welcome such contacts.

References

ANDERSON, D.C., 'The formal basis for a contextually sensitive classroom agenda', *Instructional Science*, 8, 1979a.
'The classroom as a context for health education', in ANDERSON, D.C., ed., *Health Education in Practice*, Croom Helm, 1979b.
Evaluating Curriculum Proposals – A Critical Guide, Croom Helm, 1980.
ATKINSON, M.A., CUFF, E.C., & LEE, J.R.E., 'The Recommencement of a Meeting as a Member's Accomplishment', in SCHENKEIN, J., ed., *Studies in the Organization of Conversational Interaction*, Academic Press, New York, 1978.
BAR-HILLEL, Y., 'Indexical Expressions', *Mind*, 63, July 1954.
BARNES, D., *Language, the Learner and the School*, rev. ed., Penguin, 1971.
Communication and Learning in Small Groups, Routledge and Kegan Paul, 1977.
BENNETT, N., *Teaching Styles and Pupil Progress*, Open Books, 1976.
et al., *Journeys into Space*, Department of Educational Research, University of Lancaster, 1976.
BERGER, P., and LUCKMANN, T., *The Social Construction of Reality*, Doubleday, New York, 1967.
BERNSTEIN, B., 'Open schools, open society', *New Society*, 14 September 1967.
CUFF, E.C. (ed.), *Story-Time in an Infant Classroom – Seven Initial Responses to Transcribed Materials*, Didsbury School of Education, Manchester Polytechnic, July 1979.
CUFF, E.C., and FRANCIS, D.W., 'Some features of "invited stories" about marriage breakdown', *International Journal of the Sociology of Language*, vol. 18, 1978, pp. 111–133.
DENSCOMBE, N., 'The work context of teaching', *British Journal of the Sociology of Education*, vol. 1, No. 3, 1980, pp 279–290.
EBEL, R.L., *Essentials of Educational Measurement*, Prentice Hall, New Jersey, 1972.
EDWARDS, A.D. and FURLONG, A.V., *The Language of Teaching*, Heinemann, 1975.
EVANS, Kate, 'The spatial organization of infant schools', *Journal of Architectural Research*, vol. 13, no. 1, January 1974a.
'The head and his territory', *New Society*, 24 October 1974b.
FARRAR, Mary, 'The effects of conversational structures on children's story comprehension' (unpub. doctoral dissertation), Department of Educational Theory, University of Toronto, forthcoming.

References

FRENCH, P., and McCLURE R., eds., *Adult-Child Conversations: Studies in Structure and Process*, Croom Helm, 1981.

GALLAGHER, J.J., NUTHALL, G. and ROSENSHINE, B., *Curriculum Evaluation*, AERA Monographs on Curriculum Evaluation, Rand McNally, Chicago, 1970.

GARFINKEL, H., *Studies in Ethnomethodology*, Prentice Hall, New Jersey, 1968.

GOFFMAN, E., *The Presentation of Self in Everyday Life*, Penguin, 1971.

GUION, R.M., *Standards for Educational and Psychological Tests*, American Psychological Association, Washington, 1974.

HAMMERSLEY, M. 'The organization of pupil participation', *Sociological Review*, 22, no. 3, 1974, pp. 355–68.

'The mobilization of pupil attention', in HAMMERSLEY M. and WOODS, P., eds., *The Process of Schooling*, Routledge and Kegan Paul, 1976.

'School learning: the cultural resources required to answer a teacher's question', in WOODS, P., and HAMMERSLEY, M., eds., *School Experience*, St. Martin's Press, 1977.

HARGREAVES, D., HESTER, S.K., MELLOR, F.J., *Deviance in Classrooms*, Routledge and Kegan Paul, 1975.

HEAP., J.L., 'Rumpelstiltskin: the organization of preference in a reading lesson', *Analytic Sociology*, vol. 2, no. 2, card 1, 1979.

JEFFERSON, G., 'Side sequences', in SUDNOW, D., ed., *Studies in Social Interaction*, Free Press, New York, 1972.

JOINER, D., 'Social ritual and architectural space', in PROSHANSKY, H., RIVLIN, G., and ITTLESON, W., eds., *Environmental Psychology: People and their Physical Settings*, Holt, Rinehart and Winston, New York, 1976.

LABOV, W., 'The logic of non-standard English', in WILLIAMS, F., *Language and Poverty*, Markham, 1970.

MacKAY, R., 'Conceptions of children and models of socialization', in DREITZEL, H., ed., *Childhood Socialization*, Recent Sociology No. 5, Macmillan, 1973.

McQUADE, J., 'Practices for accomplishing displays of story comprehension', paper presented at joint session of Canadian Sociology and Anthropology Association, June 1980, Montreal, Quebec, 1980.

MALINOWSKI, B., *Argonauts of the Western Pacific*, Routledge and Kegan Paul, 1922.

MARSH, P., ROSSER, E., and HARRÉ, R., *The Rules of Disorder*, Routledge and Kegan Paul, 1978.

MEHAN, H., 'Accomplishing classroom lessons', in CICOUREL A. et al., eds., *Language Use and School Performance*, Academic Press, New York, 1974.

Learning Lessons, Harvard University Press, London, 1979.

NIXON, J., ed., *A Teachers' Guide to Action Research: Evaluation Enquiry and Development in the Classroom*, Grant McIntyre, 1981.

PAYNE, G.C.F., 'Making a lesson happen: an ethnomethodological analysis', in HAMMERSLEY M., and WOODS P., eds., op. cit.

PAYNE, G.C.F., and HUSTLER, D.E., 'Teaching the class: the practical management of a cohort', *British Journal of Sociology of Education*, vol. 1, 1980, pp. 49–66.

PLOWDEN REPORT, *Children and their Primary Schools*, Report of the Central Advisory Council for Education, HMSO, 1967.

RINTOUL, K., and THORNE, K., *Open-Plan Organization in the Primary School*, Ward Lock Educational, 1975.

ROSENTHAL, R., and JACOBSON, L., *Pygmalion in the Classroom*, Holt, Rinehart and Winston, Eastbourne, 1968.

RYAVE, A., and SCHENKEIN, J., 'Notes on the art of walking', in TURNER, R., ed.,

References

Ethnomethodology: Selected Readings, Penguin, 1974.
SACKS, H., Unpublished Lectures, University of California, Los Angeles, mimeo., 1964–1972.
'Aspects of the sequential organization of conversation', unpub. MS, 1970.
'On the analyzability of stories by children', in TURNER, R., ed., op. cit., 1972.
SACKS, H., JEFFERSON, G., SCHEGLOFF, E., 'A simplest systematics for the organization of turn-taking in conversation', *Language*, vol. 50, December 1974; also in SCHENKEIN, J., ed., op. cit.
SCHENKEIN, J., ed., *Studies in the Organization of Conversational Interaction*, Academic Press, New York, 1978.
SHARP, R., and GREEN, A., *Education and Social Control: A Study in Progressive Primary Education*, Routledge and Kegan Paul, 1975.
SIMPSON, R.H., *Teacher Self-Evaluation*, Macmillan, New York, 1966.
SPEIER, M., 'The child as conversationalist: some culture-contact features of conversational interactions between adults and children', in HAMMERSLEY M., and WOODS, P., op. cit., 1976.
STAUFFER, R.G., *Directing the Reading-Thinking Process*, Harper and Row, New York, 1975.
STUBBS, M., *Language, Schools and Classrooms*, Methuen, 1976.
STUBBS, M., and DELAMONT, S., *Explorations in Classroom Observation*, Wiley, New York, 1976.
TROTT, A.J., ed., *Selected Microteaching Papers*, Kogan Page, 1977.
TURNER, R., 'Words, utterances and activities', in DOUGLAS, J.D., ed., *Understanding Everyday Life*, Aldine, Chicago, 1970; Routledge and Kegan Paul, 1971.
WERTHMAN, C., 'Delinquents in schools: a test for the legitimacy of authority', in COSIN, B.R., et al., eds., *School and Society*, Routledge and Kegan Paul, 1971.
WILLIS, P., *Learning to Labour: How Working Class Kids Get Working Class Jobs*, Saxon House, 1977.
YOUNG, M.F.D., 'Curriculum change: limits and possibilities', in YOUNG, M.F.D., and WHITTY, G., *Society, State and Schooling*, Falmer Press, Ringmer, 1977.
ZANER, R., 'The phenomenology of epistemic claims: and its bearing on the essence of philosophy', in NATANSON, M., ed., *Phenomenology and Social Reality*, Martinus Nijhoff, The Hague, 1970.
'Examples and possibles: a criticism of Husserl's theory of free-fantasy variation', *Research in Phenomenology*, vol. 3, 1973, pp. 29–43.

Index

accounts, 12, 15ff, 110, 131, 137, 175
  and accountability, 59, 91
Anderson, D.C., 8, 128, 131, 148
Anderson, R.J., 129, 185
anthropologically strange, 8, 21, 150
Atkinson, M.A., 25

Baker, C., 89
Bar-Hillel, Y., 46
Barnes, D., 133
Bennett, N., 6, 63, 85, 86
Berger, P., 104, 109
Bernstein, B., 70
Bruner, J., 19

categorization, 13, 131
  of locations, 64, 71ff
  of age, 109ff
  of phases of lessons, 175ff
competence, 55, 63, 76–7, 89, 156
  of pupils and teachers, 14–38 *passim*
  of adults and adolescents, 104–125 *passim*
  of children's reading, 39–59 *passim*
content analysis, 135–7
context, 5, 19, 20–2, 28–9, 46ff, 73, 113–14, 122, 129, 136, 170, 172, 174
  and wider social setting, 179f
control, 80–81, 88, 123, 152, 154, 179, 182
counselling, 89, 122
Cuff, E.C., 12, 14, 24
Cummings, C., 128, 184

Delamont, S., 133
Denscombe, N., 172
discipline, *see* control

Ebel, R.L., 41
Edwards, A.D., 172
ethnography, 61ff
ethnomethodology, 12, 21, 50, 128, 185, 186
  definition, 3ff
  criticisms, 7, 185
Evans, K., 73
expertise, 21, 29, 57

Farrar, M., 54
Francis, D.W., 24
Furlong, A.V., 172

Gallagher, J.J., 133
Garfinkel, H., 3
Gates-MacGinite Reading Test Technical Manual, 57

Index

generalizing, generalizations, 5–7, 75, 129, 133, 141, 172ff
Goffman, E., 66, 77
Green, A., 85
Guion, R.M., 41

Hammersley, M., 117, 123, 124, 172
Hargreaves, D., 175
Harré, R., 121
Heap, J.L., 12, 44
Hitchcock, G., 13
Hustler, D.E., 12, 96, 123

identities, 12, 30, 31, 74, 89, 92–3, 95
  of adolescents and adults, 104–125 *passim*
indexicality, 46

Jackson, L., 6
Jefferson, G., 101
Joiner, D., 66
joint productions, 27, 30, 54, 56

Kohlberg, L., 19

Labov, W., 133
Luckman, T., 104, 109

MacKay, R., 116, 124
Malinowski, B., 61
Marsh, P., 121
McQuade, J., 47
Mehan, H., 43, 47, 117
membership, 4, 5

Nixon, J., 130, 185
normalization, 1, 13, 76ff
  norm, 69, 77

participant observation, 13, 60–85 *passim*

Payne, G.C.F., 54, 88, 96, 123
phasing, 174–8
Piaget, J., 19
Plowden Report, 63
professionalism, 12, 14, 15, 30, 78, 146, 147
professional ideologies, 13, 75–6
professional expertise, 20
professional commitment, 22

question, question and answer, 16, 17, 25, 92–100, 130, 131, 134, 137, 139, 140, 141, 151, 153–6, 170, 173, 180
  on assessment, 42–55 *passim*
  concerning adolescence, 104–125 *passim*

reading, assessment of, 13, 39–59
Rintoul, K., 63
Rosenthal, R., 6
Rosser, E., 121
Ryave, A., 64

Sacks, H., 1, 22, 23, 24, 25, 28
Schenkein, J., 64
Schools Council, 185
Schutz, A., 3
setting, *see* context
sequence, sequencing, 28, 47, 49, 53, 55, 84, 91, 136, 139, 140 146
  sub-sequences, 51, 54
Sharp R., 85
Sharrock, W.W., 129, 185
Simpson, R.H., 133
Speier M., 104, 106
Stauffer, R.G., 51
stories and story-time, 12, 14–38 *passim*, 88, 131, 136, 138, 140, 144, 149, 176
  basic functions, 22
  second stories, 23

invited stories, 24
jointly produced stories, 27
and reading assessment, 42ff
Stubbs, M., 133

tape-recording, 8f, 128, 130–147 *passim*, 149–150, 155, 157, 184
theory and practice, 7, 13, 20, 75–6, 80, 84, 85, 86, 130–131, 146, 183
transcripts, *see* tape-recording
Trott, A.J., 133

Turner, R., 64, 135

visibility, 29, 65, 74, 77–8
of competence, 124
of classroom organization, 177
Vygotsky, L.S., 19

Werthman, C., 124
Willis, P., 123

Young, M.F.D., 133

Zaner, R., 57, 58